D1807723

Third Language Acquisition and Universal Grammar

PEFC

PEFC/16-33-111
CATG-PEFC-052
www.pefc.org

SECOND LANGUAGE ACQUISITION
Series Editor: Professor David Singleton, *Trinity College, Dublin, Ireland*

This series brings together titles dealing with a variety of aspects of language acquisition and processing in situations where a language or languages other than the native language is involved. Second language is thus interpreted in its broadest possible sense. The volumes included in the series all offer in their different ways, on the one hand, exposition and discussion of empirical findings and, on the other, some degree of theoretical reflection. In this latter connection, no particular theoretical stance is privileged in the series; nor is any relevant perspective – sociolinguistic, psycholinguistic, neurolinguistic, etc. – deemed out of place. The intended readership of the series includes final-year undergraduates working on second language acquisition projects, postgraduate students involved in second language acquisition research, and researchers and teachers in general whose interests include a second language acquisition component.

Full details of all the books in this series and of all our other publications can be found on http://www.multilingual-matters.com, or by writing to Multilingual Matters, St Nicholas House, 31–34 High Street, Bristol BS1 2AW, UK.

SECOND LANGUAGE ACQUISITION
Series Editor: David Singleton

Third Language Acquisition and Universal Grammar

Edited by
Yan-kit Ingrid Leung

MULTILINGUAL MATTERS
Bristol • Buffalo • Toronto

Library of Congress Cataloging in Publication Data
A catalog record for this book is available from the Library of Congress.
Third Language Acquisition and Universal Grammar
Edited by Yan-kit Ingrid Leung.
Second language acquisition: 37
Includes bibliographical references.
1. Language and languages--Study and teaching.
2. Language acquisition. 3. Generative grammar.
I. Leung, Yan-kit Ingrid.
P53.T485 2009
401′.93–dc22 2008035200

British Library Cataloguing in Publication Data
A catalogue entry for this book is available from the British Library.

ISBN-13: 978–1–84769–131–6 (hbk)

Multilingual Matters
UK: St Nicholas House, 31–34 High Street, Bristol BS1 2AW, UK.
USA: UTP, 2250 Military Road, Tonawanda, NY 14150, USA.
Canada: UTP, 5201 Dufferin Street, North York, Ontario M3H 5T8, Canada.

Copyright © 2009 Yan-kit Ingrid Leung and the authors of individual chapters.

All rights reserved. No part of this work may be reproduced in any form or by any means without permission in writing from the publisher.

The policy of Multilingual Matters/Channel View Publications is to use papers that are natural, renewable and recyclable products, made from wood grown in sustainable forests. In the manufacturing process of our books, and to further support our policy, preference is given to printers that have FSC and PEFC Chain of Custody certification. The FSC and/or PEFC logos will appear on those books where full certification has been granted to the printer concerned.

Typeset by Saxon Graphics Ltd, Derby.
Printed and bound in Great Britain by MPG Books Ltd.

Contents

Acknowledgements

I thank David Singleton for inviting me to do this L3 project for his Multilingual Matters SLA series while I was working at the University of Essex, UK. I thank all the authors who have generously contributed their papers to the present volume. I thank the following colleagues (in alphabetical order) who acted as external reviewers for the papers: Mónica Cabrera, Jasone Cenoz, Joyce Bruhn de Garavito, Roger Hawkins, Britta Hufeisen, Johanne Paradis, Virginia Yip and Boping Yuan. I also thank an anonymous reviewer arranged by Multilingual Matters for reviewing the entire manuscript. Finally, I thank all the staff members at Multilingual Matters particularly Marjukka Grover and Anna Roderick for their kind editorial help and advice.

Yan-kit Ingrid Leung
June 2008

Contributors

Patricia Bayona is a Canadian researcher interested in the acquisition of Spanish as a third or additional language, and in the sociolinguistics of Spanish as a native language. Her initial theoretical training was in second language acquisition from a generative perspective, but her doctoral specialization has recently evolved toward quantitative research on trilingualism. As an active member of the International Association of Multilingualism and of the International Research Network on Multilingualism, her exploration of the Spanish language learner has focused on the effect of the integration of sociocultural and linguistic aspects.

Diana Hsien-jen Chin is Assistant Professor of Spanish at Wenzao Ursuline College of Languages, Taiwan. She received her PhD in Spanish from the University of Illinois at Urbana-Champaign in 2006. Being a language lover, she speaks Mandarin Chinese, English, Spanish, Japanese and French. Her research interests include multilingualism, second language acquisition theories, learners' motivation and learning strategies.

Vivian Cook worked at Ealing Technical College, North East London Polytechnic and the University of Essex, teaching EFL, first and second language acquisition and language teaching methodology. Since 2004 he has been Professor of Applied Linguistics at the University of Newcastle upon Tyne. He is chiefly known through his books on second language learning, Chomsky and spelling. His current interests include the English writing system and the multi-competence view of L2 acquisition. He was the founder and first president of the European Second Language Association, and is a founding co-editor of *Writing Systems Research* (OUP), to appear in 2009.

Suzanne Flynn received her PhD from Cornell University in 1983 and is Professor of Linguistics and Language Acquisition at MIT. Her research focuses on the acquisition of various aspects of syntax by both children and adults in bilingual, second and third language acquisition contexts. More recently, her work has also focused on the neural representation of the multilingual brain as well as on the phonological and acoustic underpinnings of accent. She is the author/editor of several books as well as the author of many articles published in journals and edited volumes. She is also the co-editor of the journal *Syntax* with T. Stowell.

Rebecca Foote is Assistant Professor of Second Language Studies in the Department of Linguistics and Germanic, Slavic, Asian and African Languages at Michigan State University. She received her PhD in Spanish Linguistics from the University of Illinois at Urbana-Champaign in 2006. Her research centers on psycholinguistic aspects of second language acquisition, including bilingual and multilingual language processing and production. Ongoing and future projects examine the processing and production of gender agreement in early and late language learners, the role of working memory capacity in agreement processing and production, and multilingual sentence processing strategies.

Carol Jaensch's research to date has focused on the L3 acquisition of German by native speakers of Japanese who acquired English as an L2. The particular focus has been on the role that the L2 might play in the acquisition of properties of the German Determiner Phrase. She has recently completed her PhD thesis (entitled 'The role of the L1 and the L2 in the L3 acquisition of German DP features') at the University of Essex, UK. She has presented work related to this topic at a variety of international conferences over the past four years, which has resulted in a number of publications.

Fufen Jin is currently a researcher at the Department of Scandinavian Studies and Comparative Literature, Norwegian University of Science and Technology (NTNU). She read English Language and Literature for her BA, and General Linguistics for her MA. She had subsequently worked as a lecturer at the Department of Foreign Languages, Tsinghua University (Beijing, China) for three years before she joined NTNU, pursuing her PhD in linguistics (specialized in a Generative Approach to Second Language Acquisition). She received her PhD from NTNU in 2007. Her research interests are in second/third language acquisition, mainly involving Norwegian, Chinese and English.

Yan-kit Ingrid Leung received her PhD in linguistics from McGill University in Canada. She has taught at the linguistic departments at the University of Southern California, USA and the University of Essex, UK. She is interested in second and especially third language acquisition, as well as bilingualism/multilingualism. Her research has focused on East Asian and Southeast Asian learners. She is currently affiliated with the University of Hong Kong.

Sirirat Na Ranong is currently a PhD student at the Department of Language and Linguistics of the University of Essex, UK. Before coming to Essex, she worked as a lecturer for the English Department at Thammasat University, Bangkok, Thailand. She has developed her interest in the area of third language acquisition, focusing on the case of Thai learners of Chinese. Her PhD thesis is entitled 'Investigating the lexical and syntactic transfer in L3 acquisition of Chinese: The case of L1 Thai–L2 English–L3 Chinese'.

Wai lan Tsang is Assistant Professor at the University of Hong Kong. She received her MPhil and PhD from the University of Cambridge, UK, and the focus of her doctoral research was the acquisition of English finiteness by Cantonese learners. Her research interests include syntax and morphology, contrastive analysis of Chinese/Cantonese and English, and second/third language acquisition. Her recent projects focus on teachers' language awareness, the use of implicit/explicit feedback in second language acquisition, and the acquisition of Mandarin as a third language by Japanese learners.

Introduction

Third Language Acquisition and Universal Grammar is a volume that has collected a total of nine conceptual and/or empirical chapters that look at adult third language (L3) or multilingual acquisition from the Universal Grammar (UG)/generative linguistic perspective. A variety of languages other than English are involved in the studies reported in the chapters, including Cantonese Chinese, French, German, Italian, Japanese, Kazakh, Mandarin Chinese, Norwegian, Russian, Spanish, Tagalog and Thai, with acquisition cases taking place in a number of different geographical locations, such as Canada, Germany, Hong Kong, Norway, Taiwan, Thailand, the UK, and the USA. Compared to its mother field of second language acquisition (SLA), which has flourished over the last 30 years, L3 acquisition is only a young field that is still very much in its infancy. Irrespective of theoretical framework, the number of studies on L3 is scant. This volume brings together some up-to-date research on adult L3 acquisition that borrows insights from previous descriptive studies on multilingualism particularly concerning the role of prior linguistic knowledge (Cenoz *et al.*, 2000, 2001; see also Cook, 1996 on multicompetence), and follows the important field of generative SLA (White, 1989, 2003) to seek explanatory adequacy in (adult) non-native language acquisition research by adopting the UG framework (Flynn *et al.*, 2004; Klein, 1995; Leung, 2005, 2006a, 2006b, 2007b, 2008). For a more detailed proposal on combining multilingualism, descriptive L3 and generative SLA, see Leung (2007a). It is hoped that this volume will generate more interest in the study of L3 or multilingual acquisition from both the generative linguistic perspective and other theoretical perspectives. It is also hoped that this same volume will induce more dialogue and scholarly exchange between the fields of bi/multilingualism and SLA within academia. Undeniably the world is becoming more and more multilingual. We thus believe that this work is timely and of social relevance. The following section presents an overview of the chapters collected in this volume.

Chapters in this Volume

The chapters in this volume are presented in an alphabetical order based on the last names of the contributors. A synopsis of each chapter is provided below. Chapter 1 by Bayona looks at the acquisition of the Spanish middle construction by anglophones in Canada from two perspectives:

generative SLA and generative L3. Two experimental tasks were employed in the SLA part of the study, namely a grammaticality judgment task and a truth value judgment task. The SLA analysis centers on the issue of UG access. Intermediate and advanced Spanish learners' performance on the grammaticality judgment task testing the surface structure of *se* seems to support Full Access to UG, but the results of the truth value judgment task indicate that these same learners still have problems with the abstract semantic properties related to the Spanish middle construction, as against reflexives or perfectivity. Thus overall it is unclear as to whether UG is fully available to post-critical period SLA so far as the syntax–semantics interface is concerned. A replication experiment based on the grammaticality judgment task used in the SLA study was administered on a new group of subjects who are trilinguals (L1 English–L2 French–L3 Spanish). This L3 analysis focuses on the issues of typological proximity, L2 proficiency effect, and recency. Findings suggest that higher L2 French proficiency indeed helps those Spanish learners to perform significantly better than the low L2 French proficiency group, thus providing some support for the role of typology and L2 proficiency in L3 acquisition. Recency as defined by exposure to classroom Spanish before testing has a neutral effect. Overall Bayona rejects the Full Transfer Full Access model as she observes no absolute L1 transfer in her case.

Chapter 2 by Chin also examines L3 acquisition of Spanish. She aims to pin down the source of transfer in the acquisition of aspectual contrast amongst L1 Chinese–L2 English–L3 Spanish learners in Taiwan. An experiment that comprises a proficiency test, a morphology test and an acceptability task in two language versions was devised to test learners' knowledge and interpretation of semantic contrast of perfective and imperfect aspect in English and Spanish. With respect to the acceptability task, for L2 English, group results show that learners were sensitive to the semantic contrast between perfective and imperfective aspectual marking on state, accomplishment and achievement verbs in English; on the other hand, individual results reveal that L1 Chinese influence in some of the learners' L2 English interlanguage systems cannot be ignored. For L3 Spanish, learners only recognized the perfective and imperfective contrast on accomplishment verbs despite possible positive transfer from L1 Chinese as far as state verbs are concerned and from L2 English with respect to both accomplishment and achievement verbs. Chin argues that her overall findings point to both L1 and L2 transfer in L3 acquisition, with L2 posing the dominant influence.

Building on the idea that 'language' does not refer to a single language in the Chomskyan sense and that UG is not only concerned with a single language in the mind but allows for the possibility of multiple languages, Cook claims in Chapter 3 that (post-critical period) second, third or any subsequent language learners should not be considered as 'abnormal' compared to monolingual speakers. Quite the contrary, bilingualism or multilingualism should be considered as the norm, and monolinguals should instead be regarded as individuals who have been deprived of input in order to trigger more than one languages in their minds. In his chapter, Cook presents various arguments to support his claim and discusses the consequences of such a multilingual view on the theory of UG.

Flynn also explores the relationship between the study of L3/multilingual acquisition and the theory of UG in Chapter 4. Based on the empirical findings of her experiment on relative clauses in the case of L1 Kazakh–L2 Russian–L3 English, Flynn investigates three research questions: (1) whether the properties of the L1 grammar alone determine language learning in L3 development; (2) whether grammatical properties of all prior languages known can potentially determine subsequent patterns; and (3) how the L3 results inform us concerning the nature of the initial state for language learning The first two questions relate to the cumulative enhancement model advanced by Flynn and her colleagues in their earlier work. With regard to the third question, Flynn situates her discussion in the light of two possible models of language acquisition, namely the 'at birth' model (i.e. UG matures and changes in the course of language acquisition, and ultimately evolves into the target language) and the 'constant' model (i.e. UG remains unchanged during the language acquisition process, and remains separate from the target language (or any other previously acquired language)). Flynn concludes that her L3 findings support both cumulative enhancement and the 'constant' model.

To continue with the rest of empirical studies, in Chapter 5 Foote investigates L3 acquisition of aspect in Romance languages, focusing on the role of typology in transfer. She compares learners of three language combinations: L1 English–L2 Romance–L3 Romance, L1 Romance–L2 English–L3 Romance, and L1 English–L2 Romance. Similar to Chin, perfective vs. imperfective interpretative contrast forms the focus of Foote's study. Foote assumes that the Romance languages in her case, Spanish, Italian and French, are broadly similar to each other as far as aspectual marking and semantic contrast of perfective and imperfective are concerned. The main experimental task conducted was a sentence conjunction judgment task in which learners had to judge the logicality of sentences made up of two clauses conjoined by the target equivalent of *but*, the verb of the first clause supplied in either of the two past tense forms and only the imperfective form would make the sentences logical. Results of the task on both group and individual levels suggest that the two L3 groups consistently outperformed the L2 group; they seem to have transferred knowledge of aspect from the previously known Romance language to have gained this advantage. Foote thus contends that typology plays a crucial role in determining the major source of transfer in L3 acquisition on the morpho-syntactic (and semantic) levels.

Jaensch's Chapter 6 is concerned with the case of L1 Japanese–L2 English–L3 German. Three written gap-filling tasks have been used to investigate learners' knowledge of uninterpretable features of Case and gender on articles and attributive adjectives in German. Jaensch's study is original in that instead of focusing on the issue of cross-linguistic influence or transfer, which has constituted the theme of the majority of L3 studies (whether in the lexical or syntactic domain) in the literature to date, she looks at the effect of L2 proficiency in acquiring an L3. Specifically she aims to test whether adult learners of advanced L2 proficiency are more sensitive to the properties relevant in the L3, these same properties being absent in both the subjects' L1 and L2. Jaensch's findings seem to support this idea of L2 proficiency effect: those L3 German learners who have achieved a higher proficiency in their L2 English are more target-like in their performance on Case and gender features on the determiner phrase than learners of an equivalent L3 proficiency but a lower L2 proficiency. Jaensch proposes that her L3 learners seem to have better lexical knowledge as well as superior metalinguistic and cognitive abilities, which together facilitate the setting of UG parameters in the L3.

The study that Jin conducted in Chapter 7 also involves an East Asian language, i.e. Mandarin Chinese as a source language. The objective is to examine the status of (null) objects in L1 Chinese–L2 English–L3 Norwegian interlanguage grammars. Chinese languages including Mandarin allow the dropping of objects in sentential contexts; Jin assumes this to be related to the [+zero topic] setting of the topic-drop parameter allowed by UG. On the other hand, English and Norwegian are believed not to licence null objects since both languages are assumed to instantiate the [–zero topic] parameter setting. Jin tests Chinese native speakers' intuitions of this cross-linguistic difference by employing a grammaticality judgment and correction task in both English and Norwegian. Significant differences were found between subjects' L2 and L3 responses to ungrammatical null object sentences in English and in Norwegian both on the group level and on the individual level, across all L3 proficiency groups. Subjects rejected ungrammatical null object sentences in L2 English rather successfully but failed to do so in L3 Norwegian. Jin interprets these results as indicative of a strong L1 Chinese effect and weak L2 English influence in the L3 acquisition of Norwegian objects. Jin concludes that as far as formal syntax is concerned the L1 grammar cannot be eliminated as a direct source of transfer in L3 acquisition even a typologically closer L2 has been acquired to an advanced proficiency level.

The last two chapters deal with Chinese as well (Mandarin and Cantonese respectively), both as the target language (L3), and both chapters look at binding. In Chapter 8 Na Ranong and Leung examine the interesting case of L1 Thai–L2 English–L3 Mandarin Chinese, focusing on the acquisition of the identification property of null objects (cf. Jin above, who looks at the licencing problem of the null object phenomenon). It is controversial in the theoretical syntax literature as to whether null objects in Thai and in Mandarin Chinese have the same underlying status despite surface similarity; the debate has gone on for two decades but remains unresolved. Na Ranong and Leung thus approach the problem from an empirical perspective. Using an interpretation task devised in two language versions they first tested both native speakers of Chinese and native speakers of Thai on their native grammars to establish the status of null objects (and overt objects) in either natural language. It was found that null (and overt) objects in Thai are similar to those in Chinese as far as abstract syntax is concerned. Na Ranong and Leung then tested the Thai speakers' L3 Chinese grammars to investigate the extent to which transfer (and typology) play a role in non-native acquisition of null objects. It was found that the Thai speakers who are L3 Chinese learners with an L2 English background performed in a similar way as an L2 Chinese control group (i.e. English native speakers without any prior Asian language background who are learning Chinese as a second language) on null objects in the interpretation task. However the groups differ significantly from each other in terms of how they interpret overt objects in the same interpretation task. Na Ranong and Leung therefore dismiss universal mechanism as a possible explanation of the results, and argue instead that L1 plays a privileged role in both L2 and L3 acquisition of null objects in their case.

Finally, Tsang explores the acquisition of L3 Cantonese Chinese in Chapter 9. The research focus is on the binding condition of reflexives. Her subjects were L1 Tagalog–L2 English–L3 Cantonese learners in Hong Kong. Tsang designed a timed coreference-judgment task with spoken-stimulus sentences. A group of intermediate L3 learners of Cantonese were found to have interpreted Cantonese reflexives in a non-native manner; they were observed to be less sensitive to the morphomorphemic/polymorphemic distinction, local/non-local binding and subject/object orientation in their judgments of the reflexives. Tsang discusses these results in terms of typological proximity and sociolinguistic status of a language. A proposal of 'minimal distance' to account for the predominantly local binding preference of the learners is put forward.

References

Cenoz, J., Hufeisen, B. and Jessner, U. (eds) (2000) *English in Europe: The Acquisition of a Third Language.* Clevedon: Multilingual Matters.

Cenoz, J., Hufeisen, B. and Jessner, U. (eds) (2001) *Cross-linguistic Influence in Third Language Acquisition: Psycholinguistic Perspectives.* Clevedon: Multilingual Matters.

Cook, V. (1996) Competence and multi-competence. In G. Brown, K. Malmkjær and J. Williams (eds) *Performance and Competence in Second Language Acquisition* (pp. 57–69). Cambridge: Cambridge University Press.

Flynn, S., Foley, C. and Vinnitskaya, I. (2004) The Cumulative-Enhancement Model for language acquisition: Comparing adults' and children's patterns of development in first, second and third language acquisition of relative clauses. *The International Journal of Multilingualism* 1, 3–16.

Klein, E. (1995) Second vs. third language acquisition: Is there a difference? *Language Learning* 45 (3), 419–465.

Leung, Y-k.I. (2005) L2 vs. L3 initial state: A comparative study of the acquisition of French DPs by Vietnamese monolinguals and Cantonese–English bilinguals. *Bilingualism: Language and Cognition* 8, 39–61.

Leung, Y-k. I. (2006a) Full transfer vs. partial transfer in L2 and L3 acquisition. In R. Slabakova, S. Montrul, P. Prévost and S. Slabakova (eds) *Inquiries in Linguistic Development: In Honor of Lydia White* (pp. 157–187). Amsterdam: John Benjamins.

Leung, Y-k.I. (2006b) Verb morphology in L2A vs. L3A: The representation of regular and irregular past participles in English–Spanish and Chinese–English–Spanish interlanguages. In S. Foster-Cohen, M. Medved Krajnovic and J. Mihaljevic Djigunovic (eds) *EUROSLA Yearbook 6* (pp. 27–56). Amsterdam: John Benjamins.

Leung, Y-k.I. (2007a) L3 acquisition: Why it is interesting to generative linguists. Invited review article, *Second Language Research* 23(1), 95–114.

Leung, Y-k.I. (2007b) Second language (L2) English and third language (L3) French article acquisition by native speakers of Cantonese. *International Journal of Multilingualism* 4 (2), 117–149.

Leung, Y-k.I. (2008) The verbal functional domain in L2A and L3A: Tense and agreement in Cantonese–English–French interlanguage. In J.M. Liceras, H. Zobl and H. Goodluck (eds) *The Role of Formal Features in Second Language Acquisition* (pp. 385–409). Mahwah, NJ: Lawrence Erlbaum.

White, L. (1989) *Universal Grammar and Second Language Acquisition.* Amsterdam: John Benjamins.

White, L. (2003) *Second Language Acquisition and Universal Grammar.* Cambridge: Cambridge University Press.

Chapter 1

The Acquisition of Spanish Middle and Impersonal Passive Constructions from SLA and TLA Perspectives

Patricia Bayona

Introduction[1]

This chapter is the compendium of two studies on the acquisition of middle and impersonal passive constructions in Spanish as a foreign language.[2] Initially the subject was approached from the generative perspective of second language acquisition (SLA), but later the study was framed within the newer field of third language acquisition (TLA) studies. In both cases, the question of the full transfer from the first language (L1) is approached, although with differing theoretical assumptions and implications according to each theoretical structure.

The generative perspective on SLA is a research field that has been developed based on Chomsky's proposal (1965, 1995) on the existence of a universal system of principles, called the Universal Grammar (UG), which interacts with the lexical parameters of each language. This UG, that is proper to humans only, is presumed to provide the child with a capacity to fully acquire the grammar of his L1 regardless of the poverty of stimulus encountered. The child subsequently develops the ability to gradually restructure such innate UG principles according to the different parameters of the input. Following these premises, generative SLA researchers argue that the second language (L2) learner maintains full or partial access to UG throughout the L2 acquisition process, and as he is being exposed to the L2, he develops an 'interlanguage state' consisting of a series of systematic errors that respond to a rule-governed behavior determined by UG. The concept of interlanguage was originally proposed by Adjémian (1976), Corder (1967) and Selinker (1972), and as one of the pillars of generative SLA research, it has motivated scholars to look into the UG principles evidenced in it. In the initial states of interlanguage, it is considered that UG is continuous, since it remains from the L1 acquisition process, and that it controls the L2 grammatical representations of the

1

learner. There is abundant debate regarding the nature of the interlanguage grammar in this state, although three main hypotheses lead the discussion. The Full Transfer Full Access hypothesis, proposed by Schwartz and Sprouse (1994, 1996), argues that the initial state of L2 acquisition is the final steady state of L1, which allows the learner to fully transfer from the L1 into the L2 the totality of the grammatical parameters that the L1 exhibits. This hypothesis also assumes that subsequent restructurings governed by full access to UG will take place in the interlanguage, due to the need of the learner to assign a representation to the input data, as the acquisition process evolves. A second proposal is the Minimal Trees hypothesis by Vainikka and Young-Scholten (1994, 1996), where the claim is that only lexical categories – not functional – are present in the earliest stages of both L1 and L2 acquisition, and that during the acquisition process, the functional categories may develop in succession. According to this hypothesis, the initial states of learners with different L1s may also be different, given that such states are closely determined by the lexical specifications of each language. Still, the authors fail to indicate the nature and features of what they propose as 'functional projections', which has lessened the research applications of the hypothesis. A third major proposal was made by Eubank (1996), named the Valueless Features hypothesis, according to which the initial state of L2 grammar is determined only in part by L1 grammar. Eubank maintains that there is only a 'weak transfer' of the L1 functional categories into the L2 initial state, since feature strength is to be determined at later periods of acquisition according to the input. Following to this view, we would expect to find variability in the raising of verb features such as negation, but such behavior has not yet been reported in the literature (White, 2003).

Regarding the analysis of grammars beyond the initial state, generative SLA researchers have followed two major theoretical points of view. The first deals with the breakdown of the parametric systems. For Clahsen and Hong (1995), Neelman and Weerman (1997) and Bley-Vroman (1997) there is a total lack of parameters in the interlanguage grammars, which would imply a total lack of access to UG by L2 learners. However, other researchers have found evidence that there is partial access to UG, which is reflected in the difficulties of the L2 learner to reset feature strength (Beck, 1998; Eubank, 1996). An alternative viewpoint maintains that interlanguages fully respond to UG constraints, although the resetting of the parameters is strictly determined by the properties of L1 parameters. Here, full access to UG is assumed, and transfer from the L1 is actually the point of debate. Researchers have argued for the possibility of parameter resetting due to full transfer from the L1 (Bruhn de Garavito & White, 2002; Schwartz & Sprouse, 1998) and for the impossibility of parameter resetting, due to the constraints imposed by the L1 (Hawkins & Chan, 1997; Smith & Tsimpli, 1995).

As noted above, the generative perspective on generative SLA research provides great variability in terms of premises and approaches, as it attempts to respond to the profusion of morphosyntactic variability observed across interlanguage itself. But an alternative account has recently been offered by scholars who consider that the premise of encompassing all foreign language learners in a homogeneous group needs revisiting. Within the field of TLA research, it is argued that there are substantial differences between L2 learners, L3 learners, L4 learners and so forth (Dewaele, 1998; Hammarberg, 2001). The activation of different skills and analytical methods in multilingual learners, compared to bilingual learners, provides evidence for an alternative regrouping, according to the chronological order of acquisition of any other languages additional to the L1. Apart from aiming to determine the nature of interlanguage grammars, TLA researchers focus on the cognitive, linguistic and sociolinguistic effects of multilingualism. Herdina and Jessner (2002) have pointed out the dynamic nature of multiple language acquisition processes, which may be influenced not only by the operational effects of crosslinguistic influences, but also by personal affective factors and multiple social identities that the learner is exposed to. Unlike generative SLA studies, TLA research does not assume that there is necessarily a dominant language within the linguistic spectrum of the multilingual speaker, or a weaker language. Neither is it presupposed that linguistic transfer is predetermined by the parameters of the L1 or that it is unidirectional toward the foreign languages. For TLA researchers, any language within the language spectrum of a multilingual speaker may play a dominant role according to a particular communicative function of the speaker in specific circumstances. In the same way, the multidirectional processes of crosslinguistic influences may be reflected in the foreign language performance(s) as well as in the L1 performance. Based on these foundations, the TLA research field has concentrated mainly on the areas of the psycholinguistic dynamics of multilingual language systems, crosslinguistic influences and lexical acquisition. More recently, younger scholars have embarked on the exploration of areas such as the sociolinguistics of multilingualism, the phonological aspects of trilingual speakers and the pedagogical implications of multilingual settings.

Regarding the psycholinguistic dynamics of multilingual individuals, Herdina and Jessner (2002) have proposed the Dynamic Model of Multilingualism that makes it possible to account for processes of acquisition, maintenance and/or attrition of one or multiple languages across the life span of the speaker. This model is based on sinusoidal curves, which represent the language acquisition process as a non-linear experience depending on the individual competences and life experiences, in the same way that biological developments take place. Another relevant model is the Bilingual/Multilingual Production Model (Clyne, 2003; De

Bot, 2004), which has centered on the segmentation of the acquisition process into three subsystems: the conceptualizer, the formulator and the articulator. This model assumes that the multilingual speaker may integrate multiple identities within a single framework, depending on the social and motivational factors he faces.

In the area of crosslinguistic influences, the interaction between three or more linguistic systems is being approached from a descriptive point of view. The analysis of the different types of lexical transfer lead Ringbom (2001) to identify that there are both: (1) transfers of form, expressed as language switches, and deceptive cognates; and (2) transfers of meaning, represented by calques and semantic extensions. Ringbom argues that the comprehension of the formal interlinguistic similarities is the starting point of the learning process, while the accuracy of the production involving the semantics and morphosyntax will be indicative of more developed linguistic stages.

Unlike generative SLA studies, TLA research looks into the extent of crosslinguistic influences at the morphological, lexical, semantic and cognitive levels, with the purpose of identifying the underlying principles that might determine the learner's preferences at a given time for borrowing an element crosslinguistically. In this respect, Hammarberg (2001: 22–23) specified various factors that have been subsequently taken as grounds for testing in particular cases of multilingualism:

(1) Typological similarity: Morphosyntactic as well as cultural similarities between the languages previously acquired, and the one in process of being acquired, enhance the acquisition of the L3.
(2) Proficiency: A higher level of command of the L2 seems to facilitate the acquisition of the L3.
(3) Recency: As the term implies, if the L2 has 'recently' been activated, it remains more accessible as a linguistic reference for the learner.

For Cenoz *et al.* (2001), linguistic typology proximity is the priming factor for determining crosslinguistic influences. In the case of English L3 learners with Spanish and Basque backgrounds, she found that lexical and syntactic transfers into English came invariably from Spanish regardless of whether this language was the learner's L1 or L2. Based on Kellerman and Sharwood Smith (1978, 1983, 1986) who first showed that learners tend to transfer more elements from the L1 when it is typologically close than when it is a more distant language, Cenoz points out that the crosslinguistic influences may be found along a continuum of two extremes: Interactional Strategies and Transfer Lapses. The former are conscious decisions to use a language other than the target language; the latter are non-intentional switches that the learner produces automatically. In this process, the multilingual learner may activate more than one language simultaneously with the target language as a sort of communication strategy (Cenoz *et al.*, 2001: 107). On the other hand, in a later study Bayona (2007) has found that L2 proficiency plays an important role in determining the origin of transfer into L3. In the case of Spanish L3 learners, with French L2 and English L1, it was reported that a higher L2 proficiency level would hinder the number of L1 transfers into the L3. The study also found that social factors such as being exposed to the L2 or having lived with a French family are the more relevant factors that prompt the production of crosslinguistic influences coming from the L2.

In sum, both of these approaches, generative SLA and TLA, aim to elucidate from different angles of study the principles underlying the linguistic behavior of foreign language learners. Although the two theoretical positions do not necessarily contradict each other, they do concentrate on rather different aspects of the acquisition process.

A crosslinguistic analysis of middle constructions

As noted above, this chapter concentrates on the acquisition of middle and impersonal passive constructions in Spanish as a foreign language. Middle constructions in Spanish have been defined as a notional category that employs the reflexive marker '*se*', but whose syntactic and semantic characteristics differ from the reflexive, inchoative, impersonal and passive structures that also make use of the reflexive clitic as well (Lekakou, 2003). Different researchers have approached the examination of middle constructions by taking into account crosslinguistic considerations. Lekakou (2003) looks at middles in English (1), Dutch (2), Greek (3) and Russian, considering them as unergative structures:

(1)   This book reads easily
(2)   it boek leest gemakkelijk
       'this book read-3S easily'
(3)   Afto to vivlio diavazete efxarista
       'this the book read-PASS-3S with pleasure'

Her analysis identifies the essential characteristics of middles as three semantic properties: (1) the notional object is the subject; (2) the agent receives an arbitrary interpretation; (3) the otherwise eventive verb receives a modal reading and is a derived state. Lekakou holds that the crosslinguistic variation regarding the possible unergative and passive interpretations is due to morphosyntactic properties of the languages, such as imperfectivity. For this reason, Greek allows the explicitation of the modal operator, and therefore licenses the encoding of the middle interpretation in the passives, while English needs to make use of an unergative construction where there is an implicit modal operator and a syntactically implicit agent.

Hulk and Cornips (2000) also address the issue of middle formations and, similarly to Lekakou, they look at the crosslinguistic commonalities.

Mainly, they center their attention on the fact that middles and passives share two essential properties: (1) that the logical subject argument is syntactically absent but semantically present; and that (2) the grammatical subject is indeed the logical object. These researchers (Hulk and Cornips, 2000) focus their study on English (4), French (5) and Dutch (6):

(4)   This shirt washes well
(5)   Cette chemise se lave facilement
      'This shirt CLIT. MIDDLE washes easily'
(6)   Dit hemd wast goed
      'This shirt washes well'

Hulk and Cornips stress the importance of the Affectedness Constraint condition in middles according to which, if the object is not affected by the action, the middle formation will necessarily be taken as ungrammatical. Thus, they support the hypothesis that the reflexive '*se*' plays an aspectual role in middles and relate the notion of 'affectedness' to the aspectual impact of the clitic on the state of the verb. In other words, as an outcome of the middle voice, the active voice of the verb turns into a state.

As Hulk and Cornips, Lekakou (2003) points out that middles in French behave like unaccusatives and that their agent is syntactically active:

(7)   Ce livre se lit facilement
      'This book CLIT. MIDDLE reads easily'

However, according to her approach, the notion of 'middle constructions' has to be limited to an interpretation of a particular syntactic structure, given that she finds it impossible to characterize them syntactically in a uniform way across languages. For Lekakou, middle constructions behave in either an unergative way as in English and Dutch or in an unaccusative way as in French and Greek (Lekakou, 2003).

Middles in Spanish

Middles in Spanish seem to behave in an unaccusative way like in French and Greek, although involving more subtle semantics. In Spanish, the use of the clitic '*se*' in the formation of most middle constructions makes them share some surface characteristics with reflexive and impersonal constructions. However, the semantics of middles need to be read through a series of internal properties that Mendikoetxea (1999) enumerates in the following way:

First, middle *SE* constructions involve (primarily) accomplishment (ACC) and activity (ACT) predicates (8, 9):

(8)   Este libro se lee fácilmente.   ACC
      'This book reads easily'
(9)   Este coche se conduce con facilidad.   ACT

'This car drives easily'

Second, middle *SE* constructions are generic statives with a topic-comment structure: the predicate expresses an inherent quality of the DP (10):

(10) Este libro se vende bien (porque el tema es de gran interés, porque tiene una tapa llamativa, etc.)
'This book sells well' (due to its interesting topic, or its cover design, etc.)

Third, the DP must be definite and pre-verbal (11, 12):

(11) Los pantalones de algodón no se planchan fácilmente.
'Cotton pants don't iron easily'
(12) No se planchan fácilmente los pantalones de algodón. (*middle)
'Cotton pants are not easily ironed'/*'Cotton pants don't iron easily'

Fourth, the DP is specific, or it is interpreted as 'representative of its class' (13):

(13) Una camisa se abotona por delante.
'A shirt buttons in front'

Fifth, the external argument is suppressed (14):

(14) Este libro se lee fácilmente (*para ayudar a los estudiantes)
'This book reads easily (*in order to help the students)

Sixth, the sentence has imperfective grammatical aspect (15, 16):

(15) El Quijote se lee/leía fácilmente.
'Don Quijote reads/read (imp) easily'
(16) El Quijote se leyó fácilmente. (*middle)
'Don Quijote was read easily/*read (pret) easily'

Each one of these properties was taken into account at the time of designing the grammaticality judgment as well as the truth value judgment tasks.

The Generative SLA Perspective Regarding the Acquisition of Middles and Impersonal Passive Constructions

The initial approach reported in this chapter examines the acquisition of middles and impersonal passives from the generative SLA perspective, in the case of participants who were in the process of acquiring Spanish as an L2. This criterion assumed Spanish as 'second language' in the sense formerly proposed by Sharwood Smith (1994), where it functions as a cover term for any additional language acquired after the first one. According to this viewpoint, the status of middle constructions in any non-L1 language(s) that might be part of the linguistic repertoire of the subjects is irrelevant since what is tested is the accessibility to the syntactic and semantic features of the construction in the target language. Under this assumption, the learnability problem would be that Spanish middles are distinguishable by context only, since the morphosyntactic markers may represent grounds for semantic misinterpretation, if a crosslinguistic analogy was established.

On the other hand, the possibility of transfer from L1 may be considered since the study bases the prediction based on the Full Transfer Full Access hypothesis (Schwartz & Sprouse, 1994, 1996). Most of the participants have English as an L1, which makes the comparison of the status of the structure in English and Spanish relevant for the analysis. In particular, these languages share the fact that the logical subject is syntactically absent but semantically present, and the grammatical subject is actually the logical object. However, the languages differ radically in the sense that English does not make use of clitics or any other morphological marker in order to mark middles as does Spanish. It would be possible to say that the middle clitic is null in English, and overt in Spanish. In other words, these two languages behave rather differently with respect to middles, given that English exhibits an unergative structure, while Spanish displays unaccusativity (17, 18):

(17)   This book sells well
(18)   Este libro se vende bien
       'this book CLIT MIDDLE sells well'

The study includes as well three participants who do not have English as L1. One subject has Cantonese L1, another has Russian as L1 and the third has French as L1. These subjects were included in the study to test if full access to UG would allow them to acquire the structure in the L2, regardless of the status of the construction in their L1. As has being noted above, Lekakou (2003) argues that the structure of middles in Russian is similar to that in English, in the sense that they are unergative constructions. From this perspective, the situation of the L1 Russian speaker would be comparable to that of English L1 speakers regarding transfer processes. The French L1 speaker would be facing surface similarities between French and Spanish structures, due to the use of the clitic '*se*' in both languages, but not in both cases. While Spanish maintains the same clitic for both structures, but assigning it different semantics, French uses the clitic '*se*' only for middles since the clitic 'on' is used for impersonals. In fact this difference might constitute a misleading reference when distinguishing the internal features of Spanish middles. As for the Cantonese L1 speaker, Yu (2006) has argued that this language has indeed a system of clitics in place, but these are not accepted as grammatical at the time of expressing middles. From this perspective, the subject would initially have difficulties when acquiring the Spanish clitic system used in middles, if no UG access allows him to reset the parameters. But it is important to remember that according to Schwartz and Sprouse (1994, 1996) full transfer from the L1 pertains to the *initial* states of acquisition only, and that full access to UG is understood to function as a 'reshaping mechanism' of the learner's interlanguage in order to attain the features and feature strength exhibited in the target language. Therefore, only advanced learners will exhibit a full acquisition of the middle clitic in Spanish, demonstrating a more accurate understanding of its morphological and semantic particularities, while the learners with lower proficiency levels will exhibit some optionality in their responses. As a result, for the present study, that the status of middle constructions is in the subjects' L1 is not relevant, since the study focuses on intermediate stages of acquisition, where they may have already overcome the initial stages of full transfer.

In contrast, other scholars (Müller & Hulk, 2001; Paradis & Navarro, 2003; Sorace, 2003, 2004) have found that 'interfaces between syntax and other cognitive systems (i.e. discourse pragmatics, lexical semantics) exhibit more developmental instability than narrow syntax' (Sorace, 2004: 143). In other words, the recurrent optionality of L2 learners' grammars may be due to an actual indetermination at the interfaces level. For this reason, both the inconsistent performance and the judgments that L2 acquirers reveal in language tasks, which are different than those produced by native speakers, may actually be reflecting a representational deficit to synchronize different types of knowledge (Sorace, 2004).

Methodology

Given that variability in the learners' performance seems to be the rule among L2 acquirers, this study assumed the working hypothesis that Spanish L2 learners will exhibit some difficulty in the recognition and acceptance of middle constructions, thus differing from native speakers' linguistic behavior.

The participants in this study were 15 adult learners of Spanish L2, who had been exposed to the L2 mainly in post-secondary academic settings, for an average of five hours a week, for at least two academic years. These participants followed a series of Spanish language classification tests that included a Spanish cloze test and a test on Spanish grammar. The results placed eight participants within the advanced group and the remaining seven as high intermediate. The L1 of the subjects was mainly English, although one French, one Russian and one Cantonese L1 subjects were also included. The inclusion of these subjects was intended to allow for the examination of the full accessibility to the acquisition of Spanish middles, regardless of the status of the structure in their L1 as Duffield and White (1999) propose. Fifteen adult Spanish native speakers who represent different Spanish dialects composed the control group. All the participants were exposed to two sets of tasks in order to assess their acceptance and recognition levels regarding Spanish middle constructions with the clitic *se*, a grammaticality judgment task with 48 sentences and a true value judgment task, which included 35 items.

Grammaticality Judgment Task

This task was based on single sentences that the learner had to rate on a scale of –2 to 2 according to acceptability. The sentences sampled the criteria that, according to Mendikoetxea (1999) and Kempchinski (2004), characterize middle constructions in Spanish. In this way, the test included, in random order, the following groups of sentences.

Sentences with middle constructions with the clitic *se*

These were grammatical sentences that showed middle constructions with the use of the clitic (19). They were contrasted with sentences like (20) in which the sentence does not show the clitic:

(19)   Yo compro blusas de seda porque se lavan fácilmente
       'I buy blouses of silk because CLIT wash easily'
(20)   *En la casa de mi abuela aprendí que el pan corta con la mano
       'In the house of my grandmother I learned that the bread cuts with the hand'

Sentences with stative verbs

These sentences tested the comprehension of statives (21). They were designed with the intention of contrasting the ungrammatical statives with the clitic (22) and ungrammatical statives without the use of the clitic (23):

(21)   María posee una finca
       'Mary owns a farm'
(22)   *La casa se tiene fácil
       'The house CLIT owns easily'
(23)   *El dinero quiere frecuentemante
       'The money wants frequently'

Sentences which included specific DPs with the use of the clitic

This group of sentences was intended to test the perception of the need for a specific DP in order to obtain grammatical middle constructions. For this reason, a group of sentences with a non-specific quantifier (algún/a) (24) was included in order to contrast the reactions of participants:

(24)   *Algun condimento se digiere bien

'Some spice CLIT digests well'

Truth value judgment task

This questionnaire was designed keeping in mind the semantic–syntax interface in which the middle *se* is found. For this reason, each item of the questionnaire consisted of a short paragraph whose semantics forced the middle interpretation or ruled it out. The participant would have to choose, from two options, a subsequent sentence that best followed the semantic implications of the specific context of the paragraph. Participants had to choose between two sentences that would be grammatical in isolated contexts, but whose grammaticality in this case depended on the context of the paragraph. The test included the following type of paragraphs.

Paragraphs that contrasted middles vs. reflexives

These paragraphs contrasted the middle interpretation to the reflexive interpretation. Both types of constructions exhibit in their surface structure the clitic se, with the sole difference of the optionality of the overtness of the subject in the reflexives. In other words, in middle constructions the clitic is placed pre-verbally with an obligatory overt patient in subject position, while in reflexive constructions the clitic still maintains the pre-verbal position, but the subject is covert (25, 26):

(25) Luisa y Ana están preparando un almuerzo rápido. Luisa le pregunta a Ana: -¿Qué le agrego a la pasta?
'Luisa and Ana are making a fast meal. Luisa asks Ana: What do I put in the spaghetti?'
(a) La pasta se come con salsa. (Expected answer/middle)
'(One) eats spaghetti with sauce'
(b) Se come con salsa la pasta. (Unexpected answer/reflexive)
'REFLEX eats spaghetti with sauce'
(26) A Luisa le parece que Pedro come muy extraño porque
'Luisa thinks that Pedro eats in a strange way because'
(a) El arroz se come con mayonesa (Unexpected/middle)
'The rice has to be eaten with mayonaisse'
(b) Se come el arroz con mayonesa (Expected answer/reflexive)
REFLEX eats the rice with mayonaisse'

Paragraphs that contrasted middles vs. [±perfective] ASP

According to the analysis of Kempchinski (2004), in Spanish middles the feature [–perfective] is essential for the middle interpretation, while the opposite turns out to be an impediment to it. Therefore middles involve primarily activities rather than achievements in order to convey the lack of an end point for the event. To test the comprehension of this aspect, the task included a series of paragraphs where the semantics of [±perfective] would sanction or reject the middle analysis and therefore determine the choice of [±perfective] sentence to appropriately follow the story (27, 28). There were two groups of these paragraphs as shown here.

Paragraphs with [+perfective] context and therefore *middle interpretation

(27) Luisa preparó un pastel de manzana, pero no lo pudo servir porque:
'Luisa made an apple pie but she could not put it on the table because':
  (a) El pastel se quemó en el horno. (Expected answer [+perfective] ASP)
        'The pie got burned in the oven'
  (b) El pastel se quema en el horno. (Unexpected answer middle[-perfective] ASP) 'The pie gets burned in the oven'

Paragraphs with [–perfective] ASP context and therefore middle interpretation

(28) Ana *se* dió cuenta de que su saco estaba mojado y lo colgó a la sombra porque:
'Ana realized her jacket was wet and she hung it in the shade because':
  (a) La lana se seca a la sombra. (Expected answer [–perfective] ASP)
        'Wool has to be dried in the shade'
  (b) 'La lana se secó a la sombra' (Unexpected answer [+perfective] ASP)
        'The wool got dried in the shade'

These two paragraphs present an interesting learnability problem given that no formal instruction in the classroom will make explicit the syntactic or semantic differences between the constructions in question, and the availability of negative evidence is unlikely. In essence, the contrast of these syntactic structures (middles vs. reflexives and middles vs. active/ passive aspectuality) would constitute a clear example of the poverty of stimulus problem, where the accessibility to UG principles would be the only tool that learners were left with in order to achieve proper L2 competence.

Results and discussion

The answers obtained through the grammaticality judgment task were tabulated following the [–2 to 2] scale that the participants used to express their acceptability of the grammaticality of the sentence. (See examples of sentences 19–24.) A series of tests of means and an ANOVA statistical analysis (where appropriate) were performed on the acceptance level to each group of phrases, in order to determine if the linguistic behavior of both the intermediate and advanced Spanish L2 learners was similar to that of the native speakers.

We measured the acceptance by each group of participants to phrases where middle constructions exhibited the clitic *se*, and to phrases with middle constructions that did not include the use of the clitic. No statistical difference was reported. Through the comparison of means it is possible to see how the three groups of participants clearly preferred the phrases with the clitic, and how advanced students followed closely the behavior of native speakers. As expected, natives and advanced learners rejected the phrases without the clitic, although not as categorically.

Intermediate students tended to accept the phrases with the clitic, and this tendency diminished in the case of phrases without the clitic, revealing intuitions similar to those of natives (Figure 1.1).

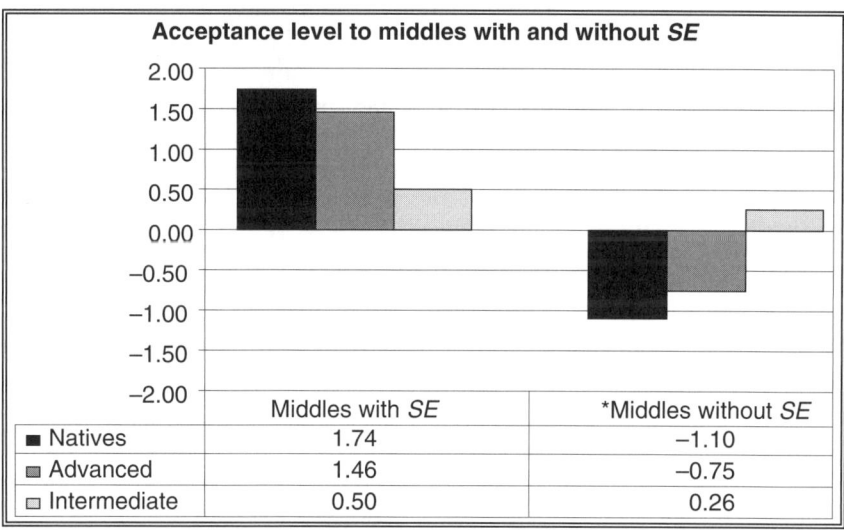

	Middles with *SE*	*Middles without *SE*
■ Natives	1.74	−1.10
▨ Advanced	1.46	−0.75
▢ Intermediate	0.50	0.26

Figure 1.1 ANOVA for acceptance to middles with and without *SE* – considering the advanced and intermediate groups grammaticality judgment task

Table 1.1 Acceptance to middles with and without *SE*

			Sum of squares	df	Mean square	F	Sig.
Natives 1/2 with *SE* GJT * interm 1/2 with *SE* GJT	Between groups	(combined)	0.058	4	0.015	1.717	0.512
	Within groups		0.008	1	0.008		
	Total		0.066	5			

From the ANOVA test (Table 1.1) we can see that both the intermediate and advanced groups showed answers highly similar to the natives in the case of acceptance of middles with *se*, to the extent that an ANOVA considering the advanced group was not possible due to the data proximity between the two groups.

Regarding the phrases that considered statives, Figure 1.2 compiles the average of acceptance per individual of grammatical phrases with statives, ungrammatical stative phrases that included the use of the clitic, and ungrammatical phrases with statives that did not include the clitic. The acceptance level to grammatical phrases with statives is high in the three groups, which allows us to think that they do understand the meaning of this type of verb. Also, the three groups of participants rejected categorically the ungrammatical stative phrases without the clitic, while some uncertainty was registered by the three groups concerning the ungrammatical phrases with statives that did include the clitic. This may be due to the fact that middles are perceived as [–perfective] ASP, as well as statives. The statistical analysis of the responses of these groups in the case of statives with *se* shows a small standard deviation for both, the intermediate group (s.d. 0.74) and the advanced group (s.d. 1.24), which reveals that the judgments are unified for the same criteria. In the case of statives without se, both the intermediate and advanced groups show a standard deviation of 0.24. An ANOVA revealed a non-significant difference within the groups (Table 1.2). Again, the advanced participants reveal intuitions similar to those of native speakers only.

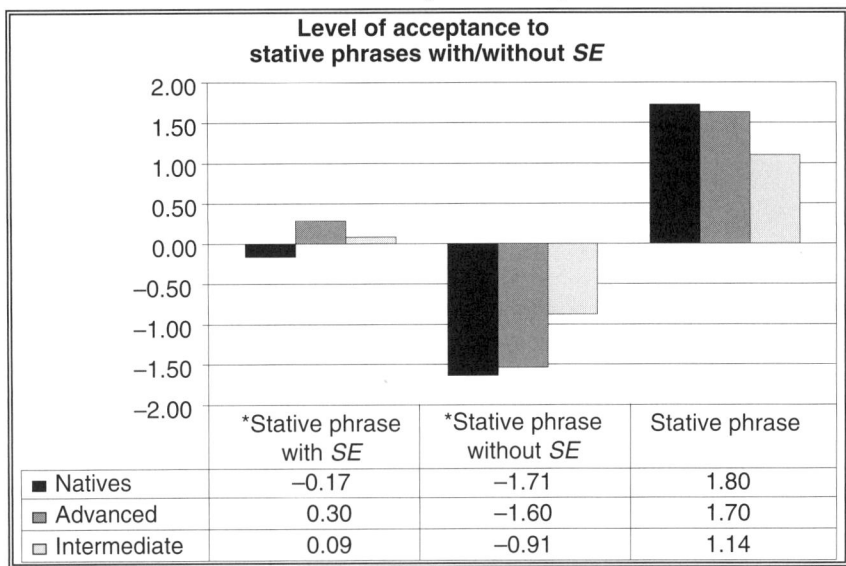

	*Stative phrase with *SE*	*Stative phrase without *SE*	Stative phrase
■ Natives	−0.17	−1.71	1.80
▨ Advanced	0.30	−1.60	1.70
☐ Intermediate	0.09	−0.91	1.14

Figure 1.2 Acceptance to statives with and without *SE* grammaticality judgment task

Table 1.2 ANOVA test for rejection to ungrammatical statives without *SE* by native and advanced groups

			Sum of squares	df	Mean square	F	Sig.
Natives * statives without *SE* GJT * adv. *statives without *SE* GJT	Between groups Within groups Total	(combined)	0.191 0.054 0.246	3 1 4	0.064 0.054	1.172	0.576

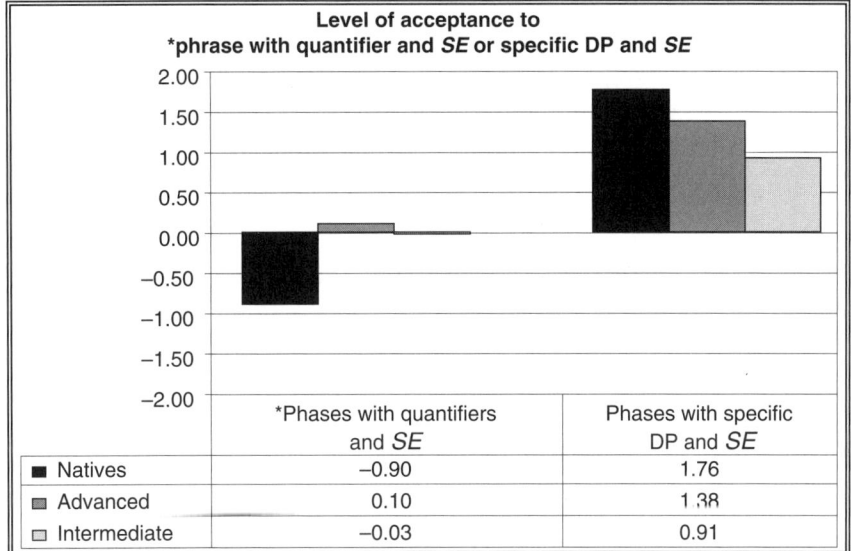

Figure 1.3 Acceptance to quantifiers with *SE* and specific DPs with *SE* grammaticality judgment task

Figure 1.3 reveals a much higher preference by all three groups of participants for phrases with middle constructions that included a specific DP. On the other hand, natives were the only ones who were certain about the rejection of those phrases with middle constructions that used the quantifier 'algún/a'. Advanced and intermediate learners showed some insecurity regarding this type of constructions judging them almost neutrally.

The ANOVA test on the results regarding the comparison of the groups in the acceptance of specific DPs and quantifiers with *SE* and specific DPs with *SE* showed no statistical significance (Table 1.3)

Table 1.3 ANOVA for acceptance to phrases with specific DPs and quantifiers with *SE* and specific DPs with *SE* by the native and intermediate groups

			Sum of squares	df	Mean square	F	Sig.
Natives specific DP GJT * interm. specific DP GJT	Between groups	(combined)	0.094	3	0.031	0.390	0.793
	Within groups		0.080	1	0.080		
	Total		0.174	4			

Table 1.4 ANOVA for acceptance of sentences with quantifiers by native and intermediate groups

			Sum of squares	df	Mean square	F	Sig.
Natives quantifiers GJT * interm. quantifiers GJT	Between groups	(combined)	0.429	3	0.143	58.371	0.096
	Within groups		0.002	1	0.002		
	Total		0.431	4			

Table 1.5 ANOVA for acceptance of sentences with quantifiers by native and advanced groups in the grammaticality judgment task

			Sum of squares	df	Mean square	F	Sig.
Natives quantifiers GJT * adv. quantifiers GJT	Between groups	(combined)	0.128	2	0.064	0.423	0.703
	Within groups		0.303	2	0.152		
	Total		0.431	4			

In the same way, the ANOVA analysis did not show a significant difference between the responses of the groups in the case of sentences with quantifiers. However, the intermediate group's (Table 1.4) answers seemed to be further apart from those of natives ($p = 0.096$) than the advanced group's answers ($p = 7.03$) (Table 1.5), which indicates that the advanced group preferences were closer to those from the native group, than the intermediate responses.

Regarding the truth value judgment task the participants were given paragraphs that portrayed a context where the reflexive or the middle interpretation would require a subsequent reflexive or middle phrase respectively. The participants had to be able to recognize this precise aspect of the semantics of the paragraph, since the phrases to choose from were always grammatical by themselves, but not necessarily as subsequent phrases to the paragraph in particular. In other words, grammaticality would be determined by the semantics of the paragraph only (see 23–26 for examples). The tabulation was based on the [0, 1] values for unexpected and expected answers respectively.

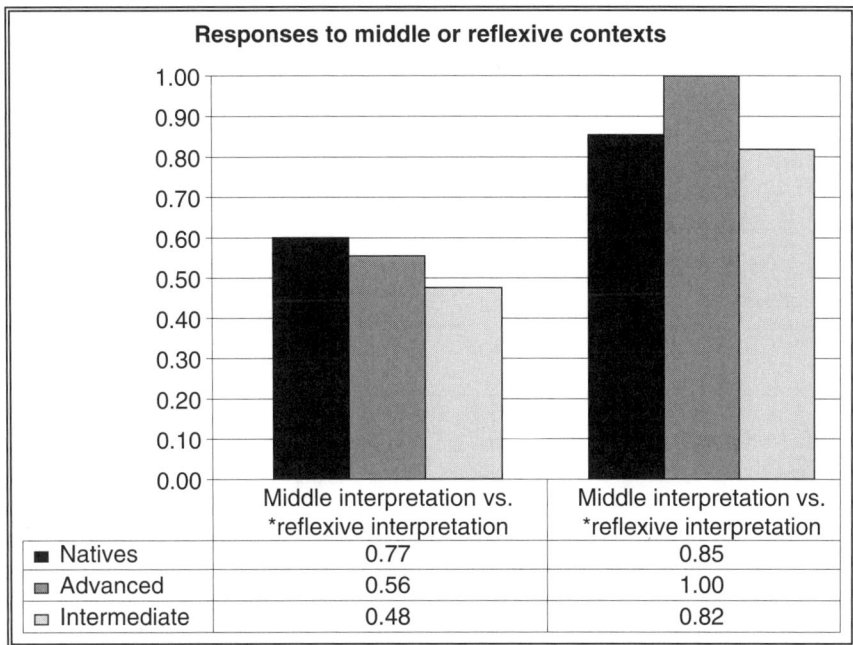

Responses to middle or reflexive contexts

	Middle interpretation vs. *reflexive interpretation	Middle interpretation vs. *reflexive interpretation
Natives	0.77	0.85
Advanced	0.56	1.00
Intermediate	0.48	0.82

Figure 1.4 Responses to middle or reflexive contexts in the truth value judgment tasks

Figure 1.4 shows the participants' reactions regarding the choice between a subsequent phrase with a reflexive construction or a middle construction, according to a reflexive or middle context in the preceding paragraph.

Comparing the means of the groups, it can be said that it was easier for all participants to recognize the contexts that implied a reflexive interpretation than the paragraphs that implied a middle interpretation. It is interesting to note how natives did not react as categorically as expected, and even produced a lower number of expected responses than advanced students in the case of recognition of reflexives. This may be attributable to possible regional differences between the Spanish dialects included in the control group, which in turn may conflict with the regional dialect of the test designer. This particular set of results is puzzling and calls for further research.

The ANOVA analysis of the responses indicates that the intermediate group (Table 1.6) behaves statistically differently from the natives ($p = 0.009$) while the advanced group (Table 1.7) showed similar behavior to that of natives ($p = 0.433$).

Table 1.6 ANOVA for responses to middle or reflexive contexts by native and intermediate groups

			Sum of squares	df	Mean square	F	Sig.
Natives 1/2* ref TVJT * interm. 1/2* ref TVJT	Between groups	(combined)	0.568	3	0.189	115.935	0.009
	Within groups		0.003	2	0.002		
	Total		0.571	5			

Table 1.7 ANOVA for responses to middle or reflexive contexts by native and advanced groups

			Sum of squares	df	Mean square	F	Sig.
Natives 1/2* ref TVJT * adv. 1/2* ref TVJT	Between groups	(combined)	0.391	3	0.130	1.433	0.433
	Within groups		0.180	2	0.090		
	Total		0.571	5			

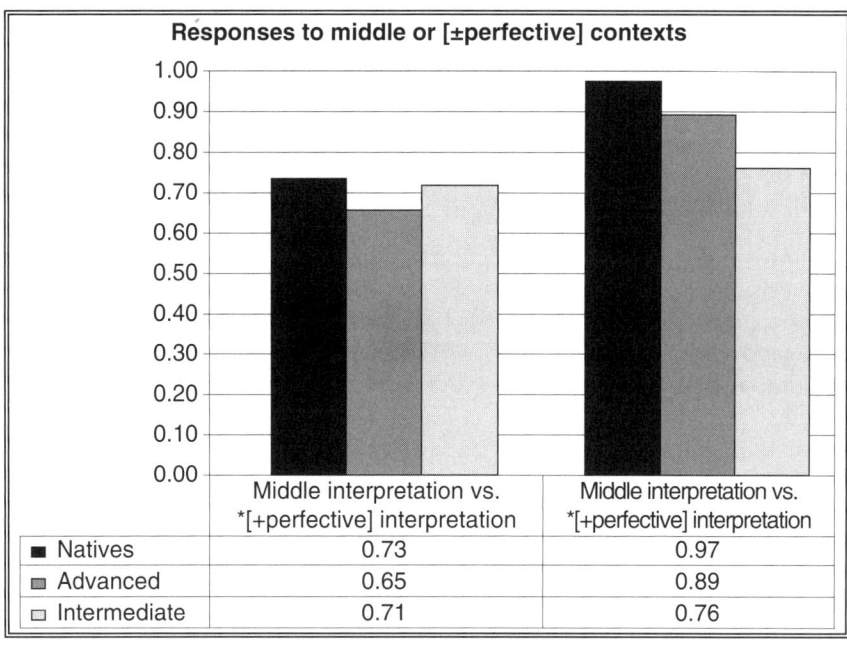

Figure 1.5 Responses to middle or [±perfective] contexts in truth value judgment tasks

The second set of results includes paragraphs with [± perfective] ASP. In the case of [–perfective] contexts, it was expected that the participants would prefer a subsequent middle sentence instead of a [+perfective] phrase. The contrary scenario ruled out the middle interpretation and called for a [+perfective] subsequent phrase. Figure 1.5 shows a higher

Table 1.8 ANOVA for responses to middle or [±perfective] contexts by native and intermediate groups

			Sum of squares	df	Mean square	F	Sig.
Natives 1/2* active ASP TVJT * interm. 1/2* active ASP TVJT	Between groups	(combined)	0.582	2	0.291	38.889	0.007
	Within groups		0.022	3	0.007		
	Total		0.604	5			

Table 1.9 ANOVA for responses to middle or [±perfective] contexts by native and advanced groups

			Sum of squares	df	Mean square	F	Sig.
Natives 1/2* active ASP TVJT * adv. 1/2* active ASP TVJT	Between groups	(combined)	0.575	2	0.288	29.641	0.011
	Within groups		0.029	3	0.010		
	Total		0.604	5			

number in the case of recognition of [+perfective] contexts for all three groups, which allows us to deduce that these were easier to recognize than the middle contexts.

The ANOVA reveals that in both cases, the intermediate and advanced groups showed statistically different behaviors from that of natives. In the case of the intermediate group, $p = 0.007$, and for the advanced, $p - 0.011$ (Tables 1.8 and 1.9 respectively).

However, in the case of the acceptance of contexts where the middle interpretation was expected, and the aspectual interpretation had to be ruled out, the intermediate group does not show a statistically significant difference in their responses compared to those of natives (Table 1.10), while the data from the advanced group (Table 1.11), indicate that they do have different judgments than those of natives. In this case, the intermediate group seems to exhibit closer intuitions to natives than the advanced group, which again turns out as a challenging scenario for future research.

Table 1.10 ANOVA for responses to ungrammatical aspectual interpretations by native and intermediate groups

			Sum of squares	df	Mean square	F	Sig.
Natives 1/2* (ASP) TVJT * intrm. 1/2* (ASP) TVJT	Between groups	(combined)	0.008	2	0.004	1.714	0.290
	Within groups		0.010	4	0.002		
	Total		0.018	6			

Table 1.11 ANOVA for responses to ungrammatical aspectual interpretations by native and advanced groups

			Sum of squares	df	Mean square	F	Sig.
Natives 1/2* (ASP)	Between groups	(combined)	0.016	2	0.008	12.857	0.018
TVJT * adv. *1/2	Within groups		0.002	4	0.001		
(ASP) TVJT	Total		0.018	6			

The set of analysis of this study points to conflicting conclusions. In general the comparison of the means in the grammaticality judgment support the Full Access hypothesis (Schwartz & Sprouse, 1996, 1998) given that the participants had a broadly successful recognition of the syntactic characteristics of middle constructions. In most cases, the reactions of advanced students were close to those of native speakers, while the intermediate students usually showed more gradient assessments. This fact may be interpreted as the representation of a gradual process of the acquisition of middle constructions, where in the initial stages of the IL only some sensibility to the new morphology in middles is registered, with a higher degree of optionality.

On the other hand, the responses to the truth value judgment are consistent with (Müller & Hulk, 2001; Paradis & Navarro, 2003; Sorace, 2003, 2004), since they illustrated that middle semantics are harder to recognize in the case of reflexive or [+perfective] contexts. The mixed results indicate that in some cases the intermediate group reflects closer intuitions to those of natives than the intuitions revealed by advanced students. In other instances, both the intermediate and advanced groups showed different tendencies than the ones shown by the native speakers. These results may be attributable to a state of permanent indetermination of IL grammars, given that participants did reveal a representational deficit at the time to synchronize syntactic and semantic knowledge (Sorace, 2004). This study should only be taken as exploratory given the small number of subjects involved, which also affected the statistical significance of the testing. For the same reason, the conclusions are only tentative and invite to further investigation.

The TLA Perspective Regarding the Acquisition of Middles and Impersonal Passive Constructions

An alternative reading of the results of the study reported above suggests that previously acquired foreign languages might indeed be a variable that influences the participants' perception of middles and impersonals in Spanish, throughout all the stages of acquisition beyond the initial. In order to look into this, part of the study was replicated, this time giving a closer look at the linguistic history of the subjects, and necessarily questioning the globalizing status of 'L2' assigned to any (or all) languages acquired after the first one.

The learnability problem for Spanish L3 learners

From this new perspective, the learnability of Spanish L3 implies other considerations. On the one hand, the screening of the subjects needed to follow stricter criteria regarding the linguistic background of the participants. Therefore, in this second stage of the study,[3] all the subjects had English as L1, French as L2 and Spanish as L3 only (see below). In addition, the consideration of the learnability problem would necessarily include a contrastive analysis of the middle structure as it is exhibited in the languages of the subjects. It has been said that middle constructions exhibit some common syntactic and semantic characteristics crosslinguistically (Hulk & Cornips, 2000; Lekakou, 2003). In the case of either unergative or unaccusative types of constructions, the logical subject is syntactically absent but semantically present, and the grammatical subject is actually the logical object. However, contrasting the French and Spanish structures with the English structure, the use of overt clitics in the former two languages appears to be the surface difference with the latter. In other words, in the former languages, the clitic 'se' may explicit the presence of middles while in the latter there are no overt morphological markers for middles. This may cause problems for the L1 English learners of Spanish if we assume that they will undergo a full transfer process from the L1 at the time of acquiring an L3.

On the other hand, if the learner is to transfer the knowledge from a previously acquired language other than the L1, in this case French L2, it may also constitute a confusing scenario. The surface similarity between French and Spanish may turn out to be deceptive since both employ the clitic 'se' for middle constructions (29 French, (Hulk & Cornips, 2000) 30 Spanish). However, French does exhibit the use of a different morphological marker 'on' for impersonal constructions (31) – unlike Spanish (32):

(29) Ce livre se lit facilement
     'This book CLIT. MIDDLE reads easily'
(30) Este libro se lee fácilmente
     'This book CLIT. MIDDLE reads easily'
(31) On travaille toute la semaine.
     CLIT. IMPER work all week.
     '(We) work all week.'
(32) Se trabaja toda la semana
     CLIT. IMPER work all week
     '(We) work all week.'

Thus, the learner of Spanish L3, whose linguistic background is English L1 and French L2, faces a challenging scenario of discerning the particular

traits of Spanish semantic features between middle and impersonal constructions, given that in this latter language the overt use of the clitic in
both cases disguises the internal syntactic differences between them. In
other words, the semantic features that differentiate middles from impersonals in Spanish have to be recognized through context only.

Methodology

According to the Full Access hypothesis (Schwartz & Sprouse, 1996,
1998; White, 2003) the learner would utilize the L1 grammar as a basis to
acquire the full set of morphological and syntactic characteristics of the
L2. It is also assumed that there will be a gradual process of parameter
resetting of the L2 features and eventually the learner will fully converge
on the L2 grammar. In this sense, only advanced learners would exhibit a
full acquisition of middles in Spanish, disregarding of the linguistic history
of the participants.

On the other hand, in the newer research field of TLA, a more detailed
picture of the role of the previously acquired languages is considered. In
1998, Williams and Hammarberg proposed the Role-Function model
according to which previously acquired languages may play an instrumental or supplier role in L3. They found that these roles might shift over
time, interacting in the acquisition and development of L3. More recently,
Hammarberg (2001) identified a number of factors that have been found
to affect the acquisition of a third or subsequent language:

(1) Typological similarity between the languages: Morphosyntactically
    and culturally.
(2) Proficiency level in each of the previously acquired languages.
(3) Recency of use of any language in the linguistic repertoire of the
    speaker.

In sum, this partial replication of the first study aimed to test if, as the
Full Transfer Full Access hypothesis proposes, it is the L1 from which the
learners derive their assumptions regarding the syntactic characteristics
of the language being acquired, or if, on the other hand, the principles of
typological similarity and proficiency allow the learner to discriminate
between the previously acquired languages in order to choose the source
language (L1 or L2 in the case of trilinguals) that would facilitate the
acquisition process.

The participants in the study were all adult students of an intensive
intermediate–advanced Spanish summer session offered by the University
of Western Ontario. They completed a language profile questionnaire
where they provided information about their linguistic background as to
the time and conditions in which they acquired their foreign languages.
This language profile also included a section in which they self-assessed
their competence in French and Spanish in all the four communicative

skills. According to Marian *et al.* (2006) self-assessment has been proven as an effective tool of measurement in the evaluation of language profiles of multilingual populations in research and clinical settings. The answers to the language profile allowed us to select 13 subjects whose age ranged from 19 to 40 years of age, and who had exclusively English L1, French L2 and Spanish L3. The answers to this questionnaire also revealed that most of the subjects started acquiring French during elementary school, and that all the participants had started their Spanish L3 acquisition in their late puberty or adult years. According to the self-assessment of French proficiency, the subjects were classified into two groups, a classification that was subsequently used for the analysis of the results:

Lower French command (LowerFR): $n = 7$
Higher French command (HigherFR): $n = 6$

The Spanish self-reported measures were consistent with the intermediate Spanish course level that all participants were attending. This course was focused on the learning of reading and writing skills, with a reduced percentage of the class dedicated to oral production and listening comprehension. This facilitated the completion of the grammaticality judgment task for data collection, since it was administered in writing only.

The replicated section of the study was based on the same core design of the grammaticality judgment task used in the previous study, where the subjects were required to interpret a given paragraph and then choose the most suitable sentence to follow the meaning of the paragraph. Each paragraph included a short description of a scene, but this time it was followed by *three* sentences – instead of two as in the previous study – that the subject would choose from in order to conclude the context scenario. These sentences exhibited the overt morphological characteristics of the three languages of the participants.

In other words, each questionnaire item would be composed of:

- A paragraph portraying a particular context (33.a).
- A short question that would make reference to the paragraph and would ask for a concluding sentence that logically followed the context of the paragraph (33.b).
- Three sentences: (1) a sentence that would imitate the surface structure proper of middles in English, without clitic, and morphosyntactically and semantically unacceptable in Spanish (33.c); (2) A sentence with the use of the clitic '*se*' – as in French middles – but whose syntactic structure would imply different semantics in Spanish. This sentence would be unacceptable for following the context initially presented in the item of the questionnaire (33.d); (3) a sentence that employed the middle '*se*' of Spanish structures, that would match

syntactically and semantically the context initially presented for each item – the expected answer (33.e).

(33.a) Luisa y Ana están preparando el almuerzo. Luisa le pregunta a Ana:
        'Luisa and Ana are making lunch. Luisa asks Ana:'
(33.b) ¿Qué le agrego a la pasta? Y Ana le responde:
        'What do I add to the spaghetti; and Ana answers:'
(33.c) La pasta come con salsa
        'Spaghetti eat with salsa'
(33.d) Se come la pasta con salsa
        CLIT REFLEX eats spaghetti with sauce
(33.e) La pasta se come con salsa
        Spaghetti CLIT MIDDLE eat with sauce
        '(One) eats spaghetti with sauce'

Results and discussion

The tabulation of the responses took into account the full identification of the morphosyntactic and semantic features of Spanish middles, as well as the preferences of the participants regarding the other two structures presented to them in each questionnaire item.

As can be seen in Figure 1.6 the data showed that the HigherFR participants tended to select the expected answer in a preponderant 66% of the cases, compared to 34% of the remaining answers in which undecided judgments between the rest of the structures were equally noted.

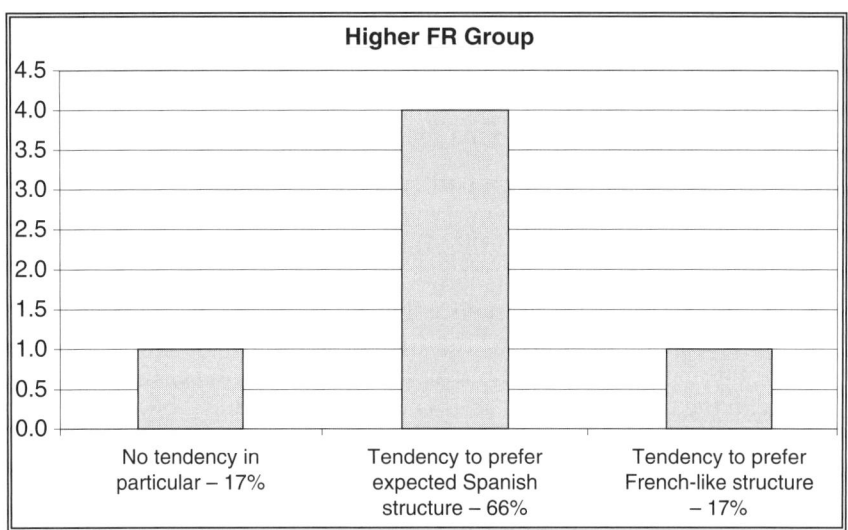

Figure 1.6 Computed answers of the HigherFR group

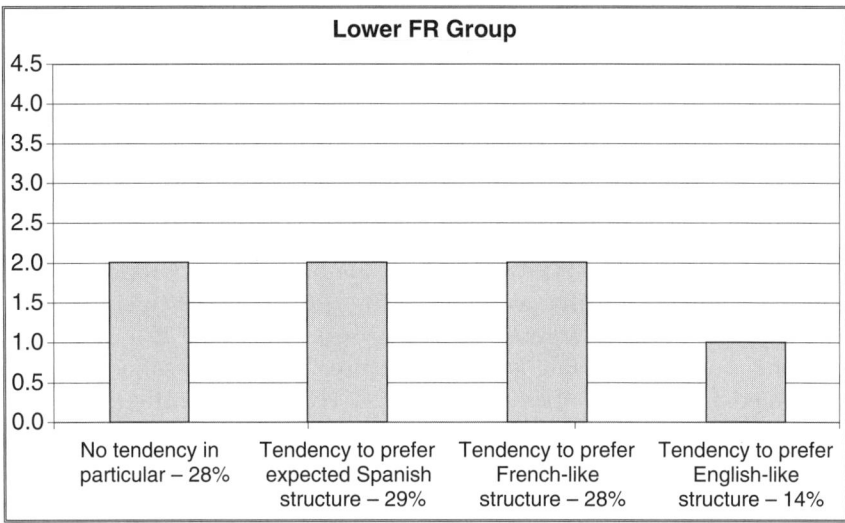

Figure 1.7 Computed answers of the LowerFR group

On the other hand, the LowerFR participants oscillated evenly between the structures that mimicked the French surface form, and the actual Spanish expected answers (28% and 29% respectively), with a high percentage of participants still opting for the structures that mimicked the English surface form (Figure 1.7).

In other words, the participants with a higher proficiency in French demonstrated more confidence and accuracy in their choice of the expected answer, whereas those with lesser command of the L2 were uncertain in their choice between the sentence that imitated the French middle structure and the one that actually portrayed the Spanish middle. In addition, these observations were confirmed by positive correlations between L2 proficiency and the level of expected answers. The participants with HigherFR showed a correlation of $r = 0.38$ between their self-assessment of FR proficiency and their test responses, while the correlation for the same factors in the case of LowerFR participants was $r = 0.32$.

The interpretation of these results suggests a number of observations. In the first place, it was observed that the principle of typological similarity stated by Hammarberg (2001) is applicable to the analysis of these data. According to this principle, typological proximity from previously acquired languages, French in this case, contributes effectively in the Spanish L3 acquisition process. Moreover, Cenoz *et al.* (2003: 104) adds that when there is a typologically closer L2, the learner tends to take it as a default supplier in the L3 acquisition process, over a typologically distant first language. In other words, having English L1 and French L2 in their linguistic background forced the participants to select the typologically closer language, French, as a resource language in the process of identification of the proper Spanish middle structure, and to discard the English reference due to the typological distance between this language and Spanish. It can be said that the supplier role of French played a part in the identification of the overt use of the clitic, against the covert clitic feature of English language.

It was also found that a higher level of L2 proficiency facilitates the successful recognition of the morphosyntactic and semantic features of the target L3 structure, as Hammarberg (2001) had initially proposed. This can be seen in the fact that over 65% of the HigherFR participants tended to choose the Spanish target structure, while less than the 20% of the participants preferred the English-like structure. These observations are corroborated by the fact that the statistical correlations between the L2 proficiency self-reports and the responses to the grammaticality judgment task turned out higher in the case of the HigherFR group, which suggests that there is indeed a relationship between L2 proficiency and L3 functioning. In addition, the principle of recency was also considered in the sense that the tasks were conducted after the totality of the subjects had been exposed to Spanish for a period of three hours. In this sense, the variable was neutral as an influential factor over the subjects' performance.

Following these results, it can be concluded that the Full Transfer Full Access hypothesis cannot be confirmed in this case of L3 acquisition process, since the learners did not seem to use the L1 to derive their assumptions regarding the characteristics of the language being acquired. Apparently, a more detailed explanation is needed on the subject of the specific function of previously acquired languages in L3 acquisition, than the one offered by the generative SLA framework. It would be worth considering if indeed there is an effect of previously acquired foreign languages, the same one that is producing the degree of indetermination in the syntax–semantics interface reported by Müller and Hulk (2001), Paradis and Navarro (2003), Sorace (2003, 2004) in the first study reported here. Unfortunately, the set of subjects involved in the first study was unavailable for such inquiry. However, as observed in the second set of subjects, the grouping of all the languages acquired after the L1 under a single umbrella called 'L2' turns out to be inadequate in the case of studies in trilingualism. The second study reported in this chapter shows how the participants discern between each of the previously acquired languages at the time of using them as resources in the acquisition of a new language. The results call for the use of a more precise terminology regarding the linguistic history of the participants in acquisition studies.

It is necessary to point out that both studies count on a rather small sample of subjects. This factor calls for caution in generalizing the results to other populations. In addition, it needs to be acknowledged that there are other variables that may have affected the results of the studies, for instance, the fact that the questionnaires were administered in writing only may have affected the preferences of the participants, since reading strategies and learning styles are involved. In sum, these studies appear as preliminary explorations of the nature of interlanguage performance, and constitute only an invitation to more elaborate and comprehensive research.

Notes

1. My sincere thanks to Dr Joyce Bruhn de Garavito and Dr Jeff Tennant for their support and direction in the production of this work. I am also very thankful to B. White for her comments on the editing of this chapter. All remaining mistakes are mine.
2. An earlier version of this study was published in the conference proceedings of the 2005 Annual Conference of the Canadian Linguistic Association.
3. A previous report of this study was presented at the 4th International Conference on Third Language Acquisition and Multilingualism. Fribourg, Switzerland, 2005.

References

Adjemian, C. (1976) On the nature of interlanguage systems. *Language Learning* 26, 297–320.

Bayona, P. (2005) Acquisition of middle constructions in Spanish L2. In Claire Gurski (ed.) *Proceedings from the Combined Session of the Canadian Linguistics Association Session and the Asociacion Canadiense de Hispanistas*. The University of Western Ontario, London, Ontario: Congress of Arts and Humanities, Canadian Linguisitics Association.

Bayona, P. (2007) Crosslinguistic influence in the acquisition of Spanish as a third language. PhD thesis, The University of Western Ontario, London, Ontario.

Beck, M.L. (1998) *Morphology and its Interfaces in Second Language Knowledge*. Amsterdam: John Benjamins.

Bley-Vroman, R. (1997) Features and patterns in foreign language learning. Second Language Research Forum, Nijmegen.

Bruhn de Garavito, J. and White, L. (2002) L2 acquisition of Spanish DPs: The status of grammatical features. In A.T. Perez-Leroux and J.M. Liceras (eds) *The Acquisition of Spanish Morphosyntax: The L1/L2 Connection* (pp. 151–176). Dordrecht: Kluwer.

Cenoz, J., Hufeisen, B. and Jessner, U. (2001) *Cross-linguistic Influence in Third Language Acquisition: Psycholinguistic Perspectives*. Clevedon: Multilingual Matters.

Cenoz, J., Hufeisen, B. and Jessner, U. (2003) The role of typology in the organization of the multilingual lexicon. In B. Hufeisen, U. Jessner and J. Cenoz (eds) *The Multilingual Lexicon* (pp. 103–116). Dordrecht: Kluwer Academic Publishers.

Chomsky, N. (1965) *Aspects of the Theory of Syntax*. Cambridge, MA: MIT Press.

Chomsky, N. (1995) *The Minimalist Program*. Cambridge, MA: MIT Press.

Clahsen, H. and Hong, U. (1995) Agreement and null subjects in German L2 development: New evidence from reaction-time experiments. *Second Language Research* 11, 57–87.

Clyne, M. (2003) *Dynamics of Language Contact*. Cambridge: Cambridge University Press.

Corder, S. (1967) The significance of learners' errors. *International Review of Applied Linguistics* 5, 161–170.

De Bot, K. (2004) The multilingual lexicon: Modelling selection and control. *International Journal of Multilingualism* 1 (1), 17–32.

Dewaele, J.M. (1998) Lexical inventions: French interlanguage as L2 versus L3. *Applied Linguistics* 19, 471–490.

Duffield, N. and White, L. (1999) Assessing L2 Knowledge of Spanish clitic placement: Converging methodologies. *Second Language Research* 15 (2), 133–160.

Eubank, L. (1996) Negation in early German–English interlanguage: More valueless features in the L2 initial state. *Second Language Research* 12, 73–106.

Hammarberg, B. (2001) Roles of L1 and L2 in L3 production and acquisition. In B. Hufeisen, U. Jessner and J. Cenoz (eds) *Cross-linguistic Influence in Third Language Acquisition: Psycholinguistic Perspectives* (pp. 21–41). Clevedon: Multilingual Matters.

Hawkins, R. and Chan, Y.H.C. (1997) The partial availability of the Universal Grammar in second language acquisition: The 'failed functional features hypothesis'. *Second Language Research* 13, 187–226.

Herdina, P. and Jessner, U. (2002) *A Dynamic Model of Multilingualism*. Clevedon: Multilingual Matters.

Hulk, A. and Cornips, L. (2000) Reflexives in middles and the syntax–semantics interface. In H. Bennis and M. Everaert (eds) *Interface Strategies* (pp. 207–222). KNAW series. Amsterdam: Elsevier.

Kellerman, E. (1978) Giving learners a break: Native language intuitions as a source of predictions about transferability. *Working Papers on Bilingualism* 15, 309–315.

Kellerman, E. (1983) Now you see it, now you don't. In S. Gass and L. Selinker (eds) *Language Transfer in Language Learning* (pp. 112–134). Rowley, MA: Newbury House.

Kellerman, E. and Sharwood Smith, M. (eds) (1986) *Crosslinguistic Influence in Second Language Acquisition*. New York: Pergamon Institute of English.

Kempchinski, P. (2004) Middles are not passives. Paper presented at LSRL XXXIV: University of Utah.

Lekakou, M. (2003) Middle semantics and its realization in English and Greek. *UCL Working Papers in Linguistics* 14, 399–416.

Marian, V., Blumenfeld, H.K. and Kaushanskaya, M. (2006) *The Language Experience and Proficiency Questionnaire (LEAP-Q): Assessing Language Profiles in Bilinguals and Multilinguals*. Toronto: Conference on Second Language Acquisition and Multilingualism, York University.

Mendikoetxea, A. (1999) Construcciones con se: Medias, pasivas y reflejas. In I. Bosque and V. Demonte (eds) *Gramática descriptiva de la Lengua Española* (Vol. 2, 1631–1722). Madrid: Espasa-Calpe.

Müller, N. and Hulk, A. (2001) Crosslinguistic influence in bilingual language acquisition: Italian and French as recipient languages. *Bilingualism: Language and Cognition* 4, 1–21.

Neelman, A. and Weerman, F. (1997) L1 and L2 word order acquisition. *Language Acquisition* 6, 125–170.

Paradis, J. and Navarro, S. (2003) Subject realization and crosslinguistic interference in the bilingual acquisition of Spanish and English: What is the role of the input? *Journal of Child Language* 30, 1–23.

Ringbom, H. (2001) Lexical transfer in L3 production. In B. Hufeisen, U. Jessner and J. Cenoz (eds) *Cross-linguistic Influence in Third Language Acquisition: Psycholinguistic Perspectives* (pp. 59–68). Clevedon: Multilingual Matters.

Schwartz, B.D. and Sprouse, R. (1994) Word order and nominative case in nominative language acquisition: A longitudinal study of (L1 Turkish) German interlanguage. In T. Hoekstra and B.D. Schwartz (eds) *Language Acquisition Studies in Generative Grammar* (pp. 317–368). Amsterdam: John Benjamins.

Schwartz, B.D. and Sprouse, R. (1996) L2 cognitive states and the full transfer/full access model. *Second Language Research* 12, 40–72.

Selinker, L. Interlanguage (1972) *International Review of Applied Linguistics* 10, 209–31

Sharwood Smith, M. (1994) *Second Language Learning.* London: Longman.

Smith, N. and Tsimpli, I.M. (1995) *The Mind of a Savant.* Oxford: Blackwell.

Sorace, A. (2003) Near-nativeness. In C. Doughty and M. Long (eds) *The Handbook of Second Language Acquisition* (pp. 130–151). Oxford: Blackwell.

Sorace, A. (2004) Native language attrition and developmental instability at the syntax–discourse interface: Data, interpretations and methods. *Bilingualism: Language and Cognition* 7, 143–145.

Vainikka, A. and Young-Scholten, M. (1994) Direct access to X'-theory: Evidence from Korean and Turkish adults learning German. In T. Hoekstra and B.D. Schwartz (eds) *Language Acquisition Studies in Generative Grammar* (pp. 265–316). Amsterdam: John Benjamins.

Vainikka, A. and Young-Scholten, M. (1996) The early stages of adult L2 syntax: Additional evidence from Romance speakers. *Second Language Research* 12, 140–176.

White, L (2003) *Second Language Acquisition and Universal Grammar.* Cambridge: Cambridge University Press.

Williams, S. and Hammarberg, B. (1998) Language switches in L3 production: Implications for a polyglot speaking model. *Applied Linguistics* 19, 295–333.

Yu, D. (2006) Relative clauses and nominal modifiers in Cantonese. University of Berkeley, Linguistics department. On www at http://www.linguistics.berkeley.edu/~dom/cantonese-rc.pdf. Accessed September 2007.

Chapter 2

Language Transfer in the Acquisition of the Semantic Contrast in L3 Spanish

Diana Hsien-jen Chin

Introduction

This chapter investigates the effect of language transfer on the acquisition of the semantic contrast between the Preterit and Imperfect marking in third language (L3) Spanish by Chinese (L1)–English (L2) learners. It examines whether the L3 learners transfer the semantic interpretation from their first language (L1) or the second language (L2) interlanguage when acquiring the aspectual contrast in an L3. Although many studies have demonstrated that the learner's native language influences the perception of the aspectual contrast in the L2 (e.g. Chin, 2006; Gabriele, 2005; Slabakova, 1999, 2000, 2001, 2005), how multilingual learners acquire the semantic interpretation of the aspectual marking in an L3 has not been thoroughly explored.

Recent studies on L2 learners acquiring the semantic contrast in L2 aspect suggest that the learners' L1 has a strong influence on their recognition of the semantic contrast between the perfective and imperfective aspect (e.g. Chin, 2006; Gabriele, 2005; Slabakova, 1999, 2000, 2001, 2005). However, L3 acquisition is more complicated. There are two possible sources for transfer: the L1 and the interlanguage of the L2 (Leung, 1998, 2002). An issue of L3 acquisition is to identify the source language for transfer. In order to explore the effects of language transfer on acquiring the semantic contrast in an L3, it is essential to explore how learners interpret the different aspectual markings in both their L2 and L3. This will reveal which of the previously acquired languages is the source for transfer in L3 acquisition. Therefore, the present study recruited Chinese native speakers who had learned English as their L2 and were learning Spanish as their L3.

This study is unique, because it investigates a topic that has been underexplored – the crosslinguistic effects on the acquisition of L3 aspectual contrast. Moreover, the participants' recognition of the aspectual contrast was assessed by an acceptability test, which is a method that has not been implemented in the research on L3 acquisition. In the following sections, I will first review some relevant studies and present the past tense aspectual contrast in Chinese, English and Spanish. Then, I will propose the research question and the hypotheses. Afterwards, I will present the results. Finally, I will discuss the findings.

The Aspectual Contrast in the Past Tense in Spanish, English and Chinese

Aspectual contrast in Spanish

The distinction between the perfective and imperfective aspect in the past tense is marked by overt tense morphology in Spanish: the Preterit and the Imperfect. In general, the Preterit marking in Spanish expresses an event as an unanalyzable action. The Imperfect presents an event as an ongoing action or habitual activity in the past.

With respect to the interpretation signaled by these markings, both telic and atelic events are compatible with Preterit and Imperfect in Spanish, depending on the speaker's point of view on the event and the context. State verbs such as '*saber* (to know)', '*querer* (to want)' change their inherent lexical aspect value with different aspectual markings. The Preterit marking on these verbs switches their inherent lexical aspect from states to achievements. This is illustrated in (1a, b):

(1) (a) Ella   sabía   el secreto.
         she   know-Imperf.-3SG   the secret
         'She knew the secret.'
    (b) Ella   supo   el secreto.
         she   find out-Pret.-3SG   the secret.
         'She found out the secret.'

As shown in (1a), the state verb '*saber* (to know)' with the Imperfect marking denotes the state of knowing something. When it is marked with Preterit, it becomes an achievement (i.e. to find out), like the sentence in (1b).

There are some other state verbs in Spanish that do not change their inherent aspect value for different grammatical aspectual markings, such as '*sentirse* (to feel)', '*estar* (to be)'. The Imperfect marking on these verbs denotes a stable situation, but the Preterit marking indicates a momentary state or a state with a definite endpoint, as shown in (2a, b):

(2) (a) Linda estaba   triste   y   siempre
         Linda be-Imperf.-3SG   sad   and   (she)   always
         se sentía   triste.
         Pron. feel-Imperf.-3SG   sad
         'Linda was sad and she always felt sad.'

(b) (*?) Linda estuvo   triste y   siempre
     Linda   be-Pret.-3SG   sad   and   (she)   always
     se   sentía   triste.
     Pron.   feel-Imperf.-3SG sad
     'Linda became sad and she always felt sad.'

In (2a), the Imperfect marking indicates that Linda's being sad was a state in the past; therefore, it is possible to combine the phrase '*Linda estaba triste* (Linda was sad)' with sentences that express a durative or stable situation, such as '*siempre se sentía triste* ([she] always felt sad)'. On the other hand, the Preterit marking in (2b) expresses the state of being sad as a momentary feeling. Hence, it is not possible to combine the phrase '*Linda estuvo triste* (Linda became sad)' with sentences that have a permanent or stable interpretation.

As for the aspectual marking on accomplishments and achievements, the Imperfect marking emphasizes the continuous phase of the event, and it presents an event in progress.[1] As presented in (3a), since the focus is on the continuation of the action, it is possible that the goal was not achieved in the end. By contrast, Preterit denotes completion of the action, as shown in (3b). In this example, the Preterit marking indicates that the action is completed; so it is impossible to combine the event with sentences such as '*pero no terminaron la construcción* (but they did not finish the construction)':

(3) (a) Ellos construían   una   casa,   pero   no
          they build-Imperf.-3PL   a   house,   but   no
          terminaron   la   construcción.
          finish-Pret.-3PL the   construction
          'They were building a house, but they didn't finish the construction.'
     (b) (*) Ellos construyeron   una casa,   pero no
          they build-Pret.-3PL   a house,   but no
          terminaron   la   construcción.
          finish-Pret.-3PL the   construction.
          (*) 'They built a house, but they didn't finish the construction.'

Aspectual contrast in English

Like Spanish, the perfective and imperfect aspect in the past tense is also presented by tense-aspect morphology: the simple past inflection '-*ed*' and the progressive marker '-*ing*'. With regard to the aspectual marking on verb predicates, it is generally accepted that English state verbs are not always compatible with progressive marking, as shown in (4):

(4) (*?) John was knowing Mr Peterson.

(5) (a) John was being stupid at the party, actually, he was not a stupid guy.
     (b) (?) John was stupid at the party, actually, he was not a stupid guy.

However, native speakers of English do mark some state verbs with the progressive marker '*-ing*', this is illustrated in (5a, b).The progressive marking on the verb '*to be*' in (5a) denotes a temporary state. It does not refer to John's intelligence, and it only indicates John's behavior at a certain point in the past. On the other hand, the perfective aspectual marking in (5b) presents the action of being stupid as part of John's personality. It refers to John's intelligence level, which is a stable state of John. Therefore, it contradicts the description 'he was not a stupid guy'.

With respect to the aspectual marking on accomplishments and achievements, the imperfective aspectual marking focuses on the successive phase of the event. By contrast, the perfective aspectual marking expresses the event as a completed action. The examples are presented in (6a, b):

(6) (a) Mary was reading a book.
     (b) Mary read a book.

'Reading a book' is expressed as a progressive event in (6a). It is the stage before the agent completely accomplished the goal. On the other hand, the perfective aspect marking in (6b) indicates that the agent has completed the action.

The aspectual contrast in English and Spanish is marked by overt tense morphology. On the contrary, such contrast is marked by aspectual markers in Chinese.

Aspectual contrast in Chinese

Since Chinese does not have tense morphology, the semantic contrast between the perfective and imperfective aspect is marked by the aspectual markers. The perfective marker '*le*' denotes the perfective aspect, and the imperfective aspect is signaled either by the progressive marker '*zai*' or the durative marker '*zhe*'.[2] The progressive marker '*zai*' is placed preverbally, and it focuses on the progressive phase of an event. On the other hand, the durative marker '*zhe*' emphasizes the duration of an event, and it appears post-verbally.

As for the interpretation denoted by these markers, it is illustrated in (7a–c):

(7) (a) State with perfective marker '*le*'
         Xiaoming you-le   yi-ge   xiangfa.
         Xiaoming have-Perf.   one-Quantifier   thought
         'Xiaoming got an idea.'
     (b) (*) State with progressive marker '*zai*'

Xiaoming zai-you   yi-ge   xiangfa.
Xiaoming Prog.-have   one-Quantifier   thought
(?) 'Xiaoming is having an idea.'

(c)   State with durative marker '*zhe*'
Xiaoming you-zhe   yi-ge   xiangfa.
Xiaoming have-Durative   one-Quantifier   thought
'Xiaoming has an idea.'

The perfective marker '*le*' in (7a) indicates the initiation of the state 'having an idea'. The progressive marker '*zai*' is not compatible with states, as shown in (7b). Finally, the durative marker '*zhe*' in (7c) presents the event 'having an idea' as a stable state, it lasts up until and includes the time of speech.

Turning now to accomplishments, which are compatible with the perfective '*le*' and the progressive '*zai*', but not the durative marker '*zhe*', as illustrated in (8a–c):

(8)   (a)   Accomplishment with perfective marker '*le*'
wo   gai-le   yi-dong   fangzi.
I   build-Perf.   one-Quantifier   house
'I was engaged in building a house.'

(b)   Accomplishment with progressive marker '*zai*'
wo zai-gai   yi-dong   fangzi.
I   Prog.-build   one-Quantifier   house
'I am building a house.'

(c)   (*) Accomplishment with durative marker '*zhe*'
(*?) wo   gai-zhe   yi-dong   fangzi.
I   build-Durative   one-Quantifier   house
'I am building a house.'

The perfective marker '*le*' on accomplishments signals termination of the event. As illustrated in (8a), the action of building a house has terminated, but whether the construction has been completed or not is unknown.[3] With respect to the progressive marker '*zai*', as shown in (8b), it emphasizes that 'to build a house' is an action in progress.

Let us now turn to achievements. Achievements are only compatible with the perfective marker '*le*', as presented in (9a–c). The perfective marker '*le*' in (9a) expresses the completion of falling:

(9)   (a)   Achievement with perfective marker '*le*'
wo   diedao-le.
I   fall-Perf.
'I fell.'

(b)   (*) Achievement with progressive marker '*zai*'
(*) wo   zai-diedao.
I   Prog.-fall

'I am falling.'
(c)   (*) Achievement with durative marker '*zhe*'
      (*) wo   diedao-zhe.
        I   fall-Durative
      'I am falling.'

The differences and similarities in the semantic interpretation between Chinese, English and Spanish are summarized in Tables 2.1–2.3.[4] In the next section, I will discuss the studies on the acquisition of aspect and language transfer in L2 and L3 acquisition.

Table 2.1 Semantic interpretation of the aspectual markings on states in Spanish, English and Chinese

State		
	Imperfective	*Perfective*
Spanish	State	Change of state/ Temporary state
English	Temporary state	State
Chinese	State	Initiation of State

Table 2.2 Semantic interpretation of the aspectual markings on accomplishments in Spanish, English and Chinese

Accomplishments		
	Imperfective	*Perfective*
Spanish	Accomplishment in progress	Completed event
English	Accomplishment in progress	Completed event
Chinese	Accomplishment in progress	Terminated action

Table 2.3 Semantic interpretation of the aspectual markings on achievements in Spanish, English and Chinese

Achievements		
	Imperfective	*Perfective*
Spanish	Achievement in progress	Completed event
English	Achievement in progress	Completed event
Chinese	Incompatible	Completed event

Language Transfer in Acquiring the Aspectual Contrast in L2 vs. L3

Although language transfer has been widely explored in L2 acquisition, the effects of L1 transfer in acquiring L2 aspectual contrast has not been explored by scholars until the recent decade. Chin (2006), Gabriele (2005) and Slabakova's (2000, 2001, 2005) studies on language learners with different language backgrounds (i.e. Chinese, Spanish, Bulgarian, Japanese and English) acquiring the aspectual contrast in an L2 indicate that the learners transfer the aspectual interpretation in their L1 to the L2 at the initial stage of acquisition. As the learners' L2 proficiency improves, they start to adopt the native-like interpretation in the L2. In addition, Slabakova (2001, 2005) found that the responses from the participants at the advanced level approximate the pattern of the native speakers, which suggests that acquiring native-like sensitivity to the aspectual contrast in an L2 is possible.

However, the case of acquiring the aspectual contrast in a language beyond the L2 is more complicated, because both the L1 and the L2 interlanguage are possible sources for transfer in L3 acquisition (Leung, 1998). As presented in Figure 2.1, Leung (1998) states that multilingual learners may transfer from their native language or the interlanguage grammar of the L2 or the target L2 grammar (i.e. the L2 input). In addition, the L2 interlanguage grammar is constructed by transferring from L1 and language universals. Learners transfer both the lexicon and the syntactic structure from their L1 to the L2, which is the basis of the L2 interlanguage grammar at the initial stage of language acquisition.

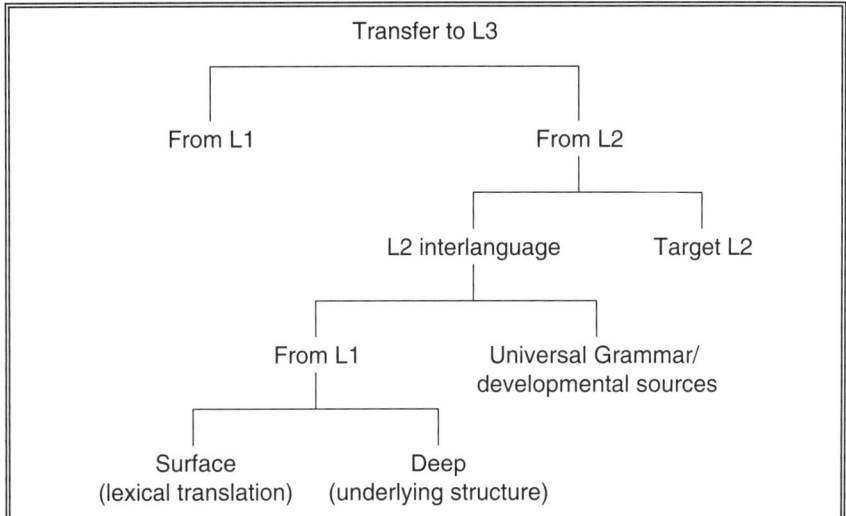

Figure 2.1 Transfer in L3 acquisition
Source: Adapted from Leung (1998: 478, Figure 1)

Leung (1998, 2002, 2005, 2006a) conducted several studies on language transfer in the acquisition of L3 French by Cantonese(L1)–English(L2) learners. The general findings of these studies show evidence of L2 inter-language transfer in word order (i.e. adjective and adverb placement), verb morphology (i.e. tense and person/number agreement) and articles (e.g. specific vs. non-specific and agreement with Determiner Phrase (DP)).

Leung's (2006b) recent study on the acquisition of L2 vs. L3 Spanish past tense verb morphology provides further evidence to the claim that L2 interlanguage is the main source for language transfer in L3 acquisition. Leung (2006b) reported that there was no major difference between the English (L1)–Spanish (L2) and the Chinese (L1)–English (L2)–Spanish (L3) learners regarding the accuracy in supplying the appropriate past tense marking in writing. Moreover, the findings of the follow-up experiment on the L3 learners' English demonstrate that the Chinese (L1)–English (L2)–Spanish (L3) participants mark past tense in a similar pattern to native speakers, which suggests that L2 plays a crucial role in L3 acquisition.

Although Leung's (1998, 2002, 2005, 2006a, 2006b) studies suggest that L2 interlanguage is the main source in L3 acquisition, her studies only investigate the acquisition of form (i.e. morphology and syntax), therefore the acquisition of meaning (e.g. semantics) in an L3 is not explored. In order to investigate language transfer in acquiring L3 semantics, Salaberry (2005) investigated English (L1)–Spanish (L2) learners acquiring the aspectual distinction between telic and atelic events in L3 Portuguese.

The participants' responses show that there was no difference between the L3 learners with advanced Spanish proficiency and Portuguese native speakers. Moreover, the English (L1)–Spanish (L2)–Portuguese (L3) learn-ers of lower proficiency in Spanish tended to make more non-categorical selections of past tense marking on states than accomplishments and achievements. Salaberry (2005) concluded that the English (L1)–Spanish (L2)–Portuguese (L3) learners' knowledge of the L2 Spanish has great influence on the acquisition of L3 Portuguese.

Although Salaberry's (2005) study examined language transfer in the acquisition of the aspectual contrast in the L3, the participants' knowledge of the aspectual system in L2 Spanish was not tested. Furthermore, the tasks implemented in his study required the participants to supply the correct aspect marking based on the context. These tasks only access the participants' knowledge of the aspect morphology, not their semantic interpretation of different aspectual marking.

In order to further explore language transfer in L3 acquisition, it is nec-essary to investigate how L3 learners acquire not only the form (i.e. syntax, morphology), but also the meaning (i.e. semantics). Moreover, it is essen-tial to examine the L3 learners' language knowledge in both the L2 and the

L3. Therefore, the present study examines the Chinese (L1)–English (L2)–Spanish (L3) learners' perception of the aspectual contrast between the perfective and imperfective aspect in both the L2 English and the L3 Spanish, with which we expect to investigate how L3 learners' L2 interlanguage affects the acquisition of the semantic contrast in the L3.

The Study

The present study aims to explore the sources of language transfer in acquiring the aspectual contrast between the Preterit and Imperfect marking in L3 Spanish by Chinese (L1)–English (L2) learners. Therefore, I propose the following research question: Which language is the source for transfer in the acquisition of the aspectual contrast in an L3? The general hypotheses are:

(1) If L1 is the source for transfer, the Chinese (L1)–English (L2)–Spanish (L3) learners will transfer the semantic interpretation from Chinese to both L2 English and L3 Spanish.

(2) If the L2 interlanguage is the source for transfer, the Chinese (L1)–English (L2)–Spanish (L3) learners will transfer their responses to the semantic contrast in English to Spanish.

Methods

Participants

There were three groups of participants involved in this experiment: the Chinese (L1)–English (L2)–Spanish (L3) group (i.e. the L3 group), the Spanish natives and the English natives. The L3 group consisted of 32 participants. They were all students taking intermediate level Spanish courses in a five-year foreign language program at a college in Taiwan. Twenty-one participants were eliminated from the study due to one of the following reasons: (1) since there were only two options for each answer in the morphology test, participants who scored just at 50 were eliminated (because the participant could get 50% of the answers correct just by guessing); (2) participants who could not detect the contrast in the distracters in one of the acceptability tests (i.e. English or Spanish) were excluded, because this indicates that they did not understand the instructions; (3) participants who did not complete the whole material packet were eliminated from the experiment as well. This resulted in 11 participants in this group.

The 11 participants in the L3 group were 10 females and 1 male, the average age was 16.7 (ranging between 16 and 17). They were all Chinese native speakers who started to learn English as the L2 after the age of 10 in an English as a foreign language environment. In addition to English, all participants began to learn Spanish as the L3 after the age of 15 in a five-year intensive language program at a college of foreign languages in Taiwan. The students received 10 to 12 hours of Spanish instruction per week. All of them were taking the intermediate level Spanish classes at the time of participation. Furthermore, they were also taking English courses as part of the program's requirements. Seven of them reported that they scored within the range of the intermediate level on the standardized national English proficiency exam (i.e. from 190 to 220 out of 300). The remaining four participants did not take the exam. None of them have lived in any English- or Spanish-speaking countries.

There were 12 participants in the English native speaker group. One of them was eliminated, because he/she did not complete the acceptability test. The 11 participants (5 females and 6 males) who remained were all English native speakers living in the US, with an average age at 24.27 (ranging from 19 to 47).

Eleven volunteers (7 females and 4 males) from a variety of Spanish-speaking countries (i.e. Colombia, Mexico, Peru, Spain, and Uruguay) participated in the Spanish native speaker group. The average age of this group was 29.45 (ranging from 23 to 38).

Materials

The materials included a background questionnaire and two test packets: one in English and the other in Spanish. Each packet included a proficiency test, a morphology test and an acceptability test. All the tests were piloted with five native speakers to ensure that there was no ambiguity in the test items, and to obtain consensus on the answers.

All participants completed the questionnaire in their L1. The native speakers were asked to complete all the tests in their L1, and the L3 learners completed both packets. All instructions were given in the participants' native language.

Background questionnaire

The background questionnaire consists of questions regarding gender, age, the participant's native language, experience in learning non-native language(s), proficiency level in all non-native languages and frequency of exposure to the languages tested.

The English packet
English proficiency test

The English proficiency test was a one-page cloze test created by deleting every seventh word in the text. If the word to be deleted was a specific name, the next one was deleted, and the counting started from the word after the deleted one. Forty fill-in-the-blanks were on the test, and there were three options for each blank. The participants had to circle the correct answer for each blank on a separate answer sheet.

English morphology test

The morphology test consists of 30 verbs appearing in both simple past and past progressive markings. The verbs covered both eventive and stative verbs and the answers were balanced in both markings. The participants were required to choose the appropriate verb form based on the contexts.

English acceptability test

The acceptability test was created following the format used in Montrul and Slabakova's (2002, 2003) studies. Each question consisted of a sequence of two sentences. The first sentence described an event, and the verb predicate was marked with either imperfective or perfective aspect. The second sentence described a situation that was acceptable for the imperfective aspect, but unacceptable for the perfective aspect. The participants were asked to rate the acceptability level of each sequence on a five-point scale: 5: acceptable, 4: somewhat acceptable; 3: neutral; 2: somewhat unacceptable; 1: unacceptable. This is illustrated in examples (10) and (11).

(10) The man was dying. The doctor cured him.

1	2	3	4	<u>5</u>
Unacceptable			Acceptable	

(11) The man died. The doctor cured him.

<u>1</u>	2	3	4	5
Unacceptable			Acceptable	

The past progressive marking in (10) indicates that 'to die' was an achievement in progress; therefore, it is logical that the doctor cured the dying man. So, the expected answer is 5. By contrast, the simple past marking in (11) signals that the man had died, thus, it is illogical to say that the doctor cured him, and the expected answer is 1.

There were sentences with both perfective and imperfective aspect marking in each verb category. Five verb predicates were chosen for each category. In addition, five logical and illogical distracters were also included to test whether the participants understood the instructions, which resulted in 40 test items in total.

The Spanish packet

Spanish proficiency test

A multiple-choice cloze test served as the Spanish proficiency test. There were 36 fill-in-the-blanks on the test, and three options for each blank. The participants were asked to mark one of the options on a separate answer sheet.

Spanish morphology test

The Spanish morphology test was created following the same format as the English morphology test, and there were 30 questions on the test.

Spanish acceptability test

The Spanish acceptability test was created in the same format as the English acceptability test.

Results

English

English proficiency test

The L3 group's average score on the English proficiency test was 48.4, and the English native speaker group's grade was 94.55. The differences between these two groups' average grades was statistically significant ($t(1,20) = 16.84$, $p < 0.0001$). The results of the proficiency test indicate that the English proficiency of the L3 group was far below native-like.

English morphology test

The native speakers scored 93.79 on the English morphology test, and the L3 learners' score was 68.42. The English native speakers' score was significantly higher than that of the Chinese (L1)–English (L2)–Spanish (L3) learner ($t(1,20) = 8.16$, $p < 0.0001$).

English acceptability test
Predictions

Since the previous studies on language learners acquiring the L2 aspect have shown evidence of L1 transfer, we propose the following predictions:

(1) The L3 learners will not accept the sentences with past progressive marking on states, because state verbs with the imperfective aspectual marking in Chinese do not denote temporary states. Furthermore, the learners will reject the sentences with simple past marking as well, since the sequence is illogical based on the context. To be specific, the Chinese (L1)–English (L2)–Spanish (L3) participants will not recognize the aspectual contrast on state verbs.

(2) Although the imperfective aspectual marking on accomplishments denotes an incomplete event in both Chinese and English, the perfective aspectual marking does not indicate the completion of an event in Chinese.[5] Therefore, these participants will accept the sentences with both aspectual markings on accomplishments. In other words, the L3 learners will not detect the semantic contrast on accomplishments.

(3) Achievements are not compatible with imperfective aspect in Chinese; consequently, these participants will reject the sentence sequences with past progressive marking on achievements. In addition, since the sequences with simple past marking are illogical, the learners will reject these sentences as well. Thus, the Chinese (L1)–English(L2)–Spanish (L3) learners will not be sensitive to the semantic contrast on achievements.

Group results
States

The participants' responses to state verbs are presented in Figure 2.2. Both the native speakers and the L3 group rated the sentence sequences with past progressive marking (e.g. John was being silly at the party. John was not a silly guy) between 3 and 4 (i.e. Natives: 3.85, SD = 1.45; L3 group: 3, SD = 0.64). As for the simple past marking on states (e.g. John was silly. John was not a silly guy), both groups rated theses sentences at 1.6 (i.e. Natives: SD = 0.31, L3: SD = 0.59). This indicates that even though the L3 learners were uncertain about the sentences with past progressive marking (i.e. the average rating was 3), they did think the sentence sequences marked with simple past less acceptable than those with past progressive.

Whether the participants were sensitive to the aspectual contrast on the verb predicates was determined by the paired sample t-test. If there was a statistically significant difference between the participants' acceptance rates for the acceptable and unacceptable sentence sequences, then it would suggest that the participants were aware of the aspectual contrast on these verb predicates.

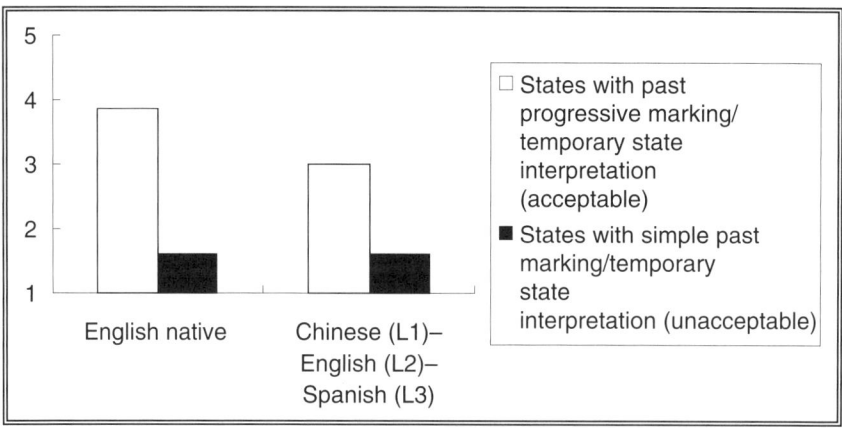

Figure 2.2 Acceptability for state verbs in English

The analysis of a paired sample *t*-test shows that both the English native speakers and the Chinese (L1)–English (L2)–Spanish (L3) groups recognized the contrast between the past progressive and simple past marking on English state verbs (Native: *t* (1,10) = 5.77, *p* = 0.0002; Chinese (L1)–English (L2)–Spanish (L3): *t* (1,10) = 5.96, *p* = 0.0001).

This finding does not support our hypothesis on L1 transfer in the acquisition of L2 aspect. Since the temporary interpretation for progressive marking on state verbs is not initiated in Chinese, we predict that the Chinese (L1)–English (L2)–Spanish (L3) learner will not detect the semantic contrast on state verbs. However, the results demonstrate that these learners were sensitive to such contrast as a group.

Accomplishments

The participants' responses to the sentences with accomplishments are presented in Figure 2.3. The natives accepted the imperfective interpretation for accomplishments with past progressive marking (e.g. Jenny was building a house. Jenny gave up building the house in the middle of construction) at 4.24 (SD = 0.77), while the Chinese (L1)–English (L2)–Spanish (L3) learners rated these sentences at 3.76 (SD = 0.68). As for the sentences with simple past, the native speakers rated these sentences at 1.89 (SD = 0.31), and the L3 group rated them at 2.85 (SD = 0.84).

The paired sample *t*-test indicates that both the native speakers and the Chinese (L1)–English (L2)–Spanish (L3) learners were sensitive to the semantic contrast between the past progressive and simple past marking on accomplishments (English: $t(1, 10)$ = 6.32, p <0.0001; Chinese (L1)–English (L2)–Spanish (L3): $t(1,10)$ = 2.64, p = 0.02). This finding contradicts the prediction previously proposed. According to the hypothesis that

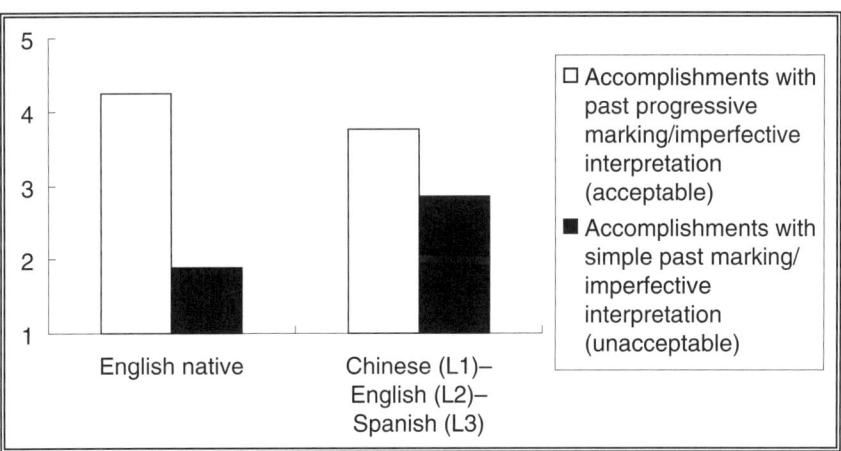

Figure 2.3 Acceptability for accomplishments in English

learners transfer the L1 to the L2, they will not recognize the aspectual contrast on accomplishments, because both the imperfective and perfective aspect markings on accomplishments denote incomplete events in Chinese. Even though the group results indicate that the L3 learners detected the aspectual contrast on accomplishments, the participants rated the sentences with past progressive marking at 3.76. This suggests that they were uncertain about the interpretation for accomplishments with imperfective aspectual marking. However, they did consider the sentences with past progressive more acceptable than those with simple past. I will leave this for later discussion.

Achievements

The data for English achievements are shown in Figure 2.4. The native speakers rated the sentences with past progressive marking (e.g. The plane was arriving in New York. The plane exploded before landing) at 3.93 (SD = 0.97), and the Chinese (L1)–English (L2)–Spanish (L3) learners rated these sentences at 2.85 (SD = 0.87). On the other hand, the natives' acceptance rate for the simple past (e.g. The plane arrived in New York. The plane exploded before landing) was 1.68 (SD = 0.19), and the L3 group's was 1.98 (SD = 0.78). The statistical results indicate that both groups detected the semantic contrast on achievements (English: $t(1, 10) = 6.17$, $p = 0.0001$; Chinese (L1)–English (L2)–Spanish (L3): $t(1, 10) = 3.17$, $p = 0.01$).

Back to our prediction, we expected that the L3 learners would not recognize the semantic contrast on achievements, due to the fact that achievements are only compatible with perfective aspect in Chinese. However, our results demonstrate that although the L3 learners' acceptance rate for the acceptable sentence sequences was below 3, they still were sensitive to the aspectual contrast between the past progressive and past simple.

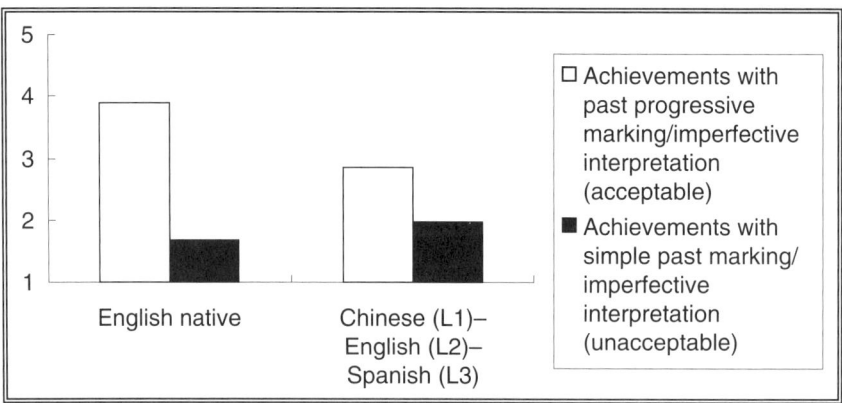

Figure 2.4 Acceptability for achievements in English

In sum, the Chinese (L1)–English (L2)–Spanish (L3) learners' responses on the English acceptability test show that they were able to detect the semantic contrast between the past progressive and the simple past marking. However, the L3 learners' low rating for the acceptable sentences in all three experimental conditions reveals that they were uncertain about the imperfective interpretation for the past progressive marking in English. In order to further investigate whether the Chinese (L1)–English (L2)–Spanish (L3) learners were sensitive to the contrast between past progressive and simple past, it is essential to look at the individual data.

Individual results
States
A paired sample *t*-test analysis was conducted to analyze each participants' acceptance rates on the acceptability test. The statistically significant difference between the individual's acceptance rates for the past progressive and the simple past marking indicates that this participant was sensitive to the semantic contrast. The percentage of participants who detected the semantic contrast on states is presented in Table 2.4.

Table 2.4 Percentage of the participants who recognized the semantic contrast on state verbs in English

Group	Contrast (%)	No contrast (%)
English native	55 (6/11)	45 (5/11)
Chinese (L1)–English (L2)–Spanish (L3)	45 (5/11)	55 (6/11)

The percentage of individuals who recognized the semantic contrast on states was close in these two groups. However, the percentage of the native speakers who recognized the contrast was low (i.e. 55%). This is because the past progressive marking on states sounds awkward to some native speakers. This finding corresponds to the group results. Recall that the native group rated the acceptable sentences at 3.85. This indicates that the natives knew that the past progressive marking on states denote a temporary state, but such marking is unusual according to English grammar.

Accomplishments
The number of participants who were sensitive to the semantic contrast on accomplishments is presented in Table 2.5. The results reveal a discrepancy between the individual and the group data. Although the L3 learners were sensitive to the semantic contrast between the past progressive and simple past marking on accomplishments as a group, only three participants actually recognized such contrast. This suggests that the rest of the

Table 2.5 Percentage of the participants who recognized the semantic contrast on accomplishments in English

Group	Contrast (%)	No contrast (%)
English native	82 (9/11)	18 (2/11)
Chinese (L1)–English (L2)–Spanish (L3)	27.27 (3/11)	72.73 (8/11)

participants in this group were still in the process of acquiring the interpretation for the past progressive and past simple marking.

Achievements

Table 2.6 presents the percentage of the participants who were sensitive to the semantic contrast on achievements in each group. There were only two Chinese (L1)–English (L2)–Spanish (L3) learners who detected the semantic contrast. The discrepancy between the group and the individual results suggests that although the Chinese (L1)–English (L2)–Spanish (L3) learners recognized the semantic contrast as a group, the influence of L1 transfer still cannot be ruled out. Let us now turn to the data in the L3 Spanish.

Table 2.6 Percentage of the participants who recognized the semantic contrast on achievements in English

Group	Contrast (%)	No contrast (%)
English native	55 (6/11)	45 (5/11)
Chinese (L1)–English (L2)–Spanish (L3)	18.18 (2/11)	82.82 (9/11)

L3 Spanish

Predictions

Based on Leung's (1998) model on language transfer in L3 acquisition, we propose the following predictions:

(1) If the Chinese (L1)–English (L2)–Spanish (L3) learners transfer from the L1 to the L3, they will accept these sentences, and will reject those with Preterit marking. This is because the imperfective marking on states denotes steady states in both Chinese and Spanish. On the other hand, these learners will not recognize the semantic contrast on accomplishments. The contrast between the perfective and imperfective aspect on accomplishments is not marked by the aspectual markers in Chinese (see endnote 1). In addition, achievements are only compatible with perfective aspect. Hence, the L3 learners will not recognize the semantic contrast on accomplishments and achievements.

(2) If the Chinese (L1)–English (L2)–Spanish (L3) learners transfer from the L2 English to the L3 Spanish, they will not recognize the contrast

on states, since the imperfective marking on states does not signal temporary state in English. However, they will detect the semantic contrast on accomplishments and achievements as a group, because the semantic interpretations for the aspectual marking on these events are similar in English and Spanish. In addition, the group results in English indicated that these participants were sensitive to such contrast.

Spanish proficiency test

The Spanish native speakers scored at 94.7 on the proficiency test, and the Chinese (L1)–English (L2)–Spanish (L3) learners scored at 46.71. The L3 group's proficiency score was significantly lower than the natives' ($t(1,20) = 21.56$, $p < 0.0001$).

Spanish morphology test

The natives' score on the morphology test was 96.9, and the L3 group scored 67.57. The native's score was significantly higher than the L3 group ($t(1,20) = 9.11$, $p < 0.0001$).

Spanish acceptability test
Group results
States

The results of state verbs are presented in Figure 2.5. The Spanish native speakers rated the sentences with Imperfect marking (e.g. *La fiesta era a la 1 de la tarde. Al final, la fiesta empezó a las 2.* [The party was (Imperf.) at 1 in the afternoon. In the end, the party started at 2]) at 4.83 (SD – 0.28), while the L3 learners rated these sentences at 3 (SD = 0.78). On the other hand, the native speakers rated the sentences with Preterit marking (e.g. *La boda de Sofía y Juan fue a las 3 de la tarde. Al final, la boda empezó a las 4.* [Sofía and Juan's wedding was(Pret.) at 3 in the afternoon. In the end, the wedding started at 4]) at 1.65 (SD = 0.52), and the L3 group's acceptance rate was 2.2 (SD = 0.66).

The paired sample t-tests show that the natives were sensitive to the aspectual contrast on state verbs ($t(1,10) = 17.31$, $p < 0.0001$), but the L3 learners were not ($t(1,10) = 2.03$, $p = 0.07$). The results of the state verbs support our second hypothesis. Although the semantic interpretations for states are similar in Chinese and Spanish, the L3 learners did not detect this similarity. On the other hand, the semantic interpretation for states in English differs from Chinese and Spanish. Furthermore, the results from the English acceptability test showed that the L3 learners were not sensitive to the aspectual contrast between the imperfective and perfective marking on states in English either. Thus, the L3 group's responses to states in Spanish suggest an influence of L2 interlanguage grammar.

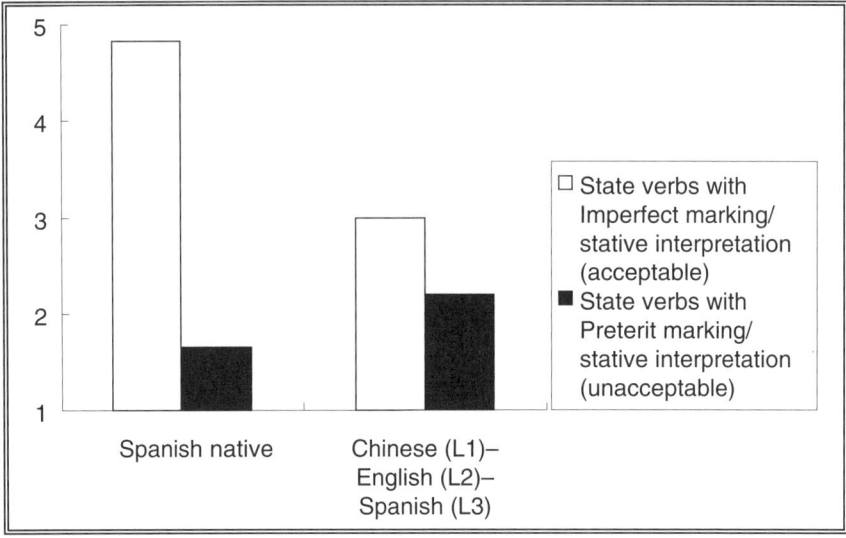

Figure 2.5 Acceptability for state verbs in Spanish

Accomplishments

Figure 2.6 shows the participants' acceptance rates for the sentences with accomplishments. The acceptance rate from the native speaker group for the Imperfect marking was 4.7 (SD = 0.53) (e.g. *Escribía una novela. No terminé la novella.* [I was writing a novel. I did not finish the novel]), and the rate from the Chinese (L1)–English (L2)–Spanish (L3) groups was 3.8 (SD = 1.04). As for the unacceptable sentence sequences (e.g. *Escribí una carta. No terminé la carta.* [I wrote a letter. I did not finish the letter]), the native speakers rated them at 1.4 (SD = 0.56), and the L3 group's acceptance rate was 2.43 (SD = 0.87).

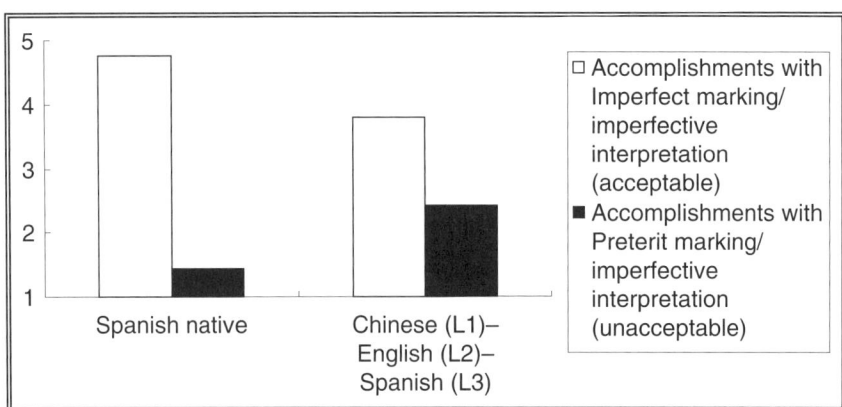

Figure 2.6 Acceptability for accomplishments in Spanish

Regarding the recognition of the semantic contrast on accomplishments, a paired sample *t*-test analysis indicates that both groups perceived the contrast between the Imperfect and Preterit markings (Spanish native: $t(1,10) = 16.3$, $p < 0.0001$; Chinese (L1)–English (L2)–Spanish (L3): $t(1,10) = 4.13$, $p = 0.002$). This confirms our hypothesis on L2 interlanguage transfer. Although the aspectual contrast on accomplishments is not initiated in the learners' L1, they were sensitive to such contrast in both the L2 English (see Figure 2.3) and the L3 Spanish. This suggests transfer from the L2 English.

Achievements

The participants' acceptance rates for achievements were demonstrated in Figure 2.7. The natives rated the sentences with Imperfect marking (e.g. *Su abuelo se moría. El médico lo curó.* [His/Her grandfather was dying. The doctor cured him.]) at 4.45 (SD = 0.6), while the L3 group rated them at 2.7 (SD = 0.86). The Spanish native rated the sentences with Preterit marking on achievements (e.g. *El hombre se murió. El médico lo curó.* [The man died. The doctor cured him.]) at 1.05 (SD = 0.09), and the L3 group's acceptance rate was 2.29 (SD = 0.58).

Paired sample *t*-tests show that the native speakers recognized the aspectual contrast on achievements (Spanish native: $t(1,10) = 18.75$, $p < 0.0001$), but the Chinese (L1)–English (L2)–Spanish (L3) group did not ($t(1,10) = 1.96$, $p = 0.77$). In addition, the L3 group's acceptance rate for the sentences with Imperfect marking was below 3. Since achievements are incompatible with the imperfective aspect in Chinese, this result might suggest direct L1 transfer.

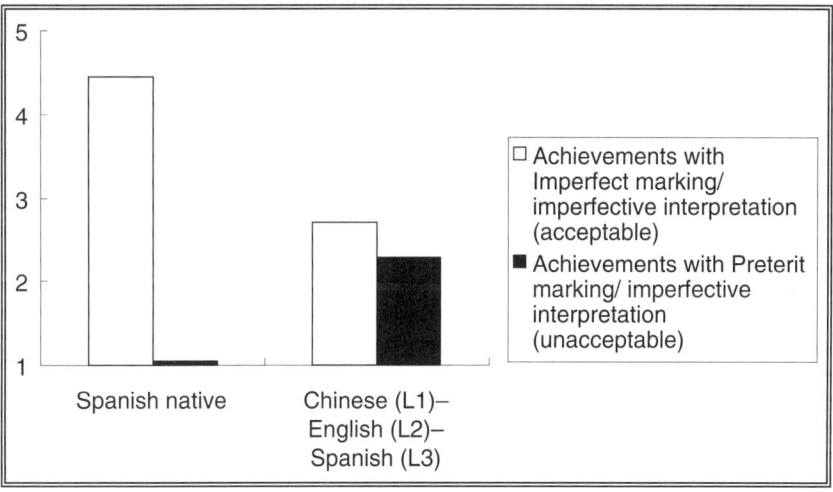

Figure 2.7 Acceptability for achievements in Spanish

Table 2.7 Percentage of the participants who recognized the semantic contrast on state verbs in Spanish

Group	Contrast (%)	No contrast (%)
Spanish native	91 (10/11)	9 (1/11)
Chinese (L1)–English (L2)–Spanish (L3)	18.18 (2/11)	81.82 (9/11)

Individual results
States

The analysis of individual responses to the sentences with state verbs corresponds with the group data. More than 90% of the participants in the native group detected the contrast, while only less than 20% of the participants were sensitive to such contrast in the L3 group. The results are presented in Table 2.7.

The results of state verbs supports our hypothesis that the Chinese (L1)–English (L2)–Spanish (L3) learners transferred from the L2 English to L3 Spanish. Despite the similarity between the semantic interpretation for states in the L1 Chinese and the L3 Spanish, the learners did not detect the semantic contrast on states in Spanish. Recall that these participants were uncertain about the acceptability of the sentences with past progressive marking on state verbs in the L2 English (see Figure 2.2). Therefore, it is possible that the L3 learners transferred the semantic interpretation for the aspectual marking on states from the L2 English to the L3 Spanish.

Accomplishments

Table 2.8 presents the individual data in each group. Even though the percentage of the L3 learners who recognized the semantic contrast was still low, there were more participants who recognized such contrast on accomplishments than on states (see Table 2.7). The semantic interpretation for the imperfective and perfective marking on accomplishments is similar in English and Spanish, thus, these findings suggest L2 interlanguage transfer for the participants who detected the contrast on accomplishments. As for the learners who were not sensitive to such contrast, a possible L1 influence cannot be ruled out.

Table 2.8 Percentage of the participants who recognized the semantic contrast on accomplishments in Spanish

Group	Contrast (%)	No contrast (%)
Spanish native	100 (11/11)	0 (0/11)
Chinese (L1)–English (L2)–Spanish (L3)	36.36 (4/11)	63.64 (7/11)

Table 2.9 Percentage of the participants who recognized the semantic contrast on achievements in Spanish

Group	Contrast (%)	No contrast (%)
Spanish native	100 (11/11)	0 (0/11)
Chinese (L1)–English (L2)–Spanish (L3)	9.1 (1/11)	81.9 (10/11)

Achievements

The individual data for achievements is presented in Table 2.9. Only one participant in the Chinese (L1)–English (L2)–Spanish (L3) group detected the semantic contrast on achievements. The individual results correspond with the group data presented in Figure 2.7. The L3 participants were not sensitive to the contrast on achievements as group either. Since achievements are not compatible with imperfective aspect in Chinese, this suggests a possible transfer from the L1.

In summary, the group and the individual results in Spanish indicate that both the L1 and the interlanguage L2 are sources for transfer. This finding seems to coincide with the results of the studies by Leung (1998, 2002, 2005, 2006a, 2006b) and Salaberry (2005). That is, the L3 participants' knowledge of the semantic interpretation of the aspectual marking in the L2 English has a strong influence on the acquisition of the L3 aspect. In the next section, I will discuss the relevance between the findings of the present study and the previous studies on L3 acquisition.

Discussion and Conclusion

The findings of this study show that the L2 interlanguage is the main source for language transfer in L3 acquisition, and the influence of the learners' L1 also affects the acquisition. Although the Chinese (L1)–English (L2)–Spanish (L3) group recognized the semantic contrast on all three verb categories in English, the individual data reveals that more than 50% of the participants in this group did not recognize the aspectual contrast.

Recall that the L3 group scored 68.42 on the English morphology test. In Montrul and Slabakova's (2002, 2003) studies, they set 75% as the cut-off point to select the learners who had acquired the aspect morphology. Following this standard, the L3 participants in the present study have not completely acquired the aspect morphology in the L2 English. This also explains why only a very small number of participants detected the semantic contrast in English. Furthermore, due to the small number of participants, the participants who were sensitive to the contrast had greater influence on the group results than we expected, which resulted in the discrepancy between the group and the individual data. In sum, the semantic interpretations of the perfective and imperfective aspectual marking in Chinese and English are different; nevertheless, the individual results on the English acceptability test confirm the L1 influence on the learners' perception of the aspectual contrast in the L2 English.

The participants' responses in the L3 Spanish reveal a different result from the previous studies on language transfer in L3 acquisition (e.g. Leung, 2005, 2006a, 2006b; Salaberry, 2005). The data of the present study showed evidence for both L1 transfer and interlanguage transfer from the L2.

The L3 group's average score on the Spanish morphology test was close to that on the English test (i.e. 67.57). This suggests that the L3 learners were also in the process of acquiring the tense-aspect morphology in Spanish. There were more participants who detected the aspectual contrast in all three experimental conditions on the English acceptability test than the Spanish test, which suggests that the participants who were sensitive to the contrast in the L2 English might not transfer the interpretation to the L3 Spanish, at least for accomplishments and achievements. Hence the semantic interpretations are similar in English and Spanish, for the participants who were sensitive to the contrast in both languages, the transfer from the L2 to the L3 was successful. By contrast, those who detected the contrast in English but did not detect such contrast in Spanish seem to transfer the semantic interpretation from the L1 Chinese to the L3 Spanish.

As for states, the interpretations in Chinese and Spanish are similar, but this similarity did not facilitate the participants' perception of the semantic contrast on states in the L3 Spanish. On the other hand, the interpretation for states is different in English; thus, the fact that the L3 learners were not able to tell the semantic contrast on Spanish state verbs might be due to the influence of the L2 English.

Furthermore, there were participants who did not recognize the semantic contrast in both English and Spanish. The L3 group's average scores on the English and Spanish morphology tests were both below 75%, which suggests that these learners might have not fully acquired the tense-aspect morphology in both the L2 and the L3. Moreover, these participants' limited knowledge of the aspect morphology affects their perception of the semantic interpretation of the aspectual marking in the L2 and the L3.

In summary, the results of recent studies on language transfer in L3 acquisition by Leung (2006a, 2006b) and Salaberry (2005) demonstrate that the L2 interlanguage plays a crucial role in L3 acquisition, especially for learners with advanced L2 proficiency. L3 learners who are proficient in the L2 can successfully transfer their knowledge of the L2 to the L3. The findings of the present study suggest that the L2 interlanguage is also crucial for L3 learners who are not highly proficient in their L2 and the L3.

The number of L3 participants in this study was small. Studies with a larger L3 learner group are essential for future research. In addition, recruiting learners with the same L1 and L2 acquiring different L3s will provide further evidence to language transfer in L3 acquisition. Moreover, the factors that affect L3 learners' choice of the source for language transfer also need to be explored.

Notes

1. Achievements marked with the Imperfect markers may sound odd to some native speakers of Spanish. Since achievements have an inherent end point, they are incompatible with the Imperfect marking, unless the context supports an imperfective interpretation of the action.
2. The experience marker '*guo*' is not included, because it is not relevant to the semantic contrast discussed in this study.
3. The completion of an accomplishment is expressed by resultative adverbials such as 'hao (well),' and 'wan (finish)' in Chinese. The verb–adverb combination (i.e. '*gai-hao*' (build-well)) is referred as the Resultative Verb Construction (RVC) (Smith, 1991; Tai, 1984; Vendler, 1957).
4. Activity verbs were excluded in this study because the semantic contrast on activity verbs was not clear in either Spanish or English. See Chin (2006) for detailed discussion.
5. To present the completion of an accomplishment, it requires the RVC structure in Chinese, such as '*chang (to sing)-wan (finish)-ge (song)*' (sang a song).

References

Chin, H.J. (2006) Cross-linguistic effects on L2 acquisition: An investigation of aspect. PhD dissertation. University of Illinois at Urbana-Champaign.

Gabriele, A. (2005) The acquisition of aspect in a second language: A bidirectional study of learners of English and Japanese. PhD dissertation. The City University of New York.

Leung, Y-k.I. (1998) Transfer between interlanguages. *Proceedings of the Annual Boston University Conference on Language Development* 22 (2), 477–487.

Leung, Y-k.I. (2002) Functional categories in second and third language acquisition: A cross-linguistic study of the acquisition of English and French by Chinese and Vietnamese speakers. PhD dissertation. McGill University.

Leung, Y-k.I. (2005) L2 vs. L3 initial state: A comparative study of the acquisition of French DPs by Vietnamese monolinguals and Cantonese–English bilinguals. *Bilingualism: Language and Cognition* 8 (1), 39–61.

Leung, Y-k.I. (2006a) Full transfer vs. partial transfer in L2 and L3 acquisition. In R. Slabakova, S. Montrul and P. Prévost (eds) *Inquiries in Language Development: Studies in Honor of Lydia White* (pp. 157–187). Amsterdam: John Benjamins.

Leung, Y-k.I. (2006b) Verb morphology in second language versus third language acquisition: The representation of regular and irregular past participles in English–Spanish and Chinese–English-Spanish interlanguages. *EUROSLA Yearbook* 6 (pp. 27–56). Amsterdam: John Benjamins.

Montrul, S. and Slabakova, R. (2002) The L2 acquisition of morphosyntactic and semantic properties of the aspectual tenses preterite and imperfect. In A.T. Pérez-Leroux and J. Liceras (eds) *The Acquisition of Spanish Morphosyntax. The L1/ L2 Connection* (pp. 131–149). Dordrecht: Kluwer.

Montrul, S. and Slabakova, R. (2003) Competence similarities between native and near-native speakers: An investigation of the preterite/imperfect contrast in Spanish. *Studies in Second Language Acquisition* 25, 351–398.

Salaberry, R. (2005) Evidence for transfer of knowledge of aspect from L2 Spanish to L3 Portuguese. In D. Ayoun and R. Salaberry (eds) *Tense and Aspect in the Romance Languages: Theoretical and Applied Perspectives* (pp. 181–210). Amsterdam: John Benjamins.

Slabakova, R. (1999) The parameter of aspect in second language acquisition. *Second Language Research* 15 (3), 283–317.

Slabakova, R. (2000) L1 transfer revisited: The L2 acquisition of telicity marking in English by Spanish and Bulgarian native speakers. *Linguistics* 38 (4), 739–770.

Slabakova, R. (2001) *Telicity in the Second Language*. Amsterdam: John Benjamins.

Slabakova, R. (2005) What is so difficult about telicity marking in L2 Russian? *Bilingualism: Language and Cognition* 8 (1), 63–77.

Smith, C. (1991) *The Parameter of Aspect*. Dordrecht: Kluwer.

Tai, J.H. (1984) Verbs and times in Chinese: Vendler's four categories. *Papers from the Parasessions* (pp. 289–296). Chicago: Chicago Linguistic Society.

Vendler, Z. (1957) Verbs and times. *Philosophical Review* 66, 143–160.

Chapter 3

Multilingual Universal Grammar as the Norm

Vivian Cook

Introduction

The Universal Grammar (UG) tradition in linguistics and second language acquisition (SLA) research has treated monolingualism as the normal state of humankind. Yet this monolingual assumption is nowhere inherent in its avowed aims. Chomsky's questions for linguistics, for example Chomsky (1991), concern the knowledge of language in the mind and its acquisition, use and storage:

(1) What constitutes knowledge of language?
(2) How is such knowledge acquired?
(3) How is such knowledge put to use?

But what does language mean in these questions? Cook (2007) distinguishes five meanings of 'language', most of which will be referred to in the following discussion:

- $Lang_1$ – a human representation system;
- $Lang_2$ – an abstract external entity;
- $Lang_3$ – a set of actual or potential sentences;
- $Lang_4$ – the possession of a community;
- $Lang_5$ – the knowledge in the mind of an individual.

While Chomsky's questions have overtones of the general $Lang_1$ meaning, 'a human representation system', they are centrally concerned with the $Lang_5$ meaning 'the knowledge in the mind of an individual'. None of them specifically refers to knowledge of *a* language ($Lang_5$): the notion of language in general ($Lang_1$) is different from the idea of a particular language ($Lang_2$), as indeed Chomsky recognizes with his use of 'grammar' for the language in the mind: 'The grammar in a person's mind/brain is real; it is one of the real things in the world. The language (whatever that may be) is not' (Chomsky, 1982: 5).

In recent years Chomsky has turned to a new question about the perfection of language: 'How good a solution is language to certain boundary conditions that are imposed by the architecture of the mind?' (Chomsky,

2000: 17). Again this is phrased in terms of language rather than of a single language. So far as these basic questions are concerned, the knowledge of language in the mind could include as many languages as it is capable of holding.

So why is a mind that knows two languages treated as an exception rather than as the rule? The usual reason put forward, mostly in footnotes and interviews rather than argued in the UG texts themselves, is that restriction to monolinguals is a necessary simplification. Linguistics needs to work with an abstraction from which irrelevant aspects have been purged: 'Linguistic theory is concerned with an ideal speaker-listener in a completely homogeneous speech community' (Chomsky, 1965: 4).

Though linguistic competence has rarely been debated in the UG field since around 1970, it implicitly underpins most analysis. Given that this version of linguistic competence excludes all the other aspects of the speaker as a psychological and social being, it is a small step to eliminate knowledge of more than one language.

Not that anyone denies that many people in the world have two languages: 'In most of human history, and in most parts of the world today, children grow up speaking a variety of languages .... That is just a natural state of human beings' (Chomsky, 2000: 59). It seems that the analyst cannot cope with the complexity of the bilingual situation.

But do second language users (henceforward L2 users) think of themselves as native speakers of one language with another language added on? Let us hear from two of them. First Edward Said, a Palestinian in exile:

> I have never known what language I spoke first, Arabic or English, or which one was really mine beyond any doubt. What I do know, however, is that the two have always been together in my life, one resonating in the other, sometimes ironically, sometimes nostalgically, most often each correcting, and commenting on, the other. Each can seem like my absolutely first language, but neither is. (Said, 1999: 4)

Next from Suresh Canagarajah, a Sri Lankan Tamil living in New York:

> In South Asian communities, such as mine we grow up with two or more languages from childhood, developing equal competence in all of them, fluidly moving between each of them in our everyday life according to the different domains of family (regional dialect of Tamil), school (English), neighbourhood (Muslim dialect of Tamil) and governmental institutions (Sinhala) ... One can imagine the difficulty for people in my region to identify themselves as native speakers of 'a' language. (Canagarajah, 2005: 16–17)

Neither of them accepts that they have added one language to another to become L2 users. Rather the two or more languages have always been interwoven into their lives.

We shall first review some of the arguments for a multilingual UG and then look at the consequences for UG theory.

Arguments for Multilingual UG

The arguments for a multilingual UG come from a variety of sources, some directly within UG, some general issues. Some of these have been presented in a slightly different context in Cook and Newson (2007).

The argument of independence from environmental variation

One of the key elements in UG theory is the vast range of circumstances in which human children acquire language. In some cultures children are literally not spoken to, in others they are bombarded with speech; some parents speak to their toddlers in baby-talk, others refuse to adapt. It doesn't seem to matter what kind of upbringing the child encounters: the sole requirement for learning a human language is to be human, as Lenneberg (1967) observed. Only a handful of children fail to learn language. But of course language acquisition fails in the rare cases when children do not encounter speech at all, such as the extreme deprivation suffered by Genie (Curtiss, 1977). The theory assumes nothing more about the child's language environment than the sheer availability of language input.

So whatever UG theory proposes for language acquisition has to be robust enough to work whatever the conditions that the child encounters. Language acquisition cannot depend on particular properties of the input, say, the frequency of this or that feature; it cannot depend on particular types of interaction, whether recasts, corrections or whatever, simply because children acquire language regardless. The powerful device for acquiring language in the child's mind is omnivorous rather than being fussy about its diet. Any theory of UG must postulate mechanisms for learning that will work in any possible human child-rearing situation short of total deprivation. It has to see language knowledge as triggered by ubiquitous properties of language and of the child-rearing situation, not by accidental features of some individual or cultural situation.

Yet children exposed to two or more languages acquire all of them – childhood simultaneous bilingualism. The mental device for acquiring language can cope with two or more languages, at least in the early years.

So why don't monolinguals speak two languages? For the reason that, like Genie, they do not hear them. They are restricted to the knowledge triggered by the set of sentences they encounter. In other words monolingualism can be considered as a widespread form of language deprivation. A child encountering two languages acquires two languages; a child encountering one acquires one. The only thing that prevents the child from learning two languages is deprivation of a second language. It is therefore an accidental environmental feature when children are deprived of a second language. It is language deprivation in that it is deprivation of *a* language rather than linguistic deprivation when no language at all is supplied. The UG model, since it does not recognise such accidents, cannot take the acquisition of one language as the norm that it has to account for but is bound to base itself on multiple acquisition of languages, taking monolingualism as a sub-category occurring in the absence of second language input. The device for learning language in the child's mind has to be capable of handling more than one language at a time. From the beginning monolingualism needs to be seen as an input-dependent constraint on the processes of language acquisition, which are perfectly capable of handling two languages at a time.

Let us briefly look at the notion of input. Lang$_3$ is language as 'a set of actual or potential sentences'. This sense recurred throughout 20th century linguistics: '[A] set (finite or infinite) of sentences, each finite in length and constructed out of a finite set of elements' (Chomsky, 1957: 13). It was brought into SLA research via a definition of interlanguage: '[T]he utterances which are produced when the learner attempts to say sentences of a TL [target language]' (Selinker, 1972). While Lang$_3$ seems a fairly precise meaning, it is, however, difficult to operate with once two languages come into the picture: how do we know that a set of sentences contains some sentences from one language, some from another? The input to many, if not most, children contains things that belong to more than one language in a Lang$_2$ sense. The logical problem for language acquisition is not just how the child acquires language from input but how they manage to separate two languages from an input that is not tagged as being language A or language B.

The argument of integrated language systems

Weinreich (1953) described three relationships between the languages in the bilingual mind: compound, coordinate and subordinate. Current UG-oriented SLA theory assumes a compound relationship: the two grammars are independent creations, two instantiations of Universal Grammar, not a single grammar, even if they have connections and links. One mental grammar has, say, set the pro-drop parameter to pro-drop, another has set it to non-pro-drop. An L2 user has two instantiations of the parameter with different settings, not one instantiation of the parameter with a variable setting according to the language being used.

Cook (2003) proposed an integrative continuum on which the possible relationships between the two languages are spread between the two poles of total separation and total integration. That is to say, the languages are constantly related, whether at the level of vocabulary, phonology or syntax. Acquiring a second language is not propping a lean-to against an existing house; it is rebuilding the property itself. An L2 user has not just added a second language to a impervious first language; they have created a complex overall system where L1 and L2 are inextricably tied together. It would not be surprising to find that the presence of a first language affects the second (transfer) and that the presence of a second affects the first (reverse transfer and L1 attrition); see Pavlenko and Jarvis (2007) for an exhaustive account. The mental grammars of the two languages are not isolated but interact to a greater or lesser degree.

If UG theory is to account for the language in the mind, it has to be flexible enough to accommodate this overall unity from the beginning. Indeed this has sometimes been allowed within UG; Universal Bilingualism permits more than one grammar to allow for transitional L1 stages at which both are in operation (Roeper, 1999); 'whatever the language faculty is it can assume many different states in parallel' (Chomsky, 2000: 59). The human mind may contain knowledge of an indefinite number of languages. If UG takes the single grammar as the norm, it cannot account for the composite system of multiple grammars, only for a default where the mind contains a single grammar.

The argument from numbers

Once in 19th century England, it may have been easy to conclude from everyday experience that most people only speak one language. Now five minutes walking on the streets of any English city, whether Newcastle upon Tyne or London, soon shows how many other languages are being used and how many different non-native accents of English are being spoken; a survey of London uncovered 300 different languages and 32% of children who spoke languages other than English at home (Baker & Eversley, 2000): bilingualism is rife. And the same would apply to almost any city or town across the globe. In the European Union 83% of young people have studied a second language (Commission of the European Communities, 1987); in Luxembourg 53% speak more than one language with their friends, and 56% speak more than one language in their workplace (European Union, 2005).

Most modern societies are multilingual in nature, however a country may recognize many official languages. While it is impossible to count the number of L2 users in the world today, they probably outnumber monolinguals: '[E]ven in the United States, the idea that people speak one language is certainly not true … everyone grows up in a multilingual environment' (Chomsky, 2000: 59).

The invisibility of L2 users for language and linguistics is partly a product of the emphasis on double monolinguals; the people that counted are 'balanced bilinguals' that behave exactly the same in two languages, not those that use L2 effectively but differently from native speakers, perhaps the overwhelming majority.

A second group of L2 users may outnumber those living together in multilingual societies, namely those who use a language they have been taught for purposes of their own; an estimated billion people are learning English as a language (British Council, 1999). English has an international L2 user community across the world for whom the native speaker community is virtually irrelevant; it is the interaction of academics, business-people, tourists and others with each other and with non-native communities that matters; 74% of tourist use of English around the globe is between non-native speakers (Graddol, 2006). Languages such as Latin and French previously had such a global role; Chinese may come to have a similar role with the spread of the study of Chinese as a second language. These are another type of L2 users: people who function in a second language for professional reasons in countries where the second language has no official status.

Adding together the multilingual groups and the lingua franca users produces a massive grand total of people for whom second languages are an integral part of their lives. Through its simplification to monolingual native speakers, Universal Grammar is ignoring the language knowledge in the minds of probably the majority of the human race.

The argument from discrimination

The key figure in Universal Grammar is the idealised monolingual native speaker. Labov's classic argument held that one group should not be measured against the norm of another (Labov, 1969); the comparison between groups yields differences, not deficits. In principle everybody is capable of the same richness of expression albeit in different ways, regardless of the language they speak, the situation they find themselves in or the characteristics of their individual minds. Hence no group of people have a better knowledge of UG than any other group; we all share the same UG heritage.

Over the years this concept of equality has been applied by linguists to:

- *Speakers of different languages*: 'The lowliest South African bushman speaks in the forms of a rich symbolic system that is in essence perfectly comparable to the speech of the cultivated Frenchman' (Sapir, 1921: 22). There is no way in which a linguist could see one language as better than another, even if this is often the view of the person in the street and of popular pundits on language.
- *Children and adults*: Chomsky's 1960s views on the independence of children's grammars led to children being treated in their own linguistic right rather than as defective adults, with occasional exceptions such as Smith (1973). Children's grammars were not adults' grammars seen through a distorting lens but different grammars.

- *Speakers of different dialects*: In a linguistic sense all regional dialects are equal, as Trudgill (1978) argued: Geordie dialect is not better or worse than received pronunciation (RP) in a linguistic sense, merely different. Only for social reasons can a particular dialect get prestige and status over other dialects as say an RP accent has greater status than Geordie.
- *Speakers of different social dialects*: Middle-class speakers may well speak differently from working-class speakers, as Bernstein (1971) and others suggested. This does not mean that objectively one class speaks better or worse than another class (Labov, 1969).
- *Black and white speakers:* Language intervention programs from the 1960s such as *Sesame Street* were predicated on the notion that black English was defective compared to white English. Labov (1969) showed that these were two dialects of the same language and there was no reason for claiming one was more logical or better than the other, except for the social implications of high-status and low-status languages.
- *Men and women*: Attempts to make women speak like men and vice versa would now be treated as ludicrous, only surviving perhaps in well-intentioned courses in conversational assertiveness for women. Whatever language differences there may be between the sexes, no-one would claim one is worse than the other.

So people should not be expected to conform to the norm of another group to which they do not belong, whether defined by race, class, sex or whatever. People who speak differently from some arbitrary group are not speaking better or worse, just differently.

Native speakers however are treated as a case apart; it is assumed that non-native knowledge of language only exists in relation to native knowledge. Succeeding in SLA means speaking it like a native speaker (and usually a speaker of a standard status form, not a dialect): 'Relative to native speaker's linguistic competence, learners' interlanguage is deficient by definition' (Kasper & Kellerman, 1997: 5). Ultimate attainment means native-like speech; 'absolute native-like command of an L2' (Hyltenstam & Abrahamsson, 2003: 575). The older the age of the second language learner the less able they are to sound like native speakers:

> …[S]ome learners can achieve very high levels of native-like pronunciation in mostly constrained tasks but [we] have yet to show that later learners can achieve the same level of phonology as native speakers in production. (DeKeyser & Larson Hall, 2005: 96)

And so on. The only true knowledge of a language is that of a native speaker, the only pure form of linguistic competence that of the native speaker; anything else has to be measured against it. It seems strange that, step-by-step, linguists have conceded that one group does not have inferior language to another, whether by race, class and sex, but are not prepared to see speakers of two languages as people in their own right measured by their own standards rather than those of a group to which they can never belong by definition – native speakers. The counter-argument is that non-native speakers are a unique group genuinely deficient compared to another group; this last-ditch defence was doubtless put forward for all the other groups listed above, whether children, working class or black.

The argument from cultural bias

All human sciences have to try to be on their guard against projecting the values of their own societies onto others. Time and again in language-based studies some construct is shown to be the consequence of the observer's preconceptions about language, say the discovery that relative orientation is not a universal for human beings (Levinson, 1996). Indeed many of the constructs of Western linguists have been traced back to the constraints of the alphabetic writing system used by their L1 writing systems, whether the phoneme as an artifact of letters (Aronoff, 1992) or the word as the artifact of using word-spaces to help reading (Olson, 1996).

Assumptions about bilingualism often betray the monolingual societies from which linguists came, in which learning another language was either an unusual intellectual feat carried out in universities or a considerable problem when carried out by the members of a minority ethnic community or by immigrants. Feat or challenge, acquiring a second language is never something ordinary to be taken for granted, as it is in countries where daily use of multiple languages is the norm, as in India and Cameroon.

UG linguists are not immune to the general inclination for Western societies to consider bilingualism as a problem rather than an asset. Bilingual children have needed special attention in all sorts of ways, and have threatened the monolingual standards of the classroom; the threat from immigration is often perceived as a threat to the society. Linguistics shows the background of linguists. A second language is seen to confer partial membership of another monolingual community rather than full membership of a bilingual community – what Brutt-Griffler (2002) terms the 'multi-competence of the community'. The language of a mixed community 'would not be "pure" in the relevant sense, because it would not represent a single set of choices among the options permitted by UG but rather would include "contradictory" choices for certain of these options' (Chomsky, 1986: 17). An L2 user becomes a secondary member of another monolingual community rather than part of a multilingual community of L2 users. So far as our overall argument goes, UG linguists have to convince that the purity they ascribe to the monolingual is not the projection of their own cultural belief about the normalcy of monolingualism.

The argument from the uniqueness of the L2 user

If we accept that L2 users exist as people in their own right and have as much claim to know their first and second languages as a monolingual, we need to establish their characteristics. Let us review some of their differences (not deficits!) from monolingual native speakers.

Different knowledge of the second language

It hardly needs to be said that the language of L2 users differs from that of monolingual native speakers. Years of research time have been devoted to trying to find cases where ultimate attainment is the same as native speakers. Undoubtedly there are cases where, in some aspects of language, non-native speakers can have the same linguistic knowledge as native speakers, say the Dutch speakers of English studied in Bongaerts *et al.* (1997). But these people are as relevant to the study of SLA as opera singers are to the study of phonology; the vast majority of L2 users are different from native speakers, however successful they may be as L2 users. If L2 users have set the UG parameters differently from monolinguals, this reflects the constrained world of the monolingual not deficiencies in their acquisition.

Different knowledge of the first language

It does need more argument that the L1 of the L2 user differs from the L1 of a monolingual native speaker of the same language. Let us take some quick syntactic examples: French speakers who know English react against French sentences using the middle voice *Un tricot de laine se lave à l'eau froide.* (*A wool sweater washes in cold water) compared to those who don't know English (Balcom, 2003); 'near-native' Greek learners of English produce far more definite pre-verbal subjects in Greek than monolingual native speakers (Tsimpli *et al.*, 2004); Japanese, Greek and Spanish speakers of English prefer the first noun to be the subject of the sentence in *The dog pats the tree* (translated into their respective languages) to a greater extent than those who do not know English (Cook *et al.*, 2003). In other words the L1 of the L2 user differs syntactically from the L1 of monolinguals in subtle ways.

Different language uses

The language abilities of L2 users have usually been discussed in terms of what L2 users lack: anything that differs from the monolingual native speaker is a deficiency. What about the other way round? What can L2 users do that monolinguals can't? The main categories are those functions that crucially rely on the presence of two languages in the same mind.

One is the process of translation; some, but not all, L2 users can hear or read a text in one language and produce an equivalent text in another. A common situation round the world is the children of immigrants acting as translators for their parents. At the top levels this can be done professionally in the highly skilled arts of simultaneous and consecutive interpreting. Curiously enough, UG theory has taken little interest in this ability of the human mind, presumably seeing it as a specific aspect of performance. Yet the ability to function in two languages simultaneously must show both the close relationships of the languages in the mind and the ability to keep them apart. Which of course monolinguals are incapable of as they don't have two languages.

The other is the process of codeswitching. Many L2 users switch between their languages during the process of speech, from one word, clause or sentence to the next, according to a host of rules about the social situation, the topic being discussed and the grammatical overlaps between the two languages (Milroy & Muyskens, 1995). Codeswitching shows that it is perfectly possible to use two grammars in the mind simultaneously. One alternative is to see this as ultra-swift switching between the two grammars during production or comprehension. The more economical choice is to see it as switching within the single overall grammar for both languages. Codeswitching is a simple everyday activity for L2 users that monolinguals cannot do. A UG theory that cannot take this in is deficient. The argument that these skills are simply an extended version of what monolingual native speakers do when switching dialect or paraphrasing may indeed be true but here is immaterial since this could still not be accommodated with UG theory.

This is not the place to detail the other cognitive differences of the L2 user, described in say Cook (2007). The L2 user is not just a monolingual with another language but someone whose mind has been transformed by knowing two languages: bilinguals think differently.

At the moment we have no idea how much L2 it takes to affect the L1; most research has dealt with fairly advanced L2 learners. Yet primary school English children who learn Italian for an hour a week for five months learn to recognize English words better than monolinguals (Yelland *et al.*, 1993); even so small an exposure can have an effect. It is unsafe to assume that such reverse transfer only occurs at high levels of L2 proficiency.

Different knowledge of other languages

Those working in the developing area of multilingualism such as Cenoz *et al.* (2001) have shown that we should not consider only the first and second languages but also further languages. Cantonese (L1)–English (L2) speakers learn (L3) French better than Vietnamese (L1)–English (L2) speakers (Leung, 2005). English (L1)–Spanish (L2) speakers transfer 19%

of L1 function words to (L3) French, 81% from their L2; Spanish (L1)–English (L2) speakers 97% from their L1, 3% from their L2 [[author to check on proofs]] (De Angelis, 2005). The sequence of acquisition of multiple languages as well as their differences affects the resulting linguistic competence. Knowledge of language is different in trilinguals. Again there must be large numbers of people in the world who know more than two languages, particularly in countries such as India and Cameroon. A monolingual UG theory reduces multilingualism to an exception; multilingual UG treats it within the same framework as monolingualism and bilingualism.

Consequences for UG Theory

UG theory is failing if, far from accepting L2 users as having one of the basic types of language knowledge, it dismisses their knowledge as a defective version of the monolingual's. Suppose that the starting point for UG theory is not a language in the mind but language in the mind, consisting of one or more languages. What are the consequences for UG theory in general and for UG-related SLA research?

Consequences for the poverty-of-the-stimulus argument

Monolingual input can be seen as language deprivation that supplies triggers for only one parameter setting, say pro-drop. The unrestricted multilingual environment provides enough material for two or more simultaneous parameter settings, say both pro-drop and non-pro-drop. The poverty-of-the-stimulus argument describes how certain aspects of language are unlearnable from the $Lang_3$ set of sentences encountered by monolinguals, either pro-drop or non-pro-drop. With multilingual UG, the poverty-of-the-stimulus argument has to be defined as whether these aspects are learnable from a $Lang_3$ set of sentences including examples of both pro-drop and non-pro-drop. The mind does not normally have to deal with monolingual input but with multilingual input; the interesting question is how the child, who does not receive an input neatly labeled as language A and language B, manages to acquire two parameter settings from one undifferentiated input – a fascinatingly changed research question for UG theory. The problem is how the child manages to gate the languages to keep the settings etc. apart.

Consequences for the grammar

The form of the grammar now has to be such that it can simultaneously have two settings for each parameter in the same mind, not dodged by treating multilingualism as an endlessly reiterated monolingualism. The UG-based SLA research has mostly talked of two grammars, one per language; grammars clone as and when necessary. So there are two copies of the parameters; the issue becomes whether the initial setting for the second grammar parameters is neutral, default or L1, as seen in the hypothesis turf-wars of the 1990s (Cook & Newson, 2007). If the mental grammar is multilingual, the problem is how the two values for a parameter are simultaneously available to the L2 user; the monolingual is an oddity in that they are restricted to one value. (Perhaps this means the metaphor of parameter setting is too restricting; an alternative would be gearboxes, the monolingual having one gear, the L2 user two or more.) Satterfield (2003) argues on evidence from pro-drop in Spanish speakers in the USA that a level above parameter setting is involved, namely in the computational system itself where features are calculated online and the multilingual has to avoid the costliness of two operations. This must be a property of all minds that is unused by monolinguals; to account for the language faculty, UG theory has to accommodate the multilingual mind. '[B]ilingualism should stand as a rigorous barometer for measuring the feasibility of our most developed linguistic theories' (Satterfield, 1999: 137).

Consequences for research methods

The arguments have shown that people who know two languages differ in many unexpected ways from monolinguals. The straightforward consequence for UG-based research is that, to learn about pure monolingual *grammar*, you have to ask pure monolinguals. The L1 of L2 users may have been 'contaminated' by their L2: '[T]he judgements about English of Bloomfield, Halliday or Chomsky are not trustworthy, except where they are supported by evidence from "pure" monolinguals' (Cook, 2002: 23).

Indeed the research method of asking for grammaticality judgments may itself be suspect since L2 users have greater metalinguistic ability (Bialystok, 1991). Descriptions of language for monolingual UG have also to be based on the usage of these pure monolinguals; an Italian who knows English may no longer use a pro-drop Italian; in phonology Kato (2004) showed that the standard values given for Voice Onset Time for Japanese differed from those for 'pure' monolinguals because they had been measured on Japanese living in the United States. Monolingual UG has to clean up its act by ensuring that it is indeed looking at pure monolinguals of the idealised 1965 type and the researchers are either pure monolinguals themselves or are capable of distancing themselves from the effects of their L2 on their L1. But the search for pure monolinguals may be hard, given the extent to which the ability to use another language is now spread around the globe. For research comparing monolinguals and bilinguals we had to call off the search for pure monolingual Japanese (Cook *et al.*, 2006) since every Japanese child is taught English from the age of 12 on and were forced to substitute groups made up of minimal and maximal speakers of English.

The alternative is to abandon the pure monolingual and to start from the view that multilingualism is the norm. Most people are users of second languages to a greater or lesser extent. Pure monolingual sentences and pure monolingual judgments may be virtually impossible to find.

Consequences for the relevant data

Researchers have constantly striven to use performance data to justify their analyses of linguistic competence, particularly in child language (Cook, 1990), despite the 1960s arguments that you can't get there from here. We collect large corpora of sentences and texts and base our analyses upon them. As we saw earlier, the learning problem for the child is how they know which language the sentences are in. The same problem arises for the linguist dealing with corpora of L2 users' sentences. Once it was easy: 'A structuralist theory of communication which distinguishes between speech and language ... necessarily assumes that "every speech event belongs to a definite language"' (Weinreich, 1953: 7). But it doesn't. The L1 sentences a L2 user produces often differ from those of a monolingual native speaker, not just their L2 sentences, let alone sentences with overt codeswitching. The $Lang_2$ that the utterance belongs to is in the mind of the beholder. SLA research needs to consider the whole set of sentences, not rejecting some in advance; only later can the sentences be assigned to languages according to other criteria. Bilingual speech therapists have long argued that therapy should be based on the child's first language as well as their second (Duncan, 1989; Stow & Dodd, 2003).

Conclusion

This chapter has then tried to approach UG theory from the assumption that bilingualism is the norm, monolingualism the consequence of inadequate input. Doubtless much of this reasoning may be wrong. Nevertheless it is salutary to look at the language acquisition from this different perspective and to question whether UG theory can achieve its basic task of describing how human minds acquire, store and use language without taking into account the minds that cope with more than one language.

References

Aronoff, M. (1992) Segmentalism in linguistics: The alphabetic basis of phonological theory. In P. Downing, S.D. Lima and M. Noonan (eds) *The Linguistics of Literacy* (pp. 71–82). Amsterdam: Benjamins.

Baker, P. and Eversley, J. (2000) *Multilingual Capital*. London: Battlebridge.

Balcom, P. (2003) Cross-linguistic influence of L2 English on middle constructions in L1 French. In V.J. Cook (ed.) *L2 Effects on the L1* (pp. 168-192). Clevedon: Multilingual Matters.

Bernstein, B. (1971) *Class, Codes and Control* (Vol. 1). London: Routledge & Kegan Paul.

Bialystok, E. (1991) Metalinguistic dimensions of bilingual language proficiency. In E. Bialystok (ed.) *Language Processing in Bilingual Children* (pp. 113–140). Cambridge: Cambridge University Press.

Bongaerts, T., Planken, B. and Schils, E. (1997) Age and ultimate attainment in the pronunciation of a foreign language. *Second Language Research* 19, 447–465.

British Council (n.d.) Frequently asked questions. On www at http://www.britishcouncil.org/learning-faq-the-english-language.htm. Accessed 19.08.2008.

Brutt-Griffler, J. (2002) *World English: A Study of its Development.* Clevedon: Multilingual Matters.

Canagarajah, A.S. (2005) Reconstructing local knowledge, reconfiguring language studies. In A.S. Canagarajah (ed.) *Reclaiming the Local in Language Policy and Practice* (pp. 3–24). Mahwah,NJ: Lawrence Erlbaum Associates.

Cenoz, J., Hufeisen, B. and Jessner, U. (eds) (2001) *Cross-linguistic Influence in Third Language Acquisition: Psycholinguistic Perspectives.* Clevedon: Multilingual Matters.

Chomsky, N. (1957) *Syntactic Structures.* The Hague: Mouton.

Chomsky, N. (1965) *Aspects of the Theory of Syntax*. Boston, MA: MIT Press.

Chomsky, N. (1982) *Some Concepts and Consequences of the Theory of Government and Binding.* Boston, MA.: MIT Press

Chomsky, N. (1986) *Knowledge of Language: Its Nature, Origin and Use.* New York: Praeger.

Chomsky, N. (1991) Some notes on economy of derivation and representation. In R. Freidin (ed.) *Principles and Parameters in Comparative Grammar* (pp. 417–545). Cambridge, MA: MIT Press.

Chomsky, N. (2000) *The Architecture of Language.* New Delhi: Oxford University Press.

Commission of the European Communities (1987) *Young Europeans in 1987.* Brussels: EC Commission.

Cook, V.J. (1990) Observational evidence and the UG theory of language acquisition. In I. Roca (ed.) *Logical Issues in Language Acquisition.* Dordrecht: Foris.

Cook, V.J. (2002) Background to the L2 user. In V.J. Cook (ed.) *Portraits of the L2 User* (pp. 1–28). Clevedon: Multilingual Matters.

Cook, V.J. (2003) Introduction: The changing L1 in the L2 user's mind. In V.J. Cook (ed.) *Effects of the Second Language on the First* (pp. 1–18). Clevedon: Multilingual Matters.

Cook, V.J. (2007) The nature of the L2 user. In L. Roberts and A. Gurel (eds) *EUROSLA Yearbook* (Vol. 7) (pp. 205–220). Amsterdam: Benjamins.

Cook, V.J. and Newson, M. (2007) *Chomsky's Universal Grammar: An Introduction* (3rd ed. Oxford: Blackwell.

Cook, V.J., Iarossi, E., Stellakis, N. and Tokumaru, Y. (2003) Effects of the second language on the syntactic processing of the first language. In V.J. Cook (ed.) *Effects of the Second Language on the First* (pp. 214–233). Clevedon: Multilingual Matters.

Cook, V.J., Bassetti, B., Kasai, C., Sasaki, M. and Takahashi, J.A. (2006) Do bilinguals have different concepts? The case of shape and material in Japanese L2 users of English. *International Journal of Bilingualism* 10 (2), 137–152.

Curtiss, S. (1977) *Genie: A Psycholinguistic Study of a Modern-day 'Wild child'.* New York: Academic Press.

De Angelis, G. (2005) Interlanguage transfer of function words. *Language Learning* 55, 379–414.

DeKeyser, R. and Larson Hall, J. (2005) What does the critical period really mean? In J. Kroll and A. De Groot (eds) *Handbook of Bilingualism: Psycholinguistic Approaches* (pp. 88–108). Oxford: Oxford University Press.

Duncan, D.M. (1989) *Working with Bilingual Language Disability*. London: Chapman and Hall.

European Union (2005) The Luxembourg presidency. Also on WWW at: http://www.eu2005.lu/en/presidence/index.html. Accessed 11.08.2008.

Graddol, D. (2006) *English Next*. London: The British Council. Also on www at: http://www.britishcouncil.org/files/documents/learning-research-english-next.pdf. Accessed 19.08.2008.

Hyltenstam, K. and Abrahamsson, N. (2003) Maturational constraints in SLA: A test of the critical period hypothesis. In C. Doughty and M. Long (eds) *The Handbook of Second Language Acquisition* (pp. 359–588). Rowley, MA: Blackwell.

Kasper, G. and Kellerman, E. (eds) (1997) *Communication Strategies: Psycholinguistic and Sociolinguistic Perspectives*. London: Longman.

Kato, K. (2004) Second language (L2) segmental speech learning: Perception and production of L2 English by Japanese native speakers. Unpublished PhD dissertation, University of Essex, UK.

Labov, W. (1969) The logic of non-standard English. *Georgetown Monographs on Language and Linguistics* 22, 1–31.

Lenneberg, E. (1967) *Biological Foundations of Language*. New York: Wiley & Sons.

Leung, Y-k.I. (2005) L2 vs. L3 initial state: A comparative study of the acquisition of French DPs by Vietnamese monolinguals and Cantonese–English bilinguals. *Bilingualism: Language and Cognition* 8 (1), 39–61.

Levinson, S.C. (1996) Relativity in spatial conception and description. In J.J. Gumperz and S.C. Levinson (eds) *Rethinking Linguistic Relativity* (pp. 177-202). Cambridge: Cambridge University Press.

Milroy, L. and Muyskens, P. (eds) (1995) *One Speaker, Two Languages*. Cambridge: Cambridge University Press.

Olson, D.R. (1996) Toward a psychology of literacy: On the relations between speech and writing. *Cognition* 60, 83–104.

Pavlenko, A. and Jarvis, S. (2007) *Cross Linguistic Influence*. Mahwah, NJ: Lawrence Erlbaum.

Roeper, T. (1999) Universal bilingualism. *Bilingualism: Language & Cognition* 2, 169–186.

Said, E. (1999) *Out of Place: A Memoir*. New York: Vintage Books.

Sapir, E. (1921) *Language: An Introduction to the Study of Speech*. New York: Harcourt, Brace and Company.

Satterfield, T. (1999) *Bilingual Selection of Syntactic Knowledge: Extending the Principles and Parameters Approach*. Dordrecht: Kluwer.

Satterfield, T. (2003) Economy of interpretation: Patterns of pronoun selection in transitional bilinguals. In V.J. Cook (ed.) *L2 Effects on the L1* (pp. 214–233). Clevedon: Multilingual Matters.

Selinker, L. (1972) Interlanguage. *International Review of Applied Linguistics* X (3), 209–231.

Smith, N. (1973) *The Acquisition of Phonology: A Case Study*. Cambridge: Cambridge University Press.

Stow, C. and Dodd, B. (2003) Providing an equitable service to bilingual children in the UK: A review. *International Journal of Language and Communication Disorders* 38 (4), 351–377.

Trudgill, P. (1978) *Accent, Dialect and the School*. London: Edward Arnold.

Tsimpli, T., Sorace, A., Heycock, C. and Filiaci, F. (2004) First language attrition and syntactic subjects: A study of Greek and Italian near-native speakers of English. *International Journal of Bilingualism* 3, 257–278.

Weinreich, U. (1953) *Languages in Contact*. The Hague: Mouton.

Yelland, G.W., Pollard, J. and Mercuri, A. (1993) The metalinguistic benefits of limited contact with a second language. *Applied Psycholinguistics* 14, 423–444.

Chapter 4

UG and L3 Acquisition: New Insights and More Questions[1]

Suzanne Flynn

Introduction

> *The problem that has virtually defined the serious study of language since its ancient origins, if only implicitly, is to identify the specific nature of this distinctive human possession.*
>
> (Chomsky, 2007: 1)

During the last 50 years or so, generative attempts to determine the character of this language faulty (LF) have led to explosive developments in the study of natural language as well as to significant advances in the study of language acquisition. While the work in acquisition within this generative framework has traditionally focused on first language (L1) learning (see reviews of the literature in Lust, 2006 and Roeper, 2007), the field of second language (L2) acquisition has also progressed in many ways. The theoretical and empirical advances (e.g. see papers and discussion in Cook, 2002; Liceras *et al.*, 2008 among others) in L2 acquisition have demonstrated that careful investigation of the L2 process is likely to be a very fruitful and productive endeavor in understanding the cognitive processes specific to language learning or the biological endowment for language.

However, in this chapter we argue that a comparison of L1 and L2 acquisition *alone* is not sufficient in terms of our understanding of the human capacity for language. We need to investigate the acquisition of a third language (L3) in order to unconfound certain factors left confounded in an L1/L2 acquisition comparison alone (see also Flynn *et al.*, 2001, 2004, 2008; Leung, 2002, 2005, 2008). The role of the L1 in subsequent language learning is left unanswered by L1/L2 acquisition studies alone. Does all next language learning fundamentally derive from the learner's L1? That is, do the properties of the L1 grammar *alone* determine language learning in, for example, the L3? Or is it possible that language learning is a cumulative process? That is, can grammatical properties of all prior languages known potentially determine subsequent patterns? And, if so, which grammatical properties? To the degree that anyone can be introspective about one's own language representation in the mind/brain, multilinguals often anecdotally relate that they believe that there are essentially two representations for language in their mind/brain: one for the L1 and one for all other languages known. Can this be shown to be empirically true? And if it is true, what types of consequences follow from such a mind/brain representation? Alternatively, it might be the case that neither the L1 nor any other language known has a privileged role with respect to the learning of a subsequent language. That is to say, it might be the case that each language learned and represented in the mind/brain of the learner is equally important and perhaps equally available for playing some role in subsequent language learning. If we had answers to these questions, they would prove important in terms of the articulation of a theory of the mind and language. Specifically, they would be relevant with respect to the integration of hypothesized innate principles of language and language specific properties in the development of a particular language grammar. In addition, results would uniquely inform us concerning how a learner moves from an 'initial' state to an 'end' state in grammar construction. More precisely, an understanding of this development would inform what we mean by an initial state – a concept that has been the source of much confusion and misunderstanding.

Research from L3 acquisition studies could also critically inform current debates concerning how much innate structure must be posited to explain language acquisition thus providing an important test of hypotheses concerning current claims made with respect to statistical models for language learning (e.g. Saffran *et al.*, 1999). Such research also contributes to an understanding of both universal constraints and variation in human languages. The interaction of hypothesized universal constraints with language-specific features in the design and the evidence of children and adults in all forms of multilingual settings indicating knowledge of this interaction will shed light on the syntax of language itself. At a more general level, as noted by many, the study of acquisition provides insights about the structure of adult languages that would not be made available through the study of 'final-state' grammars alone (Lust, 2006; McDaniel *et al.*, 1996). The study of L3 acquisition intensifies this study.

Research Focus of this Chapter

The research that is summarized in this paper is guided by three questions:

(1) Do the properties of the L1 grammar alone determine language learning in L3 development?
(2) Can grammatical properties of all prior languages known potentially determine subsequent patterns?

(3) How can these results inform us concerning the nature of the *initial state* for language learning?

In order to answer these questions, this research has focused on the acquisition of restricted relative clauses.

Background

L1 acquisition

The L1 acquisition of relative clauses in English has a long and well-documented history. Some of the early studies to which we make critical reference in this chapter include Hamburger (1980), Hamburger and Crain (1982), Goodluck and Tavakolian (1982) and Flynn *et al.* (2005), among others. These studies have provided both natural speech samples as well as controlled experimental data.

Of particular importance to this chapter is Flynn and Lust's (1981) study of monolingual children acquiring English (3 years 0 months to 7 years 0 months). Using an elicited imitation method (Lust *et al.*, 1987; Lust *et al.*, 1996), Flynn and Lust compared children's production of three relative clause types. Table 4.1 summarizes the design for the Flynn and Lust (1981) study of L1 acquisition of English. The stimulus sentences all involved relativization of a noun phrase object; within subordinate relative clause structure, the gap varied in terms of being either the *subject* or *object* (object$_{matrix}$/ subject$_{subordinate}$ and object$_{matrix}$/ object$_{subordinate}$).

Results of this study revealed that the free relative clause structures in (c) were significantly more productive than either of the lexically headed types in (a) and (b) both overall and in the youngest age groups. *Significantly more productive* in this context means that children correctly imitated the sentences with free relative clause structures significantly more often than sentences with either the lexically headed relative clause with semantic content (sentence a) or the lexically headed relative clause with no semantic content (sentence b). In addition, in terms of the errors made on the three types of relative clause sentences, the children converted both types of the lexically headed sentence structures (sentences a and b) to a free relative clause construction significantly more often than they converted a free relative clause structure to a lexically headed clause structure. For

Table 4.1 Three types of relative clause structures tested in Flynn and Lust (1981)

(a) Lexically headed, *head* with semantic content	Big Bird pushes the balloon [which bumps Ernie]
(b) Lexically headed, *head* with no semantic content	Ernie pushes the thing [which touches Big Bird]
(c) Free relative	Cookie Monster hits [what pushes Big Bird]

example, when children were given the sentence, 'Big Bird pushes the balloon which bumps Ernie' they would often convert this sentence to 'Big Bird pushes what bumps Ernie' in their imitation of the stimulus sentence. In this regard, it is important to point out that all of the sentence structures tested were equated in syllable and word length. Thus, we cannot explain the results elicited in terms of a free relative clause structure being 'simpler' due to fewer words in the stimuli. These results are robust and replicate earlier reported findings in natural speech production (Hamburger, 1980).

To briefly summarize, these results indicate the primacy of the free relative clause construction in the early development of subordination in child L1 acquisition. Subsequently, other L1 acquisition studies have isolated a similar pattern of results across a wide range of languages (e.g. Flynn *et al.*, 2005; Lee, 1991; Packard, 1987).

L2 acquisition

The same three types of relative clause structures that were varied in terms of the semantic and syntactic status of the relativized 'head' investigated in child L1 acquisition (see Table 4.1) have been investigated in studies of adult L2 acquisition of English. Flynn (1983, 1987) investigated adult Japanese and Spanish speakers acquiring English using elicited imitation and comprehension as the experimental tasks; we will report only the production results here. Each subject was at one of three levels of English proficiency (low, mid and high) as established by the Michigan Test. In the design of this study, the same types of experimental controls implemented for the L1 studies were also implemented in the L2 studies. For example, the number of words and syllables for each stimulus sentence were precisely equated across all sentence types. Knowledge of the lexical items used in the stimulus sentences was also controlled. Each participant in the study was given a bilingual list of the words used in the stimulus sentences both in the L1 and the L2 to study well in advance of the actual study. On the day of the study, the participants were tested in terms of their knowledge of the lexical items used in English prior to testing. This was done in order to make sure that the results obtained were not due to a lack of knowledge of the English lexicon but rather were due to syntactic factors involved in the developing language specific grammars of the learners of English.

Japanese

Japanese is a head-final, left-branching language (sentence 2) and therefore does not match English (sentence 1) in head direction (head-initial, right-branching):

(1) John read [$_{head}$ the book [$_{complement}$ that Mary wrote]]

(2) John-wa   [_complement Mary-ga   kaita   [_head hon-o]]   yonda.
    John-theme   Mary-nom   wrote   book-acc   read
    'John read the book that Mary wrote'   (Saito, 1985)

Spanish

Spanish (sentence 3), in contrast to Japanese, but like English, is a head-initial, right-branching language. For example, the relative clause 'that Maria wrote' *que María escribío* follows the head NP 'book' *libro*, as in (3):

(3) Juan leyó   [el libro   [que   María escribío]].
    Juan read   the book   that   Maria wrote

Results of these studies with the Japanese and Spanish speakers indicated that for L1 Japanese/L2 English speakers, the free relative clause structure appears to be a developmental precursor to the lexically headed form, as in L1 acquisition of English.

However, unlike the L1 acquisition of English and the L2 acquisition of English by Japanese speakers, the acquisition of L2 English by Spanish speakers, the free relative is *not* a developmental precursor to the lexically headed forms. This is an extremely interesting result given the fact that the Spanish and Japanese speakers were equated at all levels of English competence as determined by the Michigan Test as well as in their knowledge of all their knowledge of the lexical items used in the stimulus sentences and the experimental task requirements. In addition, the results of these studies were analyzed in terms of an analysis of covariance (ANCOVA). This statistical analysis of the results ensured that the two language groups were equivalent both overall and at each developmental stage.

Thus, the fact that the free relative clause structure was not a developmental precursor at any level in the Spanish speakers' L2 acquisition of English is an important result that needs to be explained and understood in some principled manner. The L2 acquisition by Spanish speakers appears different from L1 acquisition of English and the L2 acquisition of English by Japanese speakers. One explanation suggested by these results is that both the L1 English-speaking children and the L2 Japanese speakers learning English had no prior grammatical experience with a head-initial, right-branching language. The L1 children needed to determine this parametric value for English as their L1 and the Japanese speakers needed to establish this parametric value for English, their L2, for the first time. Given the head-final, left-branching structure of Japanese, these L2 learners had no prior grammatical experience with a head-initial, right-branching grammar. The results suggest that both 'determining' and experience with the consequences of the parametric value of this grammatical principle is necessary in acquisition in terms of the development of a language-specific grammar. In this way, it appears that the free rela-

Table 4.2 General summary of results of relative clause studies for L1 and L2
Sources: Flynn and Lust (1981); Flynn, (1983 1987)

Target language	*Group*	*Pattern*
(a) English as L1	Children	Free relative precedes lexically headed relative clause
(b) English as L2	Adults, L1 Japanese (head-final)	Free relative precedes lexically headed relative clause
(c) English as L2	Adults, L1 Spanish (head-initial)	Free relative does NOT precede lexically headed relative clause

tive construction plays an essential role in the development of subordination and more largely in terms of the grammar as a whole. In the case of the Spanish speakers learning English as an L2, these learners have already had experience with a language-specific grammar realized as head-initial, right-branching. Further developing of this line of reasoning, it appears that the consequences of this parametric value did not need to be re-established for another language-specific grammar when such a configuration is also represented in the mind/brain in some manner. From this general hypothesis, we will generate several empirical predictions that will form the basis of the studies we summarize here in this chapter. The earlier L1 and L2 results are summarized in Table 4.2.

Predictions for L3 Acquisition Study

The results of previous studies summarized in Table 4.2 suggest the following:

(1) In L1/L2 acquisition of relative clauses there is linguistic development, a process by which the learner constructs a specific language grammar (i.e. a theory of the specific language, Chomsky, (2000)).
(2) Consistent with a theory of language within a generative framework, the importance of the variation in Complementizer Phrase(CP) architecture across languages. This variation is considered to be finite and it results from the lexical and feature differences in a universal architecture for CP.
(3) Free relatives (also called headless relative clauses) are developmental precursors to headed relatives when the learner develops a new architecture of the CP (see also Flynn *et al.*, 2008).

However, certain questions remain unanswered:

(1) Are the differences in results between Japanese and Spanish speakers due to typological variation in the CP between L1 and L2 alone?
(2) Is our conclusion with respect to the Spanish speakers a viable one?

These questions lead us to test a hypothesis by studying L3 acquisition, namely, the acquisition of English as an L3 by L1 Kazakh/L2 Russian speakers. In particular, we suggest the following:

(1) If there is a privileged role for the L1 in all subsequent language acquisition and if typological differences alone determine patterns of development then L3 acquisition of English by L1 speakers of Kazakh should resemble L2 acquisition of English by Japanese (since Kazakh is similar to Japanese in a head direction).
(2) If, on the other hand, a learner has acquired or experienced development of a grammar with a new CP then we would predict for a learner of an L3 with L1 CP distinct from the L3 but with L2 consistent with the L3, CP patterns of acquisition much like those isolated in L2 acquisition of English by Spanish.

If the assumption in (2) is correct then:

(3) Development of the CP structures in a prior language or languages determines the course of future language-specific development.
(4) Having integrated language-specific CP features with universal knowledge of CP in earlier language acquisition, the learner can draw upon that developmental process or template created by this earlier developmental experience in later acquisition.

Once again, to test these predictions, we studied the acquisition of relative clauses by Kazakh speakers who acquired Russian as an L2 and English as an L3.

Syntactic background

Kazakh is a Turkish language with primary Subject Verb Order (SVO) order and a head-final, left-branching structure, like Japanese. It does not match English in its word order or head direction. Thus, in Kazakh, relative clauses appear to the left of their heads. For example, in (4), the relative clause appears to the left of the head 'girl.' In Kazakh, as in (4), there are no overt wh-operators or overt complementizers in relative clauses. The boundary between the relative clause and the main clause is indicated in the verbal morphology – for example, in (4), by the participial form of the verb 'drink.'

Lexically headed relative clause

(4) **[Sut- isken]** **kyz** bolmege kirdi
    milk-ACC drink-PART girl-NOM room-dat enter-past
    '(A/the) girl who drank (the) milk entered (a/the) room.'

In contrast, Russian is a Slavic language, with primary SVO order and a head-initial, right-branching language. It matches English in word order and branching direction; it does not match Kazakh. This is illustrated in (5) where the relative clause appears to the right of the Noun Phrase (NP) head, 'professor'.

Lexically headed relative clause

(5) **Professor   [kotory priglasil lektora]** predstavil vraca
professor-NOM   who   invite-PAST   speaker-ACC   introduce-PA
doctor-ACC
'The professor who invited the speaker introduced the doctor.'

The L3 in our experiment, English, thus matches the L2 in branching direction, but not the L1. If the L3 learner is to draw on experience with a right-branching language in constructing relative clauses in English, this experience would have to come from Russian, and not from Kazakh.

Design, method and subjects

The design of the new study varied along three factors, as seen in Table 4.3.

The design matched that of the L1 and L2 relative clause studies summarized previously in Tables 4.1 and 4.2.

Table 4.3 Three types of relative clauses in adult L3 study
Sources: Flynn *et al. (2000, 2004, 2008)*

	Head position: Subject		Head position: Object	
Type	*Gap position: Subject*	*Gap position: Object*	*Gap position: Subject*	*Gap position: Object*
Lexically headed, specified	The lawyer who criticized the worker called the policeman.	The student who the professor introduced answered the man.	The boss introduced the gentleman who questioned the lawyer.	The woman instructed the lawyer who the policeman called.
Lexically headed, unspecified	The person who criticized the engineer greeted the man.	The person who the engineer answered criticized the man.	The boss introduced the person who instructed the lawyer.	The janitor questioned the person who the student greeted.
Free relative	Whoever entered the office introduced the professor.	Whoever the policeman greeted questioned the gentleman.	The professor introduced whoever greeted the lawyer.	The doctor answered whoever the policeman criticized.

Table 4.4 Subject information, adults. L3 study

Level	n	Mean ESL score*
Low	7	11
Mid	14	19
High	12	26
Total	33	20

Note: *ESL scores are from the Michigan Test.

Using an elicited imitation task, we tested adults ($N = 33$) at one of three levels of English as a Second Language (ESL) development (low, mid and high) as measured by the Michigan Test. Subject information is summarized in Table 4.4.

Results

Responses were coded as 'correct' if they matched the stimulus sentence, and as 'incorrect' if they significantly differed from the stimulus form. Several minor changes were viewed as insignificant (e.g. changes in pronunciation that were not grammatically relevant).

Results in Table 4.5 reveal that for adults, performance across the three relative clause types was closely matched (i.e. no significant difference in amount correct across type and developmental level), as it was for Spanish speakers acquiring L2 English. The three-way contrast across *relative clause type* is not significant for the L1 Kazakh group. This same result also characterized L1 Spanish acquisition of L2 English as noted above in the discussion of our earlier L2 studies. These results vividly contrast with the Japanese results, as did the pattern of results for the Spanish speakers as originally reported. Since Kazakh is like Japanese in its Subject Order Verb (SOV), left-branching structure, this contrast would have been surprising if these speakers had not also had experience with a right-branching language (Russian as an L2).

Table 4.5 Kazakh percentage responses without changes, by stimulus type and group

Group	Headed (semantic content	Headed (no semantic content)	Free relative
Low (n = 7)	57	50	50
Mid (n = 14)	51	45	48
Hi (n = 12)	67	66	67
Total (n = 33)	58	54	56

In addition, the results of the error analyses also suggest the fact that the free relative is *not* developmentally primary to the lexically headed relative clauses for the adult Kazakh speakers. The error data for the Japanese speakers in their acquisition of English as an L2 indicated significant conversions of the lexically headed relative clauses to free relative clause structures in the analysis of the errors. The results of L1 acquisition of English revealed a similar result. However, the results for the Spanish speakers' L2 acquisition of English indicated no such preference. The results for the adult Kazakh speakers' acquisition of English as an L3 do not indicate any preference for the free relative. These results, as hypothesized, pattern with those for L1 Spanish acquisition of L2 English.

The L1 Japanese/L2 English speakers differentiated the three types of relative clauses in their imitations in terms of the error analyses as well. In terms of the errors, speakers often changed a lexically headed relative clause to a free relative clause in their imitations of the structures. In contrast, the Japanese speakers rarely converted free relative clause structures to lexically headed relatives. This is an interesting result given the fact that the stimulus sentences were all equalized in terms of number of words and syllables. Important for the purposes of this chapter is the fact that the Kazakh speakers rarely, if ever, converted the lexically headed to free relatives or the free relatives to lexically headed in their errors. This same result characterizes the Spanish speakers' L2 acquisition of English as well.

Discussion and Conclusions

In general, the results for the adult L3 learners of English confirm our prediction. They provide evidence that patterns for the L1 Kazakh/L2 Russian/L3 English speakers match those for L1 Spanish/L2 English, rather than L1 Japanese/L2 English as hypothesized above. These results suggest that prior CP development can influence development of CP structure in subsequent language acquisition. Taken together, these results suggest that experience in any prior language can be drawn upon in subsequent acquisition. The L1 does not play a privileged role in subsequent language acquisition. However, the adult results we report here are left confounded with respect to the role of an immediately prior learned language. Could it be that the last learned language determines the next language learned in some sense? Such an explanation is compatible with the results reported here as well. Subsequent testing demands that we consider the acquisition of an L3 by a speaker in which the CP properties, for example, match in the L1 and the L3 but not the L2. For example, we need to investigate the acquisition of Japanese by a Korean speaker who has learned English as an L2. In this case, we would predict that the learner's L1 should determine patterns of acquisition in the L3 and we would additionally predict that the patterns in this case would be enhanced relative to the L1 acquisition of Japanese and the L2 acquisition of Japanese by an L1 English speaker. Assuming however that the model hypothesized in this chapter withstands analysis, the results are consistent with the minimalist emphasis on formal features of the functional category CP: UG seems to demand that learners of an L1, an L2 and beyond use these features in mapping to language-specific clausal architecture. The results have implications for the representation of knowledge in the mind. In particular, they support the view that domain-specific structure for learning may exist, and that 'movement along a domain-relevant learning path' characterizes L1, L2 and L3 acquisition. Results also suggest, in support of the basic premise of the *cumulative enhancement model* (Flynn *et al.*, 2004) for language acquisition, that developmental patterns in language learning are not redundant. Finally, language acquisition is accumulative, i.e. the prior language can be neutral or enhance subsequent language acquisition.

In addition, in contrast to language-specific knowledge, the universal knowledge underlying the free relative appears to be fully available at all points in development. The free relative again emerges as developmentally primary. These results lend support to a growing view that the free relative serves as a developmental precursor to the construction of other relative forms when no relevant experience of constructing relative forms can be drawn upon.

Finally, one of the most difficult concepts to understand in the fields of language acquisition is what we mean by an *initial state*. While we know that the initial state is common to the human species, there is considerable debate and confusion concerning what it means to be in an initial state, and fundamental questions persist. Does the initial state hypothesis apply only to the L1 acquisition process? Or, does it apply to L2 and L3 acquisition as well? Is there a way that we might formulate an hypothesis about the initial state that would empirically account for all language learning? If so, would this then allow us to develop a unified and principled account for all language acquisition?

We begin our discussion with a review of three basic assumptions.

Assumption 1: Universal Grammar (UG) is a theory of the biologically endowed faculty for language – a theory of the initial state.

Properties of this LF include that it is an autonomous, independent cognitive module that may interact with, but does not derive from other domains of human cognition. It is a 'language organ in the sense in which scientists speak of the visual system, or the immune system, or the circulatory system, as organs of the body' (Chomsky, 2000: 4). Further, we assume there must be some property of humans – a function that takes acoustic output in context and maps it to knowledge of language, e.g. third person present-tense subject-verb agreement rule – including its syntax, phonology, morphology and semantics. We assume this function must be guided by UG – a species-specific property that allows us to gain knowledge of language – while as Chomsky notes, the New York City telephone exchange – which gets more primary language data than humans *ever* will – never develops knowledge.

> *Assumption 2*: The UG principles are 'wired-in' and 'distinguished from the acquired elements of language, which bear a greater cost'. (Chomsky, 1991: 140)

This hypothesis entails that at the end-state or steady-state 'the UG principles remain distinct from language particular properties'. Chomsky suggests that 'work by Flynn (1987) suggests that at least some principles of UG remain active in adult acquisition, while parameter-changing raises difficulties' (1991: 24). Moreover, Chomsky (2000: 4) argues that we need to differentiate properties of the initial state from acquired knowledge:

> It would be pointless in fact highly confusing for a dictionary of English, Spanish, or Japanese or whatever to present the actual meanings of words, even if they had been discovered. Similarly someone studying English as an L2 would only be confused by instruction about the real properties of grammar; these they already know, being human. Though not by conscious design, dictionaries rightly focus on what a person could not know, namely superficial details of the kind provided by experience; not on what comes to us 'by the original hand of nature.' The latter is a topic of a different inquiry, the study of human nature, which is part of the sciences.

Clearly, regardless of the metaphors we use to distinguish between 'wired-in' universal principles and 'acquired' elements of language-specific grammars, we ultimately need to keep distinct two different kinds of UG principles at both the initial and final states.

> *Assumption 3*: We can characterize UG (the language-specific faculty) as a theory of the initial state,

'We can think of the "initial state" as a language acquisition device that takes experience as input and gives the language "output" that is internally represented in the mind/brain' (Chomsky, 2000:4).' More specifically, Chomsky (2000: 8) writes that the initial state can be thought of as

> a fixed network connected to a switchbox; the network is constitute of the principles of the language, while the switches are the options to be determined by experience. When the switches are set one way, we have Swahili; when they are set another way, we have Japanese. Each possible human language is identified as a particular setting of the switches.

Two possible models

Initial state *means 'at birth'*

Under these basic assumptions, we can construct at least two possible models to represent a theory of the *initial state* for language acquisition. The first of these models is schematized as Figure 4.1:

$$S_{1 \text{ (at birth)}} \rightarrow S_2 \rightarrow S_3 \rightarrow S_4 \rightarrow S_n \rightarrow CORE\ FIRST\ LANGUAGE \rightarrow L_2 \rightarrow L_3 \rightarrow L_n$$

S = Stage of Universal Grammar

Figure 4.1 Model one: 'At birth' (maturation of UG)

In this model, the initial state means the state of the mind/brain at birth. The mind/brain is in an initial state for language acquisition at only one point in time. UG, over time, actually becomes the language-specific grammar that is being acquired. Stated somewhat differently, UG and the L1 (L1s) become dissociable from each other. Under this scenario, UG itself must change in the language acquisition process. This interpretation is equivalent to what has been termed a 'maturation' theory of UG (e.g. see Chomsky, 1988) in the field of L1 acquisition.

Maturation theory, as we have defined it above, asserts that the function of mapping acoustic input to knowledge undergoes change. That is, the *function = UG* might be different at different developmental stages, e.g. at some stage it might be that *a-chain* 'noises' as primary linguistic data, e.g. the noise 'John was arrested' does *not* trigger knowledge of *a-chains*. Whereas at some later stage, the *function = UG* changes so that such primary language data exposure *does* lead to a change in the grammar. By contrast, as we will see, model two, the 'Constant Model' (Figure 4.2) hypothesizes that there is no change in the *function = UG*. We will return to a discussion of this model below.

Theoretical and empirical consequence of 'at birth' model

If we maintain the 'at birth' model, however, this will lead to a new dilemma. If, as theorists assume, UG is a discrete set of principles and parameters (or however one wants to conceive of it abstractly), *how can* we have maturation of UG as in model one? Such a characterization would be possible only if we recognize subsets of the finite set of the universal principles. But these subsets, by definition, are *not* UG; only the finite explicit set is UG. Thus, UG cannot be a model of the *initial state*. Alternatively, if UG is a model of the *initial state*, then under the 'at birth' model, we must have at least two theories of UG: a pre-matured UG and a post-matured UG. Or, alternatively stated, an *initial state-UG* and a *final state-UG*, where these two UGs differ. Moreover, more than two UGs may in fact exist. Given multiple UGs, in what meaningful sense can we say that 'UG is a model of the *initial state*'?

Empirical questions regarding L2 and specifically L3 acquisition correlate with this theoretical paradox (for a more extensive discussion of these
issues see Epstein *et al.*, 1996a, 1996b; Flynn & Lust, 2002). One such question is, 'Do the UG principles remain distinct from the language specific
properties in the *end state*?' And, as a corollary, we can ask, 'Can an adult
who approaches a new language in adulthood access UG or the LF in the
same way as the child does for L1 acquisition at the so-called "initial
state"'?

Given the 'at birth' model, the answers to both these question would
presumably be *'no'*. UG in this model is *not* distinct from the language-
specific grammar in the *end state* and consequently, the next language
learner *cannot* access UG again after the *initial state*, which is presumably
defined as S_1. New language knowledge must be accessed through the L1,
presumably in some transfer-based way. *Function = UG* would presumably not be available to anyone beyond an L1? One could not acquire this
function via the L1 as a language-specific grammar. Under this scenario,
subsequent language learning would consist only of acquisition of finite
sets of sentences, expressions, words, etc. What the subsequent language
learner came to know about the new language would presumably be
delineated by the learner's linguistic experience alone with the new target
language?

This model would be predicted to hold, for example, if maturation
under some form of genetic programming determined much of the course
of L1 acquisition. Presumably there would be actual brain change (as yet
undefined) under this model which correlates with the course of acquisition of an L1. The brain would never be in the same state again in this
model, after state at birth.

A dilemma emerges, however, when at the same time – as Chomsky
(1991: 420) also notes – we 'want to distinguish between the transition
from the *initial state* of the language faculty … to various subsequent states,
including … a steady state that undergoes only limited and marginal
change.' With the 'at birth' model, if UG is continuous between the *initial
state* and the final state (yet to be defined), then how can the distinction
between initial and final state also be maintained and in what does it
consist? Moreover, on empirical grounds, how can the wide array of subsequent language acquisition facts be related to this theory? Most specifically, how can we account for L3 acquisition? These issues concerning L3
acquisition overlap with issues current in the study of L1 and L2 acquisition regarding whether or not UG is continuous across the path of L1 and
L2 acquisition or subject to maturation of some form. Together these issues
concern the foundation of the nature of language development in real time
and the power of the theory of UG to account for this.

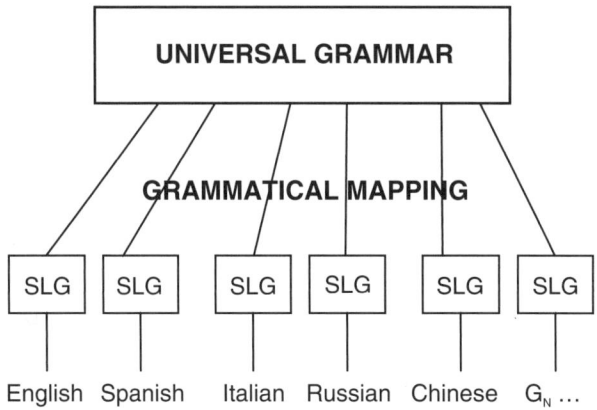

Figure 4.2 The constant model
Note: SLG = Specific Language Grammar

The constant model

On the other hand, in model two, roughly sketched out below in Figure 4.2, UG remains distinct from the language-specific grammar that is being acquired. In model two, UG remains constant over time; it is continuously available to assist in the construction of various specific grammars. This interpretation is equivalent to the 'Strong Continuity Hypothesis' in the study of L1 acquisition (e.g. Lust, 2006). Given model two, we would predict the opposite set of answers to our questions noted above. In this model, UG *does* remain distinct from the language-specific grammar and the adult can return to the so-called *initial state* (representing the LF) at the time of acquisition of the new target language. New language acquisition benefits from the language faculty, just as does L1.

However, in the 'constant' model, UG would be presumed to be biologically programmed and to remain genetically fixed and constant throughout the course of L1 acquisition and throughout one's life remain available for constant new language acquisition. We are not materialists – i.e. we do not require that every theoretical construct must be photographable, tangible. Thus, we have no problem with phonemes, trees, rules, etc. Just as mathematicians have the 'number 2' (not tangible, no surface area, no weight) and physicists talk about gravitational force – even though – no matter how much you dig – you will not find in the dirt the earth's gravitational force, we assert the following:

(1) The 'constant' model of UG is correct.
(2) UG remains distinct in the end state from the language specific grammars.
(3) UG remains available in its entirely to the adult subsequent language learner, specifically the adult L3 learner.

(4) New language knowledge in adulthood is not accessed *only* through the learner's L1, e.g. through some form of negative cross-language transfer, as the 'at birth' model would suggest. We do not propose that there are no differences between L1 and subsequent language acquisition. However, we argue that such changes are not due to changes in UG (e.g. Epstein *et al.*, 1996a, 1996b, 1998; Flynn *et al.*, 2000). The study of L3 acquisition heightens the clarity of the evidence to support this claim. Continued research investigating precisely the manner in which L1, L2 and L3 acquisition converge will continue to elucidate the fundamental nature of the human language faculty.

Note

1. The author wishes to thank the editor of this volume for invaluable comments, feedback and patience. Some of the research summarized in this chapter can also be found in Flynn *et al.* (2000, 2004 and 2008).

References

Chomsky, N. (1988) *Language and Problems of Knowledge: The Managua Lectures.* Cambridge, MA: MIT Press.

Chomsky, N. (1991) Some notes on economy of derivation and representation. In R. Freidin (ed.) *Principles and Parameters in Comparative Grammar* (pp. 417–454). Cambridge, MA: MIT Press.

Chomsky, N. (2000) *New Horizons in the Study of Language and Mind.* Cambridge: Cambridge University Press.

Chomsky, N. (2001) Beyond explanatory adequacy. *MIT Working Papers in Linguistics* 20, 1–28.

Chomsky, N. (2007) Biolinguistic explorations: Design, development, evolution. *International Journal of Philosophical Studies* 15 (1), 1–21.

Cook, V. (2002) *Portraits of the L2 User.* Clevedon: Multilingual Matters.

Epstein, S.D., Flynn, S. and Martohardjono, G. (1996a) Explanation in theories of second language. *Behavior and Brain Science* 19 (4), 677–714.

Epstein, S.D., Flynn, S. and Martohardjono, G. (1996b) Universal grammar and second language acquisition: The null hypothesis. *Behavior and Brain Science* 19 (4), 746–752.

Epstein, S.D., Flynn, S. and Martohardjono, G. (1998) Universal grammar: Hypothesis space or grammar selection procedures: Is UG affected by critical periods? Response to J. Herschensohn. *Behavior and Brain Science* 21 (4), 612–614.

Flynn, S. (1983) A study of the effects of principal branching direction in second language acquisition: The generalization of a parameter of Universal Grammar from first to second language acquisition. PhD thesis, Cornell University.

Flynn, S. (1987) *A Parameter-setting Model of L2 Acquisition: Experimental Studies in Anaphora.* Dordrecht: Reidel.

Flynn, S. and Lust, B. (1981) Acquisition of relative clauses in English. *Cornell Working Papers in Linguistics 1*, 1. Ithaca, NY: Department of Modern Languages and Linguistics, Cornell University.

Flynn, S., Foley, C. and Vinnitskaya, I. (2000) Grammatical mapping in the acquisition of a third language. Paper presented at the Annual Meeting of the Linguistics Society of America, Washington D.C.

Flynn, S. and Lust, B. (2002) A minimalist approach to L2 solves a dilemma og UG. In V. Cook (ed.) *Portraits of the L2 User* (pp. 93–120). Clevedon: Multilingual Matters.

Flynn, S., Foley, C. and Vinnitskaya, I. (2004) The cumulative-enhancement model for language acquisition: Comparing adults' and childrens' patterns of development in first, second and third language acquisition of relative clauses. *International Journal of Multilingualism* 1 (1), 3–17.

Flynn, S., Vinnitskaya, I. and Foley, C. (2008) Complementizer phrase features in child L1 and adult L3 acquisition. In J.M. Liceras, H. Zobl and H. Goodluck (eds) *The Role of Features in Second Language Acquisition* (pp. 519–533). New York: Lawrence Erlbaum Associates.

Flynn, S., Foley, C., Gair, J. and Lust, B. (2005) Developmental primacy of free relatives in first, second and third language acquisition: Implications for their syntax and semantics. Paper presented at Linguistic Association of Great Britain, Cambridge University.

Goodluck, H. and Tavakolian, S. (1982) Competence and processing in children's grammar of relative clauses. *Cognition* 11, 1–27.

Hamburger, H. (1980) A deletion ahead of its time. *Cognition* 8, 389–416.

Hamburger, H. and Crain, S. (1982) Relative acquisition. In S. Kuczaj (ed.) *Language Development* (Vol. 1, *Syntax and Semantics*). Hillsdale, NJ: Lawrence Erlbaum.

Lee, K-Y. (1991) On the first language acquisition of relative clauses in Korean: The Universal Structure of COMP. PhD dissertation, Cornell University, Ithaca, NY.

Leung, Y-k.I. (2002) Functional categories in second and third language acquisition: A Cross-linguistic study of the acquisition of English and French by Chinese and Vietnamese speakers. PhD dissertation, McGill University, Montreal, Canada. Distributed by McGill Working Papers in Linguistics. On WWW at: www.arts.mcgill.ca/programs/linguistics/mcgwpl/index.htm. Accessed 19.08.2008.

Leung, Y-k.I. (2005) L2 vs. L3 initial state: A comparative study of the acquisition of French CPs by Vietnamese monolinguals and Cantonese–English bilinguals. *Bilingualism: Language and Cognition* 8 (1), 39–61.

Leung, Y-k.I. (2008) The verbal functional domain in L2A and L3A: Tense and agreement in Cantonese–English French interlanguage. In J.M. Liceras, H. Zobl and H. Goodluck (eds) *The Role of Features in Second Language Acquisition* (pp. 378–403). New York: Lawrence Erlbaum Associates.

Liceras, J.M., Zobl, H. and Goodluck, H. (eds) (2008) *The Role of Features in Second Language Acquisition*. New York: Lawrence Erlbaum Associates.

Lust, B. (2006) *Child Languauge: Acquisition and Growth*. Cambridge: Cambridge University Press.

Lust, B., Chien, Y-C. and Flynn, S. (1987) What children know: Methods for the study of first language acquisition. In B. Lust (ed.) *Studies in the Acquisition of Anaphora*, (Vol. 2 *Applying the Constraints*, pp. 271–356). Dordrecht: Reidel.

Lust, B., Flynn, S. and Foley, C. (1996) What children know about what they say: Elicited imitation as a research method for assessing children's syntax. In D. McDaniel, C. McKee and H.S. Cairns (eds) *Methods for Assessing Children's Syntax* (pp 55–76). Cambridge, MA: MIT Press.

McDaniel, D., McKee, C. and Cairns, H. (eds) (1996) *Methods for Assessing Children's Syntax*. Cambridge, MA: MIT Press.

Mukherji, N., Patnaik, B. and Agnihotri, R. (2000) *Noam Chomsky: The Architecture of Language*. Oxford: Oxford University Press.

Packard, J. (1987) The first language acquisition of pronominal modification with *de* in Mandarin. *Journal of Chinese Linguistics* 16 (1), 6–21.

Roeper, T. (2007) *The Prism of Grammar: How Child Language Illuminates Humanism.* Cambridge, MA: Bradford Books.

Saffran, J.R., Johnson, E.K., Aslin, R.N. and Newport, E.L. (1999) Statistical learning of tone sequencs by human infants and adults. *Cognition* 70 (1), 27–52.

Saito, M. (1985) Some asymmetries in Japanese and their theoretical consequences. PhD dissertation, MIT, Cambridge, MA.

Chapter 5

Transfer in L3 Acquisition: The Role of Typology

Rebecca Foote

Introduction

Theories concerning the initial state, or starting point, of the second language (L2) learner's interlanguage range from those that propose the entirety of the first language (L1) grammar as the initial state for the L2 learner to those that claim that the L1 has no part in the L2 learner's beginning interlanguage. An example of the former, the Full Transfer Full Access (FTFA) hypothesis of Schwartz and Sprouse (1994, 1996) maintains that when confronted with the task of acquiring a second language, learners assume the whole grammar of their L1 as a starting point (Full Transfer). Upon discovering that L2 input cannot be accounted for by the L1 grammar, the L2 system then restructures itself in accordance with the L2 input based on options available from Universal Grammar (UG) (Full Access).

While there is ample evidence in support of the FTFA hypothesis based on data from L2 acquisition (see White, 2003, for a review), recent research within the field of generative approaches to third language (L3) acquisition suggests partial transfer of the L2 into the initial state of the bilingual acquiring an L3; L1 transfer does not occur, contrary to what might be predicted by a straightforward extension of the FTFA hypothesis to the case of L3 (Leung, 2005, 2006). However, research focusing on the lexical level of language acquisition suggests that one of the principal predictors of source(s) of interlanguage transfer in the L3 learner is language typology (Cenoz, 2003), or even psychotypology (Kellerman, 1983; Ringbom, 2001),[1] with transfer of word form being more prevalent between languages that are typologically similar in relation to those that are not, regardless of order of acquisition. The purpose of the present study is to determine if it is also the case for morphosyntax that language typology, or relative similarity between a multilingual's languages, influences whether transfer will come from the L1 or the L2.[2] Specifically, this chapter addresses whether there is transfer from the L1 or the L2 to the L3 when these share features and feature values, by focusing on the acquisition of the contrast in aspectual meaning in Romance past tenses by native speakers of English who have learned one Romance language as an L2 and another Romance language as an L3 in comparison to native speakers of Romance who have learned English as an L2 and a Romance language other than the L1 as an L3. It also compares these L3 learners to native speakers of English learning a Romance language as an L2. Results suggest that transfer may come from either the L1 or the L2, depending on language typology, or more specifically, whether the languages share the particular features and feature values in question; hypotheses concerning the initial state of L2 acquisition should be revised in order to account for the case of L3 acquisition.

Aspect in English and Romance

Before considering the acquisition of aspect in L2 and L3 Romance, we must briefly describe its instantiation in English and Romance past tenses. To begin with a general definition, aspect refers to the internal temporal constituency of a situation and can be classified as expressing two principal types of meaning: perfective and imperfective (Comrie, 1976). The expression of perfective meaning involves the presentation of a situation as a whole, viewed, as Comrie explains, from the outside. The expression of imperfective meaning implies the viewing of a situation from the inside, that is, it allows for reference to be made to an internal element of the situation without reference to its beginning or end. Perfective and imperfective aspect can be expressed both lexically and grammatically.

Aspect can be expressed lexically as part of the meaning of a particular lexical item, specifically the meaning of a particular verb along with its arguments and adjuncts (i.e. a particular verb predicate). Vendler (1967) classifies verbs into four aspectual categories. Activities are processes going on in time without inherent endpoints; examples in this category can include *dance* and *read*. Accomplishments are processes that do have inherent endpoints; an example in this category is shown in (1):

(1) She ate the cookie.

Achievements are like accomplishments in that they have an inherent endpoint, but the process leading up to the endpoint is immediate; an example is given in (2):

(2) They blew up the building.

States are not processes, but rather unchanging conditions or situations that do not have inherent endpoints; they include predicates containing verbs such as *know* or the existential *be*. It is important to note that verbs themselves do not inherently belong to one category or another; depending on the context, or the predicate, in which they appear, their categorization may vary.[3]

Aspect can be expressed in a language grammatically as well as lexically. In Romance languages, the perfective/imperfective distinction described above is expressed in the past by means of inflectional morphology that combines information about tense and aspect. In Italian, the *passato prossimo* expresses perfective aspect as well as past tense; in French, this is done with the *passé composé*,[4] and in Spanish with the *pretérito*,[5] as illustrated in (3). The imperfect tense expresses imperfective aspect and past tense in all three languages, and is shown in (4):

(3) Ho ballato il tango. (Italian)
    J'ai dansé le tango. (French)
    Bailé el tango. (Spanish)
    I danced (PERF) the tango.
(4) Ballavo il tango mentre Gianni cantava. (Italian)
    Je dansais le tango pendant que Jean chantait. (French)
    Bailaba el tango mientras que Juan cantaba. (Spanish)
    I danced (IMPF) the tango while Gianni sang (IMPF).

While the three Romance languages differ with respect to how the perfective tense is encoded, with Italian and French making use of compound tenses to express perfectivity and Spanish a simple tense, all three languages share the contrast in meaning between perfective and imperfective tenses. That is, perfectivity in Italian, French and Spanish is never expressed with the imperfect tense, and imperfectivity is never expressed with the *passato prossimo*, the *passé composé* or the *pretérito*.

English, on the other hand, is not like the Romance languages; the perfective/imperfective distinction is not expressed morphologically. With eventive predicates, the simple past always has a perfective reading. To express imperfectivity in the past with these predicates, English must either use the past progressive, or rely on lexical forms such as *used to* or *would*. When stative verbs are used in the simple past, they are ambiguous in that they can have either a perfective or an imperfective interpretation. For example, (5) can mean either that John became happy, referring to the starting point of his happiness (a perfective interpretation), or that he was in the condition of being happy without reference to the beginning or end of that condition (an imperfective interpretation):

(5) John was happy.

Giorgi and Pianesi (1997) analyze the syntactic difference between the English and Romance aspectual systems using the theory of features and functional categories proposed in Chomsky's (1995) Minimalist Program, according to which functional categories are made up of sets of formal features and corresponding morphophonological forms. According to Giorgi and Pianesi, the functional category AspP and its associated feature [±perfective] are instantiated in both English and Romance languages, situated between Tense Phrase (TP) and Verb Phrase (VP). In English, however, the feature value [–perfective] is irrelevant, since English associates the feature value [+perfective] with all non-stative predicates. Conversely, in Romance languages such as Spanish, Italian and French, AspP is associated with both [±perfective] features, which are checked overtly in the AspP phrase by means of *pretérito / passato prossimo / passé composé* and imperfect tense morphology according to Montrul and Slabakova (2002). In English, eventive predicates check the [+perfective] feature in AspP through English simple past morphology. Thus, when speakers of English as an L1 are presented with the task of learning how aspect is expressed in Italian, French or Spanish, they must figure out that verbs in the past are not always associated with the feature [+perfective]. They must also learn appropriate pretérito / passato prossimo / passé composé and imperfect morphology as well as the corresponding mappings of features. Knowledge of aspect in Romance therefore involves both knowledge of morphosyntax and its semantic interpretation (Montrul & Slabakova, 2002).

Previous Research: The Acquisition of Aspect in L2 Romance

Research on the L2 acquisition of aspect has been carried out from the perspective of various theoretical approaches (Salaberry & Ayoun, 2005). One characteristic that the majority of this research shares is a focus on the acquisition of tense and aspect morphology as evidenced almost exclusively by production data. However, as Montrul and Slabakova (2002) point out, these data are not reliable to test the acquisition of aspect from a UG/Minimalist perspective, as production data do not allow us to observe the acquisition of functional categories, nor the semantic interpretations of aspect in the L2 learners' interlanguage.

Montrul and Slabakova's (2002) study was the first to explore the acquisition of tense and aspect morphology as well as learners' interpretations of the preterite and imperfect tenses in L2 Spanish. This study asked whether English L1 learners of Spanish as an L2 who seem to know preterite/imperfect morphology also know the semantic implications of these forms. Participants included L1 English, L2 Spanish learners ranging in proficiency level from intermediate to advanced, and native Spanish speakers as a control group. A cloze task was used to test knowledge of preterite and imperfect morphology. Knowledge of the semantic contrast between the two tenses was tested with a sentence conjunction judgment task developed by the authors, in which participants made logic judgments about sentences consisting of two coordinating clauses that varied in logicality according to their use of the perfective or imperfective forms. Results showed that the acquisition of the semantic contrast is gradual, with emergence beginning at the intermediate level of proficiency, even if the morphology has already been acquired. The examination of individual results revealed that there is a strong relationship between acquisition of morphology and the semantic implications of the preterite and imperfect tenses, in that the morphology is acquired before the semantic functions of the tenses. As Montrul (2004: 278) observes, this implies that it is not possible to assume semantic knowledge simply from correct morphological production.

While this and other research on the acquisition of aspect conducted from a generative perspective generally shares the goal of determining whether L2 learners have access to UG in order to acquire features and feature values not present in their L1, the present study follows the methodology used by Montrul and Slabakova (2002) to investigate from a generative perspective the issue of source(s) of transfer in the L3 acquisition of aspect by looking at both the knowledge of tense and aspect morphology as well as its semantic interpretations, and relating this knowledge in L3 to similar knowledge in previously known languages.

Previous Research: Transfer in L3 Acquisition

As stated in the introduction, research within the field of generative approaches to L3 acquisition suggests that the L2 is the main source of transfer for the L3. Leung (2005) investigated transfer in L3 by examining the acquisition of the Determiner Phrase by groups of L1 Cantonese, L2 English learners of L3 French in comparison to groups of L1 Vietnamese learners of L2 French. Neither Chinese nor Vietnamese has the functional categories of Determiner (D) or Number (Num), or the formal feature [± definite] instantiated in its grammar, while English and French both do, though the feature strength of Num is weak in English and strong in French. Experimental tasks included an elicited oral production task, an elicited written production task, a grammaticality judgment and correction task, a picture identification task and a multiple choice task. Results for the L2 group supported full transfer from the L1. Results for the L3 group indicated partial transfer of the L2 steady state into the L3 initial state. The functional categories of D and Num were present in L3 French, though it appeared that there was a one-way failure of the feature [± definite] in the L3 (participants' performance was not native-like on [+definite] task items). Feature strength of Num seemed to be variable; participants accepted and produced both correct and incorrect adjective placement. Leung concluded that feature strength may not be transferred in L3 acquisition; there is partial transfer of L2 instead of L1 transfer to the L3 initial state, in contradiction of the Failed Functional Features hypothesis (Hawkins & Chan, 1997) which predicted that the L3 initial state would be the L1 Chinese final state (i.e. that functional categories, features and feature strength not instantiated in the L1 would not have been acquired in the L2, and therefore would not be available to transfer from L2 to L3), and inconsistent with a straightforward extension of the FTFA hypothesis to the case of L3, which would only allow for full transfer from L2 (or L1).

Leung (2006) came to a slightly different conclusion in her examination of the acquisition of tense and agreement and adverb placement by the same participant groups. She investigated feature strength of Tense (T) along with the presence or absence of agreement and [± past] features in L2 English and L2 and L3 French. Results from two elicited production and two preference tasks supported transfer from L2 English to L3 French of both [± past] and agreement features; adverb placement data showed that participants had already acquired the correct feature strength of T in L3 French and were able to correctly place adverbs, thus not clearly indicating a source of transfer for the L3. Leung concluded that transfer from the L1 or other known languages is present in the L3 initial state, but that some participants may have progressed beyond the stage in which full transfer was present. With respect to source(s) of transfer in L3 acquisition, in both of Leung's studies (2005, 2006) it is difficult to determine whether the partial and/or full transfer from the L2 to the L3 (instead of from the L1 to the L3) is generalizable across different language combinations, or whether it was due to the typological similarities in the participants' L2 English and L3 French. The current study will expand on Leung's findings by examining this question.

Turning for the moment from transfer at the syntactic level to transfer at the lexical level (on which most work in L3 acquisition has focused), most research that investigates L3 lexical acquisition tends to be of a case-study nature due to the difficulty in finding participants with similar L1/L2/L3 experience. According to case studies conducted by Williams and Hammarberg (1998) and Hammarberg (2001), the tendency in L3 lexical production with respect to transfer seems to be to activate an earlier L2 rather than the L1, based on factors such as (psycho)typological similarity, and the foreign language status of the earlier L2(s). Ecke (2001) found the same tendency in his L1 Spanish, L2 English, L3 German learners, to retrieve an L2 candidate in a word translation task rather than an L1 candidate. Again, the L2 and the L3 were typologically similar in Ecke's study. Cenoz (2003) also found that language typology was the main factor in predicting lexical transfer to the L3 in her study of Basque/Spanish/English trilinguals, though foreign language status may also have been a contributor. However, all of these studies centered on activation and transfer of form rather than meaning. Ringbom (1987, 2001) examined translation errors of Finnish/Swedish/English trilinguals and found that most form transfer errors came from the L2, while most transfer of meaning errors came from the L1, in spite of the typological similarity of the L2 and the L3. It therefore appears that both the L1 and the L2 play a role in transfer to the L3 at the lexical level, though this may be dependent on typological similarity as well as whether we are considering the transfer of form (which may come from either L1 or L2) or meaning (which appears to come only from L1). Taking these findings into consideration, it is an open question whether transfer of the contrast in aspectual meaning between past tenses in learners of Romance who either speak English as a native language or have studied it as a second language will come from L1, L2, or both, depending on the similarity of the languages involved (i.e. with respect to shared features and feature values).

Current Study

Given this background on the acquisition of aspect in L2 Romance as well as the L3 studies of transfer at both the syntactic and the lexical levels, the current study asks whether there is transfer of the contrast in aspectual meaning between Romance past tenses (the *pretérito* and imperfect in Spanish, the *passato prossimo* and imperfect in Italian and the *passé composé* and imperfect in French) from either L1 to L3 or L2 to L3. The two research questions posed are the following:

(1) If the L3 (a Romance language) has a semantic contrast realized grammatically in a way that differs from the L1 (English), but is the same in the L2 (another Romance language), will this contrast in meaning be transferred from the L2, or will the L3 learner have to 'relearn' this contrast for the L3, having the L1 as the initial state?

(2) If the L3 (a Romance language) has a semantic contrast realized grammatically in way that is similar to the L1 (another Romance language), but different from the L2 (English), will this contrast be transferred from the L1, or will the L2 interfere in some way?

It is hypothesized that there will be transfer of meaning from the most typologically similar language when the other language has no analogous semantic contrast available which may be used as a source of transfer, consistent with an extension of initial state hypotheses, such as the FTFA hypothesis (Schwartz & Sprouse, 1994, 1996), which allow for transfer from L2 as well as L1, but contrary to what Ringbom's (1987, 2001) findings show. Specifically, L1 Romance, L2 English learners of L3 Romance will transfer their knowledge of this contrast from the L1 without the L2 English interfering. Similarly, L1 English, L2 Romance learners of L3 Romance will transfer their knowledge of the contrast from the L2.

Method

Participants

There were 85 participants in the current study, all volunteers. Many were students at the University of Illinois, though some were also recruited from other research universities in the US. The participants were divided into four groups: native speakers of Romance (n = 34) who served as a control group, native speakers of English learning a Romance language as an L2 (n = 25), native speakers of English learning a Romance language as an L3, having already learned a Romance language as an L2 (n = 14), and native speakers of a Romance language learning another Romance language as an L3, having learned English as an L2 (n = 12). Groups were matched as follows for comparison purposes: the L1 English, L2 Romance, L3 Romance group was matched on mean time the L2 and the L3 were studied with the L1 Romance, L2 English, L3 Romance group. Both L3 groups were matched on mean time the L3 was studied with the L1 English, L2 Romance group's mean time the L2 was studied. An independent samples t-test showed no difference between the L1 English, L2 Romance, L3 Romance group and the L1 Romance, L2 English, L3 Romance group's L2 time studied [$t(23^6)$ = 0.32; p = 0.753]; a one-way ANOVA showed no differences in L3 groups' L3 time studied and the L1 English, L2 Romance group's L2 time studied [$F(2, 48)$ = 0.06; p = 0.944]. Table 5.1 summarizes information on mean time studied for each participant group. Table 5.2 summarizes by group which languages participants knew or had studied and in what order.

Table 5.1 Participant group information, mean time studied

Group	*N*	*Mean time studied (years) L2*	*Mean time studied (years) L3*
L1 Romance (L1Rom)	34	–	–
L1 English, L2 Romance (L1EngL2Rom)	25	5.42	–
L1 English, L2 Romance, L3 Romance (L1EngL3Rom)	14	12.93	5.14
L1 Romance, L2 English, L3 Romance (L1RomL3Rom)	12	12.18	4.96

Table 5.2 Number of participants by group who knew / had studied each language

	L1				**L2**				**L3**			
	Span.	Fren.	Ital.	Eng.	Span.	Fren.	Ital.	Eng.	Span.	Fren.	Ital.	Eng.
L1Rom	12	8	14	–	–	–	–	–	–	–	–	–
L1EngL2Rom	–	–	–	25	18	6	1	–	–	–	–	–
L1EngL3Rom	–	–	–	14	9	5	0	–	1	6	7	–
L1RomL3Rom	6	1	5	–	–	–	–	12	3	8	1	–

Instruments

Language history questionnaire

A language history questionnaire given to all participants requested basic information such as native language(s), as well as details concerning other languages studied.

Romance morphology tests

In order to determine whether the participants with a Romance language as L2 and / or L3 had acquired *pretérito / passé composé / passato prossimo* and imperfect morphology, morphology tests were given to all L2 and L3 participants in all Romance languages known; L1 Romance control group participants also completed morphology tests in their respective native languages. Tests in each Romance language (Spanish, French and Italian) were adapted from various language textbook texts (the Spanish test is the same one used by Montrul & Slabakova, 2002), and contained a total of 30 verbs in each for which participants were asked to choose a form, with 15 expected *pretérito / passé composé / passato prossimo* responses and 15 expected imperfect responses. Participants were asked to choose the *pretérito / passé composé / passato prossimo* or imperfect verb form to correctly complete the sentences in the text, as shown by the sample from the Spanish test given in (6):

(6) El jefe le (1) *daba/dio* el dinero a la empleada para depositarlo en el banco. La empleada (2) *trabajó/trabajaba* para la compañía pero no (3) *estuvo/estaba* contenta con su trabajo …
The boss *gave* the money to the employee to be deposited in the bank. The employee *worked* for the company but *was* not happy with her job …

Romance sentence conjunction judgment tasks

Sentence conjunction judgment tasks (SCJTs) in Spanish, French and Italian tested knowledge of the semantic implications of the uses of the *pretérito / passé composé / passato prossimo* and imperfect by the L2 and L3 participants. They were also given to the L1 Romance control group participants in their respective native languages. Derived from the same task designed by Montrul and Slabakova (2002), each SCJT consisted of a list of sentences made up of two coordinating clauses, connected with the word *but*. Participants judged the logicality of each sentence, using a scale that ranged from −2 (completely illogical) to 2 (completely logical). For each verb tested, two sentences appeared, one with the imperfect and one with the *pretérito / passé composé / passato prossimo*. The use of the imperfect made the sentence logical, while the use of the *pretérito / passé composé / passato prossimo* rendered it illogical. Examples of a logical and an illogical sentence used in the Spanish version of the task are presented in (7):

(7) (a) Le escribía (IMPF) una carta a mi amiga pero nunca la terminé.
I was writing a letter to my friend but I never finished it.

(b) La novelista escribió (PRET) una novela de fantasía pero nunca la terminó.
The novelist wrote a fantasy novel but never finished it.

Each SCJT consisted of 56 sentences, 28 logical and 28 illogical. There were 14 sentences with each type of verb (classified according to lexical aspect), accomplishment, achievement and state. As in Montrul and Slabakova, activity predicates were not included due to the difficulty in forming logical sentences with this type of verb predicate. There were also 14 distractor sentences included in each task, seven logical and seven illogical, using the *pretérito / passé composé / passato prossimo* and imperfect tenses. The distractor sentences were not only used to draw the participant's attention away from the purpose of the task, but also to test whether he or she was distinguishing between logical and illogical situations as represented by the task's sentences; these sentences also served to break up the pattern of imperfect sentences all being logical and *pretérito / passé composé / passato prossimo* illogical. Examples of a logical distractor and an illogical distractor used in the Spanish version of the task are given respectively in (8):

(8) (a) Corrí (PRET) en el maratón pero mi hermana caminó.
I ran in the marathon but my sister walked.

(b) Había (IMPF) 10 personas en la fiesta pero al final sólo vinieron 8.
There were 10 people at the party but in the end only 8 came.

All sentences in the SCJTs were presented in random order; sentences that appeared in the SCJT in one language did not also appear in the task in another language since the L3 participants had to complete the task in more than one language. However, the verb predicates used in each task were created to be very similar in order to make the tasks as equivalent as possible, with many of the same verbs appearing in each language.

Procedure

Due to the difficulty of finding and recruiting participants with these particular language combinations, all testing was completed on the internet through a website created by the author for this purpose. This allowed recruiting to extend beyond the author's immediately available participant pool, an advantage that was felt to outweigh any disadvantage associated with a loss of control over participant test-taking behavior due to the testing medium. All participants filled out the language history questionnaire. L1 Romance participants then completed the morphology test and the SCJT in their native language. L1 English, L2 Romance participants completed the morphology test and the SCJT in their L2, and L1 English, L2 Romance, L3 Romance participants completed the morphology tests and the SCJTs for both their L2 and their L3. L1 Romance, L2 English, L3 Romance participants completed the morphology tests and the SCJTs for both their L1 and their L3.[7] Participants' answers for all tasks were stored in a database associated with the website, and were subsequently downloaded for analysis.

Group Results

Results for both the morphology tests and the SCJTs were collapsed across languages for analyses.[8]

Morphology tests

Results for the morphology tests are presented first, since previous research (Montrul & Slabakova, 2002) indicates that knowledge of morphology precedes knowledge of the semantic implications of aspectual contrasts in L2 (and in extension L3) Romance. Thus, if participants have not yet acquired past tense Romance morphology, it is probable that they will not yet have acquired the semantic contrast.

In scoring the morphology test(s), the percentage of correct verb choices was calculated for each individual on each test he or she completed. The mean percentage correct was then calculated for each group, and is presented in Table 5.3.

Table 5.3 Mean percentage correct by group, morphology tests

Group	*Mean % correct*	*SD*
L1Rom	94.71	5.13
L1EngL2Rom	77.07	12.26
L1EngL2RomL3Rom (L2)	91.43	8.03
L1EngL2RomL3Rom (L3)	87.86	11.74
L1RomL2EngL3Rom (L1)	95.83	4.74
L1RomL2EngL3Rom (L3)	86.97	12.69

As Table 5.3 illustrates, both L3 groups averaged above 85% in both their L2s and L3s; the L1 English, L2 Romance group averaged above 75% in their L2. It appears that, at least at the group level, participants had generally acquired *pretérito/passé composé/passato prossimo* and imperfect morphology, though the L1 English, L2 Romance group lagged behind the other groups.

Sentence conjunction judgment tasks

SCJTs tested participants' knowledge of the semantic contrast between the *pretérito/passé composé/passato prossimo* and the imperfect. As outlined previously, the use of the imperfect rendered critical sentences logical while the use of the *pretérito/passé composé/passato prossimo* rendered them illogical. Because logicality judgments tend to be less black-and-white than grammaticality judgments, it was decided to analyze results for only the five sentences for each verb type (and for the distractors) rated by the L1 Romance group as most logical (in the case of the use of the imperfect) and most illogical (in the case of the use of the *pretérito/passé composé/ passato prossimo*). This left a total of 10 sentences for each verb type and for the distractors to be included in analyses.

For each participant, mean ratings were calculated by verb type (recall that the rating scale went from –2 for completely illogical to 2 for completely logical). Individual ratings were then combined to obtain mean ratings by verb type/distractor for each group and each Romance language within each group. Though there were no hypothesized differences in source(s) of transfer from L1 and/or L2 to L3 based on verb categorizations according to lexical aspect (Montrul & Slabakova, 2002), results are presented by verb type as a convenient way to compare across groups. First, however, participants' ratings of distractor sentences are presented, since if participants are not able to distinguish between logical and illogical sentences in general, their judgments on the critical sentences are not valid.

SCJT results: Distractors

Table 5.4 shows mean ratings for illogical and logical distractors by group, and Figure 5.1 presents the same information in graphic form.

Table 5.4 Mean ratings for distractors by group, SCJT

	Dist. (illog.)	*Dist. (log.)*
L1Rom	–1.80	1.76
L1EngL2Rom	–0.89	1.18
L1EngL2RomL3Rom (L2)	–1.71	1.49
L1EngL2RomL3Rom (L3)	–1.64	1.55
L1RomL2 EngL3Rom (L1)	–1.57	1.37
L1RomL2EngL3Rom (L3)	–1.69	1.51

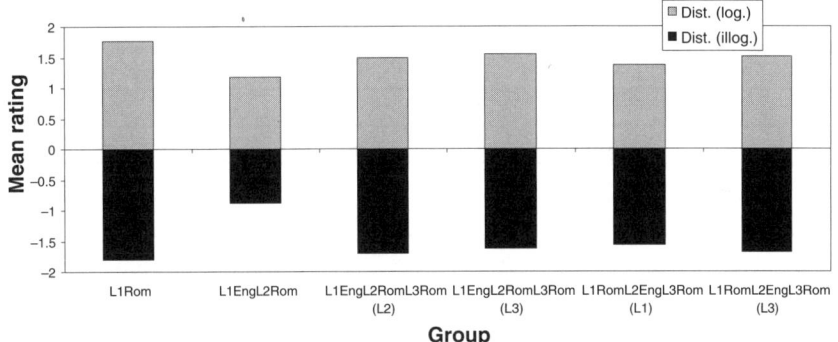

Figure 5.1 Mean ratings for distractors by group, SCJT

Table 5.5 Results of paired samples *t*-tests on ratings for distractors, SCJT

	df	*t*	*p*
L1Rom	33	47.19	<0.001
L1EngL2Rom	24	9.79	<0.001
L1EngL2RomL3Rom (L2)	13	16.68	<0.001
L1EngL2RomL3Rom (L3)	13	11.38	<0.001
L1RomL2 EngL3Rom (L1)	11	18.50	<0.001
L1RomL2EngL3Rom (L3)	11	16.25	<0.001

SCJT results: Accomplishment verbs

Table 5.6 presents mean ratings for accomplishment verbs by group; Figure 5.2 graphs the same information.

As both Table 5.4 and Figure 5.1 illustrate, all groups are able to distinguish between logical and illogical sentences, indicating that judgments on critical SCJT sentences are based on (lack of) knowledge of the semantic distinctions between the *pretérito/passé composé/passato prossimo* and the imperfect, rather than difficulties in judging between logical and illogical statements. Paired samples *t*-tests confirmed that the contrast between logical and illogical distractors was significant in each group (analyses results shown in Table 5.5). Having established that participant groups are able to make logicality judgments, we now turn to the SCJT results by verb type.

Table 5.6 Mean ratings for accomplishment verbs by group, SCJT

	Pret/PC/PP (illog.)	*Imp. (log.)*
L1Rom	−1.14	1.16
L1EngL2Rom	−0.42	0.86
L1EngL2RomL3Rom (L2)	−1.62	1.47
L1EngL2RomL3Rom (L3)	−1.53	1.09
L1RomL2 EngL3Rom (L1)	−1.14	0.74
L1RomL2EngL3Rom (L3)	−1.54	1.20

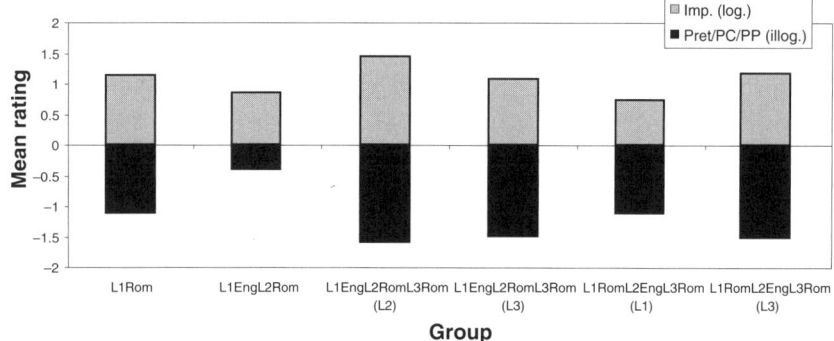

Figure 5.2 Mean ratings for accomplishment verbs by group, SCJT

Table 5.7 Results of paired samples *t*-tests on ratings for accomplishment verbs, SCJT

	df	t	p
L1Rom	33	13.41	<0.001
L1EngL2Rom	24	4.96	<0.001
L1EngL2RomL3Rom (L2)	13	15.59	<0.001
L1EngL2RomL3Rom (L3)	13	7.92	<0.001
L1RomL2 EngL3Rom (L1)	11	7.66	<0.001
L1RomL2EngL3Rom (L3)	11	9.33	<0.001

All groups differentiate between the *pretérito / passé composé / passato prossimo* and the imperfect with accomplishment verbs, though the L1 English, L2 Romance group seems to be less sure about the illogicality of the sentences with the *pretérito / passé composé / passato prossimo* tenses, as Figure 5.2 illustrates. Paired samples *t*-tests conducted on each group's mean ratings confirmed that the contrast between *pretérito / passé composé / passato prossimo* and the imperfect was statistically significant in each group. Table 5.7 presents analyses results.

In order to test whether the L1 English, L2 Romance, L3 Romance group and the L1 Romance, L2 English, L3 Romance group show an advantage over the L1 English, L2 Romance group in the acquisition of the semantic contrast between the past tenses in L3 Romance (thus indicating possible transfer from the previously acquired Romance language), these groups and the L1 Romance group were compared in a repeated measures ANOVA with logicality as a within-participant variable with two levels (Pret/PC/PP-illog. vs. Imp.-log.) and group as a between-participant variable with four levels. Analyses revealed a main effect for logicality [$F(1, 81) = 270.90; p < 0.001$], and a logicality × group interaction [$F(3, 81) = 6.58; p < 0.001$], but no main effect for group [$F(3, 81) = 1.96; p = 0.126$], indicating again that groups do distinguish between logical and illogical sentences, but that different groups make the distinction to a different degree. In order to further get at this difference, one-way ANOVAs were conducted separately on responses for logical and illogical accomplishment verb sentences. Results for illogical sentences indicated a main effect for group [$F(3, 81) = 7.59; p < 0.001$]; a post-hoc Tukey analysis revealed the differences to be between the L1 English, L2 Romance group and all other groups. Results for logical sentences showed no differences between groups [$F(3,81) = 1.01; p = 0.393$]. Both L3 groups evidence an advantage over the L1 English, L2 Romance group in judging the illogical (*pretérito/ passé composé/passato prossimo*) sentences; only the L1 English, L2 Romance group differs from native speakers.

SCJT results: Achievement verbs

Results for achievement verbs are presented in Table 5.8 and Figure 5.3.

Table 5.8 Mean ratings for achievement verbs by group, SCJT

	Pret/PC/PP (illog.)	*Imp. (log.)*
L1 Rom	−1.74	0.92
L1EngL2Rom	−0.90	0.77
L1EngL2RomL3Rom (L2)	−1.75	1.20
L1EngL2RomL3Rom (L3)	−1.60	0.85
L1RomL2 EngL3Rom (L1)	−1.71	0.34
L1RomL2EngL3Rom (L3)	−1.40	1.00

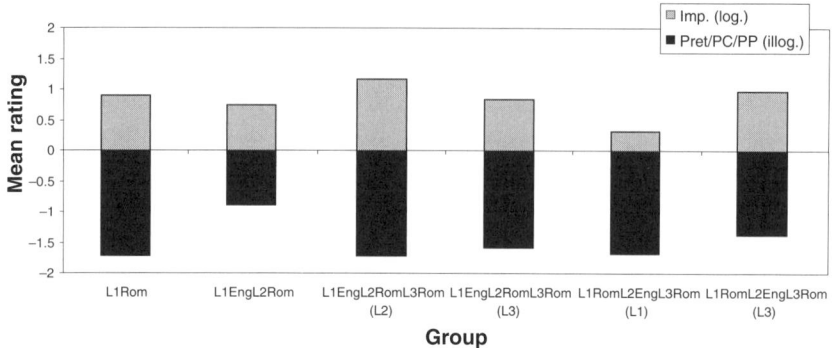

Figure 5.3 Mean ratings for achievement verbs by group, SCJT

Table 5.9 Results of paired samples *t*-tests on ratings for achievement verbs, SCJT

	df	*t*	*p*
L1Rom	33	15.18	<0.001
L1EngL2Rom	24	7.34	<0.001
L1EngL2RomL3Rom (L2)	13	12.35	<0.001
L1EngL2RomL3Rom (L3)	13	7.51	<0.001
L1RomL2 EngL3Rom (L1)	11	9.95	<0.001
L1RomL2EngL3Rom (L3)	11	5.96	<0.001

As with the accomplishment verbs, all participant groups appear to distinguish between the *pretérito/passé composé/passato prossimo* and the imperfect. Overall, ratings tended to be less distinctive with the imperfect. However, according to Giorgi and Pianesi (1997), achievement predicates may not make sense for some Romance speakers with the imperfect reading but can be expressed with the progressive. This is due to a contrast in meaning between the progressive form and the imperfect; the imperfect implies the realization of an action in the real world, while the progressive does not. The progressive also emphasizes the dynamic nature of the action, while the imperfect does not (King & Suñer, 1999: 102).[9]

Paired samples *t*-tests confirmed that the contrast between *pretérito/passé composé/passato prossimo* and the imperfect was statistically significant in each group; Table 5.9 displays the results of the analyses.

A repeated measures ANOVA with logicality as a within-participant variable with two levels (Pret/PC/PP-illog. vs. Imp.-log.) and group as a between-participant variable with four levels compared the L2 and the L3 groups' responses; a main effect for logicality was found [$F(1, 81) = 289.29$; $p < 0.001$] and a logicality × group interaction [$F(3, 81) = 4.11$; $p < 0.01$], but group only approached significance [$F(3, 81) = 2.51$; $p = 0.064$]. One-way ANOVAs conducted separately on responses for logical and illogical achievement verb sentences revealed the same pattern of results as for accomplishment verbs. The analysis for illogical verbs showed a main effect for group [$F(3, 81) = 9.29$; $p < 0.001$] with the differences being between the L1 English, L2 Romance group and all other groups. The analysis for logical verbs showed no differences between groups [$F(3, 81) = 0.45$; $p = 0.718$]. Again, the L3 groups show an advantage over the L1 English, L2 Romance group in judging the illogical (*pretérito/passé composé/ passato prossimo*) sentences.

SCJT results: State verbs

Mean ratings for state verbs are presented in Table 5.10 and Figure 5.4.

As with accomplishment and achievement verbs, all participants appear to distinguish between logical (imperfect) and illogical (*pretérito/passé composé/passato prossimo*) state verb sentences, though the L1 English, L2 Romance group seems less sure about both logical and illogical judgments. Table 5.11 presents the results of paired samples *t*-tests conducted on each group's mean ratings verifying that the contrast between *pretérito/*

Table 5.10 Mean ratings for state verbs by group, SCJT

	Pret/PC/PP (illog.)	*Imp. (log.)*
L1Rom	−1.41	1.60
L1EngL2Rom	−0.22	0.41
L1EngL2RomL3Rom (L2)	−1.38	1.04
L1EngL2RomL3Rom (L3)	−1.02	1.09
L1RomL2 EngL3Rom (L1)	−1.43	1.54
L1RomL2EngL3Rom (L3)	−1.29	1.66

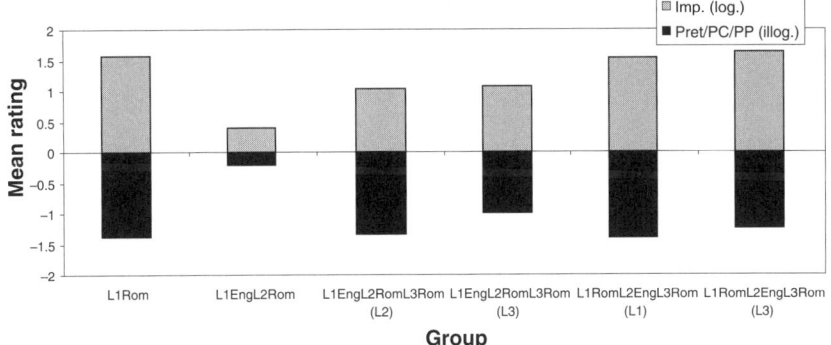

Figure 5.4 Mean ratings for state verbs by group, SCJT

Table 5.11 Results of paired samples *t*-tests on ratings for state verbs, SCJT

	df	*t*	*p*
L1Rom	33	22.81	< 0.001
L1EngL2Rom	24	2.95	< 0.01
L1EngL2RomL3Rom (L2)	13	9.32	< 0.001
L1EngL2RomL3Rom (L3)	13	7.29	< 0.001
L1RomL2 EngL3Rom (L1)	11	17.09	< 0.001
L1RomL2EngL3Rom (L3)	11	8.16	< 0.001

passé composé/passato prossimo and the imperfect was significant in each group.

The repeated measures ANOVA conducted on L2 and L3 groups' ratings with logicality as a within-participant variable with two levels (Pret/PC/PP-illog. vs. Imp.-log.) and group as a between-participant variable with four levels showed a main effect for logicality [$F(1, 81) = 333.54$; $p < 0.001$] and a logicality × group interaction [$F(3, 81) = 30.40$; $p < 0.001$], but no effect for group [$F(3, 81) = 0.77$; $p = 0.515$], patterning similarly to both other types of verbs. One-way ANOVAs were conducted separately on responses for logical and illogical state verb sentences. Results for illogical sentences indicated a main effect for group [$F(3, 81) = 13.79$; $p < 0.001$] and a post-hoc Tukey analysis again revealed the differences to be between the L1 English, L2 Romance group and all other groups. The analysis for logical sentences showed similar results, a main effect for group [$F(3, 81) = 18.63$; $p < 0.001$] with a post-hoc Tukey confirming differences between the L1 English, L2 Romance group and all other groups. Unlike results for accomplishment and achievement verbs, the L1 English, L2 Romance group appears to have difficulties with both illogical and logical judgments with state verbs, or with both *pretérito/passé composé/passato prossimo* and imperfect, possibly due to influence from the L1 English.[10] As described previously, when state verbs appear in the simple past in English, they can receive either a perfective or an imperfective interpretation. This ambiguity may make it difficult for native speakers of English to assign a perfective or imperfective reading to state verbs in Romance past tenses.

In summary, according to group results on the SCJTs, all participant groups have acquired the semantic contrast between the past tenses in Romance for all verb predicate types, though the L1 English, L2 Romance group appears to lag behind both L3 groups in the certainty of their judgments. We now turn to individual results to further explore this apparent advantage that both of the L3 groups show over the L1 English, L2 Romance group.

Individual Results

Morphology tests

One issue to consider in the interpretation of the group results for the SCJTs is whether the individual participants in each group had knowledge of past tense Romance morphology, which has been shown to precede knowledge of the semantic contrast between the past tenses (Montrul & Slabakova, 2002). Group results on the morphology tests showed a high percentage correct for all groups, though the L1 English, L2 Romance group scored lower than the other groups (75% vs. 85% and up). An examination of individual scores revealed that 11 out of 25 (44%) of the L1 English, L2 Romance group scored lower than 75% on the morphology test, a cut-off that Montrul and Slabakova used to classify participants as not having knowledge of past tense morphology. In contrast, in each of the L3 groups there was only one participant who scored below 75% on the test in the L3 (all of the L3 participants scored above 75% in the other Romance language known, the L1 or L2). These participants in all three groups scoring lower than 75% were removed from further analysis.

Sentence conjunction judgment tasks

Group results on the SCJTs suggested an advantage of the L3 groups over the L2 group in judging the semantic contrast between Romance past tenses. However, something to take into consideration when interpreting this apparent advantage as being directly related to transfer from the previously known Romance language to the L3, is whether the individual participants in the L1 English, L2 Romance, L3 Romance group had knowledge of the contrast available to transfer from L2 to L3. To determine if they did have knowledge of this contrast in the L2, each L1 English, L2 Romance, L3 Romance participant was given an overall accuracy score on the SCJT in the L2. One point was awarded for each judgment of 2 or 1 with imperfect forms, and for each judgment of –2 or –1 with *pretérito/ passé composé/passato prossimo* forms; no points were given for judgments of 0. With 10 sentences for each of the three verb types tested (five with perfective forms and five with imperfective forms), there were a total of 30 possible points for the overall accuracy score. After calculating these scores in terms of percentage accuracy, it was revealed that three of the 14 L1 English, L2 Romance, L3 Romance participants scored lower than 75% accuracy on the SCJT in the L2.

After excluding these three L1 English, L2 Romance, L3 Romance participants, and those participants in all groups who scored lower than 75% on the morphology tests, individual overall accuracy scores on the SCJTs were computed (in the same way as described above) for the remaining participants in the L2 and L3 groups. These scores computed for the L1 English, L2 Romance group in the L2 were compared with overall accuracy scores on the SCJTs computed for both L3 groups in the L3. Table 5.12 presents individual participants' accuracy scores as percentages.

According to these results, while the majority of both L3 groups scored over 75% on the SCJT, only three out of 14 participants in the L1 English, L2 Romance group did. Mean percentage accuracy for the L3 groups was relatively high, at around 85%, while the mean percentage accuracy for

Table 5.12 SCJT accuracy scores by participant, L2 group and L3 groups

Group	*Individual accuracy scores (%)*
L1EngL2Rom	60.0
	26.7
	33.3
	73.3
	53.3
	93.3
	86.7
	73.3
	80.0
	73.3
	63.3
	53.3
	66.7
	73.3
Group mean percentage	*65.0*
L1EngL2RomL3Rom	83.3
	96.7
	86.7
	93.3
	100.0
	53.3
	90.0
	73.3
	96.7
	90.0
Group mean percentage	*86.3*
L1RomL2EngL3Rom	96.7
	73.3
	93.3
	53.3
	73.3
	60.0
	93.3
	96.7
	86.7
	66.7
	100.0
Group mean percentage	*81.2*

the L1 English, L2 Romance group was approximately 20 percentage points less. The advantage found at the group level for the L3 groups over the L1 English, L2 Romance group also holds at the individual level.

Discussion and Conclusion

The purpose of the current study was to investigate transfer of the contrast in aspectual meaning between Romance past tenses from either L1 to L3 or from L2 to L3. Previous research conducted by Leung (2005, 2006) on the initial state in L3 acquisition indicated partial transfer from the L2 to the L3. However, the L2 and L3 investigated were typologically similar to each other while typologically different from participants' L1s. The present study examined whether typological similarity (in the form of shared features and feature values) determines sources of transfer in L3 acquisition. Transfer was hypothesized to come from the most typologically similar language when the other language has no analogous semantic contrast available which may be used as a source of transfer. Specifically, it was hypothesized that both the L1 English, L2 Romance, L3 Romance learners and the L1 Romance, L2 English, L3 Romance learners would transfer their knowledge of the semantic contrast between Romance past tenses from the previously known Romance language, whether L1 or L2. This hypothesis appears to have been upheld by the results.

According to results on SCJTs, all participant groups have acquired knowledge of the semantic contrast between the *pretérito/passé composé/passato prossimo* and imperfect tenses in Romance, they all judged illogical (*pretérito/passé composé/passato prossimo*) and logical (imperfect) sentences significantly differently, and in the correct manner. In other words, they have learned that in Romance, AspP is associated with both [±perfective] features in contrast to English, in which all eventive predicates are associated with [+perfective] while stative predicates are not clearly perfective or imperfective when used in the simple past. Nevertheless, though all three learner groups evidence knowledge of the semantic distinction between these tenses in Romance, both L3 groups show a significant advantage over the L2 group in consistently interpreting the contrast accurately. Results at the individual level reveal that the majority of the L2 group participants were less accurate on the SCJTs than the participants in the L3 groups. Similar to Montrul and Slabakova's (2002) findings for their intermediate L2 learners, the L2 group of the current study generally shows the correct pattern to be emerging, though in a gradual manner. Both as a group and individually, their judgments are marked by uncertainty, particularly with respect to the interpretation of the *pretérito/passé composé/passato prossimo* with accomplishment and achievement verbs, and the interpretation of both the *pretérito/passé composé/passato prossimo* and the imperfect with state verbs. One reason for the differences between the L2 group and the other groups showing up mainly in the perfective forms may be that many participants who had knowledge of the *pretérito / passé composé / passato prossimo* vs. imperfect contrast tended to rate illogical sentences more illogical than they rated logical sentences logical, while the L1 English, L2 Romance group was uncertain about both types of judgments. This seems to have been the case with both accomplishment and achievement ratings (see Tables 5.6 and 5.8). State logicality ratings were more balanced among participant groups (see Table 5.10), thus highlighting the uncertainties of the L1 English, L2 Romance group with both *pretérito / passé composé / passato prossimo* and imperfect forms. This pattern of gradual development in the L2 group rather than an abruptly acquired sharp contrast is not unexpected considering the nature of the judgments these learners are making. This contrast in meaning between perfective and imperfective forms may seem clearer to them with certain verbs or verb predicates, and less clear with others. Native speaker logic judgments of these types of sentences are not black-and-white either, as demonstrated by the less than 'perfect' ratings evidenced by the L1 Romance group in Tables 5.6, 5.8, and 5.10. This is in opposition to what might be found with a grammaticality judgment test examining a more purely syntactic characteristic of a language, such as adverb placement, for example.

Overall, group and individual results taken together suggest that L3 groups may have been able to transfer previous knowledge of the semantic contrast between Romance past tenses to the L3, while the L2 group lags behind in their development of the contrast in the L2. It seems that transfer of a contrast in meaning that is grammatically realized may come from either the L1 or the L2, contrary to what has been found in L3 research focusing on the transfer of meaning at the lexical level (Ringbom, 1987, 2001).

One alternative to this interpretation of the results that assumes transfer from L1 and L2 to L3 is that the advantage shown by both L3 groups over the L2 group is due to a higher overall proficiency level in the L3 in comparison to the L2 group's proficiency in the L2. None of the groups in the current study were tested for proficiency because of time constraints,[11] so it is not possible to rule out this interpretation of the results, though the fact that the L3 groups were matched on the mean time they had studied the L3 with the mean time the L2 group had studied the L2 suggests a somewhat equivalent proficiency level for the L2 and L3 groups. However, as described previously, participants in the L3 groups generally performed better on the morphology tests than those in the L2 group, possibly indicating a difference in overall proficiency level. Alternatively, it may be that the advantage for the L3 groups does not lie solely in transfer of knowledge of the semantic contrast from a previously known Romance language, but also in a facilitation of the learning of the morphology. The morphology is different in each of the languages investigated, so this facilitation could stem not from a similarity in form between languages, but from already having acquired one language with relatively rich verbal morphology. It could also be the case that the advantage for the participants in the L3 groups, both in acquiring the morphology and in interpreting the aspectual contrast between Romance past tenses is because they are simply better language learners than participants in the L2 group (see Cook, 1995 for a characterization of how multilingual speakers are different from monolingual speakers[12] and Klein, 1995 for empirical research supporting an advantage in language learning for multilinguals). Nevertheless, the fact that the L3 advantage held after removing L2 participants who scored lower than 75% accuracy on the morphology tests seems to imply that all other characteristics being as equivalent as possible (i.e. knowledge of past tense morphology as evidenced by scores on the morphology tests and mean time participants had studied L2 or L3), participants who did have knowledge of the aspectual contrast between Romance past tenses from previously learned languages probably transferred that knowledge and applied it to the L3, as they were more consistent in judging the contrast.

Assuming that this is the case, that transfer is at least partially responsible for the significant advantage of the L3 groups over the L2 group, present results suggest that language typology does play a role in source(s) of transfer in L3 acquisition, since both L3 groups seem to have been able to transfer their knowledge from the previously known Romance language, whether it was L1 or L2. Theories concerning the initial state in L2 acquisition that do not allow for feature values to be transferred from either the L1 or the L2 (i.e. the Valueless Features hypothesis – Eubank, 1993/1994, 1994, 1996; the Minimal Trees hypothesis – Vainikka & Young-Scholten, 1994, 1996; the Failed Functional Features hypothesis – Hawkins & Chan, 1997) cannot be extended to account for transfer of the knowledge of the aspectual contrast in Romance past tenses from either L1 or L2 to L3; these hypotheses are not supported by this interpretation of present results. The FTFA hypothesis of Schwartz and Sprouse (1994, 1996) seems to be the best candidate for extension to the case of L3 based on the current study, though the influence of typological similarity as determining sources of transfer in L3 acquisition is not addressed in the hypothesis in its present form. This conclusion differs from that of Leung (2005) who proposes that there is only partial transfer from L2 to L3 and thus not full support of an extension of the FTFA hypothesis to L3. Her conclusion is based on what appears to be the presence of variable feature strength of Num in her L3 French results. Since the current study did not look at feature strength, her finding is neither supported nor contradicted by present results.

Some future directions for research on the initial state of L3 acquisition include further examination of which aspects of L2 (and L1) can transfer to L3. The current study shows possible evidence of transfer of feature values from an L1 or an L2 to an L3, though previous studies suggest that feature strength may not be transferred. Also, while this study found evidence for the role of typological similarity in this sense, psychotypology was not taken into account. It would be beneficial to ask study participants how similar they believe their various languages to be in order to provide a richer picture of how language typology affects processes of transfer, including whether it affects all speakers in the same manner, or whether it depends upon personal beliefs about language structure. Also, is it the overall typological similarity of the languages that matters, or is it the similarity of specific properties across languages that influences where transfer comes from? Most importantly, based on the answers to these questions, how should we modify or extend existing hypotheses on the initial state of L2 acquisition to account for L3 acquisition? These are a few of the issues that need to be addressed in this relatively new area of investigation in the field of language acquisition. The present study as well as other recent L3 research makes it clear that L3 acquisition is not the same as L2 acquisition, and that it is of theoretical and practical value to investigate not only how L3 acquisition differs, but also what it can tell us about language acquisition in general.

Notes

1. Psychotypology can be defined as the multilingual's perception of the similarities and differences between his or her various languages.
2. Language or linguistic typology here is used in the same general sense that it is used in the cited literature on L3 acquisition; that is, it is intended to loosely mean a general similarity on one or more levels (lexical, morphological, syntactic, etc.) between languages usually pertaining to a common language family or background. In adapting this notion of similarities between languages to the study of L3 acquisition from a generative perspective, this study specifically explores transfer between typologically similar languages when these share particular features and feature values.
3. For example, while the verb *dance* can be classified as an activity that has no inherent endpoint, as in *She dances well*, it can also be classified as an accomplishment, as in *She danced the tango at the party*. In the second example, there is an endpoint at which the song is over and she has completed the process.
4. While there are other tenses in both Italian and French that are used to express perfective aspect in the past, we will focus on the *passato prossimo* and the *passé composé* as those commonly taught in L2 classrooms.
5. In Spain particularly, the present perfect may be used in place of the preterite to talk about a perfective event in the past; however, the aspectual contrast between the perfective tenses and the imperfect remains the same no matter which is used.
6. One participant from the L1 Romance, L2 English, L3 Romance group did not report the L2 time studied.
7. The L1 Romance, L2 English, L3 Romance participants completed the tasks in their L1 in order to verify that they were making similar judgments in both Romance languages known, L1 and L3.

8. While it would have been ideal to test only participants with the same language combinations, or to perform statistical analyses separately on participants grouped by language combination, the wide variety of combinations existing in the participant populations accessible to the author precluded this. It was therefore decided that because the three Romance languages included in the study share the same distinction in meaning between the forms used to express perfectivity and imperfectivity in the past, results would be collapsed across languages for analyses.
9. This reference to King and Suñer (1999) was added at the suggestion of an anonymous reviewer.
10. This possibility was pointed out by an anonymous reviewer.
11. Each sentence conjunction judgment task by itself took approximately 30 minutes to complete, making completion of the entire study very long for L3 participants, who had to complete two SCJTs in addition to the morphology tests and the language history questionnaire.
12. This reference to Cook (1995) was added at the suggestion of an anonymous reviewer.

References

Cenoz, J. (2003) The role of typology in the organization of the multilingual lexicon. In J. Cenoz, B. Hufeisen and U. Jessner (eds) *The Multilingual Lexicon* (pp. 103–116). Dordrecht: Kluwer.

Chomsky, N. (1995) *The Minimalist Program*. Cambridge, MA: MIT Press.

Comrie, B. (1976) *Aspect*. Cambridge: Cambridge University Press.

Cook, V. (1995) Multi-competence and the learning of many languages. *Language, Culture and Curriculum* 8, 93–98.

Ecke, P. (2001) Lexical retrieval in a third language: Evidence from errors and tip-of-the-tongue states. In J. Cenoz, B. Hufeisen and U. Jessner (eds) *Cross-linguistic Influence in Third Language Acquisition: Psycholinguistic Perspectives* (pp. 90–114). Clevedon: Multilingual Matters.

Eubank, L. (1993/1994) On the transfer of parametric values in L2 development. *Language Acquisition* 3, 183–208.

Eubank, L. (1994) Optionality and the initial state in L2 development. In T. Hoekstra and B.D. Schwartz (eds) *Language Acquisition Studies in Generative Grammar* (pp. 369–388). Amsterdam: John Benjamins.

Eubank, L. (1996) Negation in early German–English interlanguage: More value-less features in the L2 initial state. *Second Language Research* 12, 73–106.

Giorgi, A. and Pianesi, F. (1997) *Tense and Aspect: From Semantics to Morphosyntax*. Oxford: Oxford University Press.

Hammarberg, B. (2001) Roles of L1 and L2 in L3 Production and Acquisition. In J. Cenoz, B. Hufeisen and U. Jessner (eds.) *Cross-linguistic Influence in Third Language Acquisition: Psycholinguistic Perspectives* (pp. 21–41). Clevedon: Multilingual Matters.

Hawkins, R. and Chan, C. (1997) The partial availability of Universal Grammar in second language acquisition: The 'failed functional features hypothesis'. *Second Language Research* 13 (3), 187–226.

Kellerman, E. (1983) Now you see it, now you don't. In S.M. Gass and L. Selinker (eds) *Language Transfer in Language Learning* (pp. 112–134). Rowley, MA: Newbury House.

King, L. and Suñer, M. (1999) *Gramática española: Análisis y práctica*. New York: McGraw-Hill.

Klein, E. (1995) Second versus third language acquisition: Is there a difference? *Language Learning* 45 (3), 419–465.

Leung, Y-k.I. (2005) L2 vs. L3 initial state: A comparative study of the acquisition of French DPs by Vietnamese monolinguals and Cantonese–English bilinguals. *Bilingualism: Language and Cognition* 8 (1), 39–61.

Leung, Y-k.I. (2006) Full transfer vs. partial transfer in L2 and L3 acquisition. In R. Slabakova, S. Montrul and P. Prévost (eds) *Inquiries in Linguistic Development: In Honor of Lydia White* (pp. 157–188). Amsterdam: John Benjamins.

Montrul, S. (2004) *The Acquisition of Spanish: Morphosyntactic Development in Monolingual and Bilingual L1 Acquisition and Adult L2 Acquisition*. Amsterdam: John Benjamins.

Montrul, S. and Slabakova, R. (2002) The L2 acquisition of morphosyntactic and semantic properties of the aspectual tenses Preterite and Imperfect. In A.T. Pérez-Leroux and J. Liceras (eds) *The Acquisition of Spanish Morphosyntax. The L1/L2 Connection* (pp. 131–149). Dordrecht: Kluwer.

Ringbom, H. (1987) *The Role of the First Language in Foreign Language Learning*. Clevedon: Multilingual Matters.

Ringbom, H. (2001) Lexical transfer in L3 production. In J. Cenoz, B. Hufeisen and U. Jessner (eds) *Cross-linguistic Influence in Third Language Acquisition: Psycholinguistic Perspectives* (pp. 59–68). Clevedon: Multilingual Matters.

Salaberry, M.R. and Ayoun, D. (2005) The development of L2 tense-aspect in the Romance languages. In D. Ayoun and M.R. Salaberry (eds) *Tense and Aspect in Romance Languages* (pp. 1–34). Amsterdam: John Benjamins.

Schwartz, B.D. and Sprouse, R. (1994) Word order and nominative case in non-native language acquisition: A longitudinal study of (L1 Turkish) German interlanguage. In T. Hoekstra and B.D. Schwartz (eds) *Language Acquisition Studies in Generative Grammar* (pp. 317–368). Amsterdam: John Benjamins.

Schwartz, B.D. and Sprouse, R. (1996) L2 cognitive states and the Full Transfer/Full Access Hypothesis. *Second Language Research* 12, 40–72.

Vainikka, A. and Young-Scholten, M. (1994) Direct access to X'-theory: Evidence from Korean and Turkish adults learning German. In T. Hoekstra and B.D. Schwartz (eds) *Language Acquisition Studies in Generative Grammar* (pp. 265–316). Amsterdam: John Benjamins.

Vainikka, A. and Young-Scholten, M. (1996) Gradual development of L2 phrase structure. *Second Language Research* 12, 7–39.

Vendler, Z. (1967) *Linguistics and Philosophy*. Ithaca, NY: Cornell University Press.

White, L. (2003) *Second Language Acquisition and Universal Grammar*. Cambridge: Cambridge University Press.

Williams, S. and Hammarberg, B. (1998) Language switches in L3 production: Implications for a polyglot speaking model. *Applied Linguistics* 19, 295–333.

Chapter 6

L3 Enhanced Feature Sensitivity as a Result of Higher Proficiency in the L2

Carol Jaensch

Introduction

This chapter investigates the effect that level of proficiency in second language (L2) has on the acquisition of a third or subsequent language (L3), in particular with regard to morpho-syntactic features that are present in neither the first language (L1) nor the L2 but are present in the L3. The three languages under observation are Japanese (L1), English (L2) and German (L3) and the features are to be found in the German Determiner Phrase (DP).

The second section of this chapter reviews some previous research on bilingualism, third language acquisition (TLA) and the acquisition of specific features. The third section will discuss the linguistic assumptions made in the present study, describing the crosslinguistic differences between Japanese, English and German. The methodology of the study will be presented in the fourth section, followed by the results in the next section. Finally the last section will provide discussion on the results along with concluding comments.

Previous Research

Bilingualism – general cognitive advantages or disadvantages

Historical background

Up until the early 1960s the general opinion of bilingualism was not particularly positive, in fact, bilinguals were thought of as being somehow cognitively disadvantaged. This changed after research by Peal and Lambert (1962) that challenged this negative view of bilingualism. In the carefully controlled testing of verbal and non-verbal abilities of 164 10-year-old French–English bilingual schoolchildren in Montreal, the researchers found that bilinguals outperformed monolinguals in 15/18 tests – the remaining three showing no difference. They concluded that bilinguals have a 'language asset', allowing them greater mental flexibility.

Several studies followed Peal and Lambert's pivotal study that observed that bilinguals who show greater proficiency in both languages have a range of cognitive advantages. Ianco-Worrall (1972) looked at metalinguistic awareness by examining the semantic/phonetic preferences of English–Afrikaans bilingual nursery schoolchildren in South Africa. The children were asked questions such as, 'What is more like "cap" – "can" or "hat"?' The bilinguals preferred the semantic option (generally considered developmentally more advanced) 54% of the time, compared to 0% by the monolingual Afrikaans group. Kessler and Quinn (1987) argued that bilinguals, who outperformed monolinguals in their ability to formulate scientific hypotheses and express them in complex syntactic constructions, demonstrated a higher level of creativity. Whitaker *et al.* (1985) examined the effect of bilingualism of children (aged 7–8) with mild mental retardation on certain memory tasks. The high proficiency bilinguals significantly outperformed the low proficiency and monolingual groups.

However, despite the emergence of such studies extolling the virtues of bilingualism, research arguing the opposite continued to appear. For example, Japanese–English bilingual children (aged 10–11) scored lower on measures of verbal ability than monolinguals in a comparison group (Tsushima & Hogan, 1975); Spanish–English bilinguals showed some delay in acquiring vocabulary and grammatical structures (Ben-Zeev, 1977). In an attempt to explain these differing results, Cummins (1976) suggested a hypothesis – the threshold hypothesis.

The threshold hypothesis

The threshold hypothesis was proposed with bilingual children in mind and maintains that these children need to achieve a certain level of proficiency before any cognitive benefits become evident. In effect, there are two thresholds; at the lowest level up to the first threshold bilingual children have low levels of competence in both languages, and are, as such, 'limited bilinguals'; this can result in negative cognitive effects. Between the first and second thresholds are bilingual children who have 'age-appropriate competence' in one but not both languages, thus one language will be relatively weak. The cognitive effects are neither positive nor negative; in fact, cognitively, the bilingual child will show little difference from a monolingual child. However, bilingual children at the uppermost level, above the second threshold, have 'age-appropriate competence' in both languages; sometimes known as 'proficient bilinguals', these children are likely to demonstrate positive cognitive effects.

Ricciardelli (1992) set out to test this hypothesis with Australian bilingual children. She took a group of 57 Italian–English bilingual children and a group of 55 monolingual children (all aged 5–6 years). She divided these two groups into high and low proficiency English groups, the bilingual groups were further sub-divided into high and low proficiency Italian. These groups were then tested on a variety of cognitive skills, including metalinguistic awareness and creativity, non-verbal abilities and reading achievement. Ricciardelli found an overall significant difference ($p < 0.01$) between the high English/high Italian group who significantly outperformed the high English/low Italian group and the high English monolinguals. The other groups showed no such differences, a result that she considered supported the threshold hypothesis, as only those bilinguals with a high proficiency in both languages showed cognitive advantages, with the less proficient bilinguals performing no differently than the less proficient monolinguals.

L3 research – general proficiency

Whilst the threshold hypothesis was formulated with bilingual children in mind, it seems feasible to extend it to adults acquiring an L3, that they too could demonstrate similar positive linguistic effects, dependent upon the proficiency of their L2. This has been demonstrated in a number of studies, such as Cenoz and Valencia (1994) and Lasagabaster (2000), who both compared the L3 English acquisition of Basque–Spanish bilinguals with that of Spanish monolinguals; and Sanz (2000), who compared the L3 English acquisition of Catalan–Spanish bilinguals with that of Spanish monolinguals; all three studies found that bilingualism, or a good proficiency in two languages (as suggested by the 'threshold hypothesis'), was a reliable predictor of general attainment in English.

A collection of work put together by Hufeisen and Lindeman (1998) looked at a number of aspects of TLA. A number of contributors studied the attitudes and expectations of L3 learners, whilst others considered the implications of influence from L1 and L2 on the L3. One paper, by Groseva (1998), attempted to show that earlier research and studies that assumed that the L3 process repeated that of the L2 process were inaccurate. She proposed that L2 knowledge eases the process of TLA, via compensation strategies, and that the learner uses the L2 as a model, either consciously or unconsciously, for the system and acquisition of an L3.

The above studies discuss L3 acquisition with regard to general proficiency; the following section looks, however, at the acquisition of specific features in an L3.

L3 research – specific features

An important contribution to TLA studies was made by Klein's (1995) study of monolingual and multilingual immigrant schoolchildren. She looked at the acquisition of specific properties in both lexical learning (specific verbs and their prepositional complements) and syntactic learning (preposition stranding). Grammaticality judgment and correction tasks were administered orally and in written form to a group of 17 L2 learners and a group of 15 multilingual high-school learners of English, who were matched on English proficiency. The previous languages of the multilinguals varied but all were similar to English in the manner in which *wh*-questions are formed (*wh*-movement) and furthermore none of the previous languages allow preposition stranding. Subjects had to make judgments about a series of sentences from which the preposition had been omitted, and correct if necessary. Declarative sentences were used to test the lexical learning and only the interrogative sentences that had an accurate response for the matching declarative sentences were analyzed for the preposition stranding. Both groups of learners made the same types of errors, which Klein interpreted as both groups following the same route leading to the acquisition of this parameter; however, the rate at which each group progressed was significantly different.

The multilinguals significantly outperformed the monolinguals both in correct sub-categorizations and in preposition stranding (see Table 6.1), from which the author concluded that the attitude to learning, heightened metalinguistic skills, enhanced lexical knowledge and cognitive skills of multilinguals are all advantageous in triggering the setting of Universal Grammar (UG) parameters.

Recent research by Flynn *et al.* (2004) looked at the acquisition of relative clauses in L3 English by adults and children, with L1 Kazakh and L2 Russian. They compared results obtained in this study with those of an earlier study that looked at the acquisition of L2 English by Japanese and Spanish speakers. Kazakh is a Turkic language with Subject Verb Order (SVO) order and head-final, left-branching structure and is, with respect to these properties, similar to Japanese. Russian is a Slavic language with SVO order but head-initial, right-branching structure, thus structurally matching English. The researchers surmised that if the L1 holds a privileged role in the acquisition of subsequent languages and only typological differences between the L1 and the L3 determine the pattern of development, then the L3 learners should pattern with the Japanese learners of the previous study (since the head-direction is the same). However, if the L1 does not hold a privileged role in the acquisition of subsequent languages, the prediction for learning an L3 with a Complimentizer Phrase (CP)

Table 6.1 Results from Klein (1995)

Group	Sub-categorizations		Preposition stranding	
	Correct tokens/total	*%*	*Correct tokens/total*	*%*
Monolinguals	48/102	47	26/48	54
Multilinguals	68/90	75	47/68	69

different to the L1 but consistent with the L2, is a pattern of acquisition matching that of the Spanish L2 learners. The results indicated that the L1 Kazakh – L2 Russian – L3 English learners' pattern of acquisition matched that of the L1 Spanish – L2 English learners rather than that of the L1 Japanese – L2 English learners; which demonstrated that prior CP development was a positive influence in the acquisition of the CP structure in English. This allowed the authors to conclude that the L1 does not appear to hold a privileged role in the acquisition of subsequent languages.

A recent study by Leung (2005) compared the L2 and L3 acquisition of articles in French, by L1 Vietnamese speakers (L2 French) and L1 Cantonese speakers with L2 English (L3 French). Both Cantonese and Vietnamese have no articles and no marking on the DP for the [± definite] feature, however this feature is present in English and French. In the written production task, she found that the L3 group significantly outperformed the L2 group in all three areas tested; definite (suppliance of correct articles in context given, L3 33% versus L2 14%, $p < 0.05$), specific indefinite (L3 81% and L2 45%, $p < 0.0001$) and non-specific indefinite (L3 83% and L2 50%, $p < 0.0001$).

By showing that L3 learners do perform better, both in terms of general proficiency and specific features, the above studies make valuable contributions to TLA research. However the question of whether the proficiency level of an L2 can affect the performance on a specific feature in the L3, which is present in neither the L1 nor the L2, has, to the author's knowledge, not been addressed. The current study addresses this issue by examining the uninterpretable features of gender and Case on the determiner and the adjective in L3 German.

Crosslinguistic Variation

The features investigated in this study determine grammatical gender and Case marking on the determiner and the adjective in L3 German. The following section describes how these properties are realised in German, and how English and Japanese differ from German.

German

In German, the gender of a noun is grammatical in nature, and this influences the form of a number of co-occurring elements; all singular articles, attributive adjectives, adjectival pronouns, ordinal numbers, relative and question pronouns. There are three genders: masculine, feminine and neuter. German also distinguishes four Cases: nominative, accusative, dative and genitive.[1] These are signaled by inflectional endings on the determiner and the attributive adjective.

Table 6.2 German determiner paradigm by gender and Case

Case	Definite/indefinite article by gender		
	Masculine	*Neuter*	*Feminine*
Nominative	der / ein	das / ein	die / eine
Accusative	den / einen	das / ein	die / eine
Dative	dem / einem	dem / einem	der / einer

As shown in Table 6.2, the morphological forms of German determiners display considerable overlap or syncretism in their distribution. For example, the definite singular article, *die*, can encode feminine gender for two Cases, nominative and accusative, likewise *der* can encode masculine in nominative Case and feminine in dative Case. In fact, in the singular, there is only one definite article, *den*, which uniquely encodes one gender (masculine) and one Case (accusative), and two indefinite articles, *einen*, again encoding masculine and accusative, and *einer*, encoding feminine and dative.[2]

Adjectives in predicative position, as in (1), are uninflected in German; however in attributive position they decline according to the gender, number and Case of the noun they are modifying. Furthermore, there are two declensions, which are known as 'strong' and 'weak'; the choice of declension type is determined by context. Strong declension (shown in example (2) and Table 6.3) is used if there is no determiner preceding the adjective which indicates the gender, number and (generally) Case of the noun; with a few exceptions the weak declension (shown in (3) and Table 6.4) is used in all other cases:

(1) Das Auto ist rotØ   predicative
    The car is red
(2) Das ist ein rot**es**   Auto   attributive/
                                                            strong
    That is a   red$_{\text{NEUT/NOM}}$ car
(3) Ich fahre mit einem   *roten*   *Auto*   attributive/
                                                            weak
    I   travel with a   red$_{\text{NEUT/DAT}}$ car

Table 6.3 Strong adjective declension affixes

Strong adjective declension			
Case	Singular		Plural
	Masculine	*Neuter*	*Feminine*	
Nominative	-er	-es	-e	-e
Accusative	-en	-es	-e	-e
Dative	-em	-em	-er	-en

Table 6.4 Weak adjective declension affixes

Weak adjective declension			
Case	*Singular*		*Plural*
	Masculine	*Neuter*	*Feminine*	
Nominative	-e	-e	-e	-en
Accusative	-en	-e	-e	-en
Dative	-en	-en	-en	-en

German DP features and UG

In recent Minimalist Program hypotheses about grammatical represen-tation (Chomsky, 1995), it is assumed that articles and/or adjectives, are valued for gender through a feature matching/valuation process (known as concord), with the inherent gender feature of the noun, and are further valued for Case by a similar matching/valuation process with a Case assigning category (such as Tense or V). The process of concord, whereby the gender (and number) features of a noun are copied onto determiners and/or adjectives, which modify that noun *inside* a particular expression, is in contrast to Agreement, whereby the person-number features of a noun are copied onto a verb that is *outside* the nominal expression.

The assumption is that German nouns have the inherent features [mas-culine], [feminine] and [neuter], that determiners and adjectives have an 'uninterpretable' gender feature [*u*-gender], which needs to be valued by an inherent gender feature on a noun, and that this valued feature has a phonological reflex in the form that a determiner and/or an adjective takes. Num has an interpretable number feature, and Noun (N), Adjective (A) and Determiner (D) have uninterpretable number features that must agree with that feature. Further, it is assumed that Tense has an inherent nominative Case feature, V an inherent accusative Case feature and deter-miners/adjectives have an uninterpretable Case feature [*u*-Case] that, when valued, has a particular phonological realization.

This means that the derivation of a simple sentence such as *Ich sehe [das schöne Haus]*, 'I see [the beautiful house'], would be as illustrated in Figure 6.1. At the start of the derivation, the noun, *Haus*, has the inherent feature of gender valued as neuter; it also has the uninterpretable features of number and Case and is therefore active. Continuing upwards, the adjec-tive, *schön*, is also active by virtue of the uninterpretable features of gender, number and Case. Num is valued for singular. D is valued for definiteness but has gender, number and Case unvalued. Syntactic operations apply so that all unvalued uninterpretable features of the DP are valued, except for the Case feature which is determined by the DP's position in the clause. In the sentence *Ich sehe [das schöne Haus]*, this DP receives accusative Case by virtue of being the direct object of a thematic verb, as the determiner is [+definite], it is spelled out as *das*.

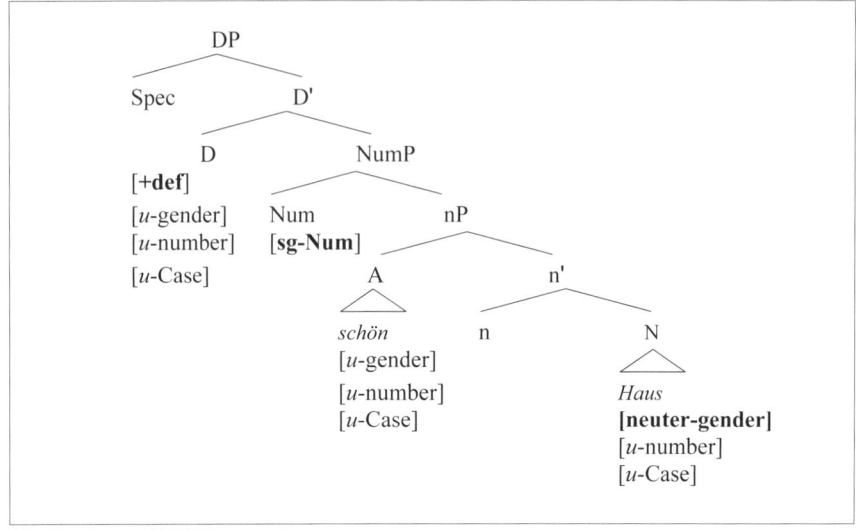

Figure 6.1 Structure of German DP – singular noun inflection

In German there are a number of prepositions that assign inherent accusative Case (for example, *bis* 'until', *durch* 'through', *für* 'for') and a number that assign inherent dative Case (such as *mit* 'with', *nach* 'to', *von* 'from'). Furthermore there are a number of prepositions that can assign either accusative or dative Case (for example, *auf* 'on (to)', *in* 'in (to)', *vor* 'in front of'). This problem is explained if it is assumed that a preposition (P) is an inherent (or lexical) Case assigner that can assign two distinct thematic roles to its complement which is accompanied by different Case realizations. When the sentence is interpreted as directional, P assigns a GOAL theta role to its complement and Case is realized as accusative. When the sentence is interpreted as stative, P assigns a LOCATIVE theta role and Case is realized as dative.

English

In English, gender contrasts are semantic in nature, determined by the sex of the referent. Grammatically, a contrast is realized between male and female on third person singular pronouns, such as *he/she him/her* and on certain nouns, such as *actor/actress*. The accusative Case is considered to be the default Case in English, as it is used in contexts where there is no overt Case assigner, for example for dislocated topics ('Me, I love cheese'), or in answer to subject questions ('Me' in answer to 'Who wants cheese?'), whilst in German the nominative Case would be used in such circumstances. In English, however, Case is only morphologically evident on personal pronouns, (*he/she/we/they* – nominative, *him/her/us/them* – accusative). There are no Case markings on determiners in English. English uses adjectives in a similar way to German; they can be both predicative and attributive. Syntactically they are in the same position – pre-nominal for attribute adjectives and post-nominal following a copula for predicative adjectives. However, neither type of adjective has markings for declension, grammatical gender or for Case.

Japanese

It is commonly accepted that Japanese does not have articles, and there can, therefore, be no grammatical gender or Case marking on the DP.[3] In fact, grammatical gender does not exist in Japanese at all; Case, however does. Morphological markers that denote Case and topicality are usually attached to the noun.[4] Other features such as tense, negation, location and direction are indicated by bound morphemes that are attached to the verb. Similarly adjectives can be combined with morphemes to denote tense and negation. These features are illustrated in the examples 4 and 5. However, Japanese adjectives are not marked for number, grammatical gender, Case[5] or definiteness:

(4) Ziroo-ga   Yoshio-ni   ringo-o   age-ta
    $Ziro_{NOM}$ $Yoshio_{DAT}$ $apple_{ACC}$ $give_{PAST}$
    'Ziro gave an apple to Yoshio.'
(5) Ano   uti-wa   ooki-i
    that $house_{TOP}$ $big_{NON-PAST}$
    'As for that house, it is big.'

Empirical Study

Japanese has no article system, whereas English does; however, English articles are not marked for grammatical gender or Case. Although Japanese may mark predicates, such as verbs and adjectives for a range of features, including tense and negation, and nouns for tense and Case, there are no markings on adjectives for gender, number or Case. This produces an interesting paradigm for the three languages under investigation. Table 6.5 illustrates that there can be no L1 or L2 transfer effect of the features (gender and Case) under investigation.

Table 6.5 Feature distribution by language

Language	Articles present	Articles marked for:			Attributive adjectives marked for:		
		Case	Num	Gender	Case	Num	Gender
Japanese	no	–	–	–	no	no	no
English	yes	no	partial	no	no	no	no
German	yes	yes	yes	yes	yes	yes	yes

Research questions

With respect to general proficiency, we have shown earlier, that bilinguals proficient in both languages seem to have an advantage over monolinguals when acquiring an L3 (Cenoz & Valencia, 1994; Lasagabaster, 2000); and we have seen that a similar advantage is found for the L3 acquisition of specific features – whether the feature is present in the L2 (Flynn *et al.*, 2004; Leung, 2005) or not (Klein, 1995). The current study aims to combine these factors; L2 proficiency, on the one hand, and, on the other, acquisition of features not present in either the L1 or the L2. The research questions that therefore present themselves are:

(1) Will the adult L3 learners of equal German proficiency *but* a higher L2 English proficiency outperform those learners with a lower L2 English proficiency on the uninterpretable features (on the determiner and adjective) investigated?
(2) If so, does this occur at all levels of German proficiency or is there a level or threshold of proficiency in the L3 that subjects need to acquire before their L2 proficiency becomes relevant?

These questions give rise to two specific hypotheses, with respect to the effects of high proficiency in the L3 *and* the L2, on the one hand, and, on the other, low proficiency in the L3.

Hypotheses
(1) L1 Japanese learners of advanced L3 German proficiency with a higher L2 English proficiency will outperform learners with a comparable L3 German proficiency but a lower L2 English proficiency on the forms that realize uninterpretable gender and Case values on the determiner and adjective. (The 'beneficial effect of bilingualism' hypothesis.)
(2) Proficiency in L2 English will have no effect on the L3 German performance (on the same forms) of L1 Japanese learners if those learners are of low German proficiency. (The 'threshold' hypothesis.)

Participants

A total of 49 (adult) subjects took part in the study, including eight German native controls who served as a baseline for comparison of the learners' results. The native controls were all students at the University of Essex (UK) and originated from different parts of Germany.[6] The experimental group consisted of 41 native Japanese speakers, who were studying or working in and around the Düsseldorf/Cologne area of Germany, where data were collected.

A personal data sheet was completed for each participant, where the following details were recorded; gender, date of birth, age at which study of English and German had begun, length of tuition time, length of immersion time, if any, for each language and in which country this had taken place. Finally the participants were asked if they had any knowledge of other languages; this resulted in the removal of two subjects, who had knowledge of French and Spanish prior to learning German. This was to ensure that the subjects' first encounter with grammatical gender was with German. The gender division and mean ages of the remaining 47 participants are shown in the appendix.

Method

All non-native speakers (NNS) completed three written tasks and two orals task in German, followed by a proficiency test in German (from the Goethe Institute) and the *Oxford Quick Placement Test* (2001) (OQPT) in English. The tasks were completed in one sitting. Native speakers (NS) of German completed the same tasks, with the exception of the two proficiency tests. This chapter will discuss results from the written tasks only, which will be described in the following sections.

Task 1 – gender

The aim of this task was to elicit gender on the determiner for 30 (real) nouns, evenly balanced for gender, definiteness and for nominative and accusative Case. The nouns were further divided according to the type of gender assignment related to the nouns; as such there were two semantically motivated gender assigned nouns for each of the three genders, (e.g. mother/female, driver/male, baby/neuter[7]); four rule-based gender assigned nouns for each gender – these nouns conform to certain morphological shapes (see Durrell, 1996: 2) which tend to correlate with a particular gender, e.g. 90% of nouns ending in *-e* are assigned feminine gender and all nouns ending in *-chen* are assigned neuter gender; and finally four nouns that were assigned gender according to neither semantic nor morphological assignment rules. A further aim was to observe the participants' gender selection for non-existent nouns. These six novel nouns were, however, morphologically similar to existing nouns, in that they exhibited certain affixes (either prefix or suffix) that are generally assigned a specific gender. The morphological tendencies used were as follows; neuter gender: multi-syllabic with prefix *Ge-* (over 90% neuter) and the diminutive suffix *-lein* (all nouns); feminine gender: suffix *-e* (over 90%) and suffix *-heit* (most nouns); masculine gender: suffix *-ling* and *-ich* (most nouns) (see Durrell, 1996: 1–14 for further information). The intention here was to observe the learners' reactions to nouns which, although unknown, did exhibit a similar morphological form to existing high frequency common nouns – in other words whether learners would match the gender to the form or simply insert a default gender. The novel nouns were once again balanced for definiteness and for target gender. Target gender was judged according to the same morphological tendencies mentioned above (prior to live testing, 20 novel nouns were pilot tested on seven natives in order to determine the most robust tokens).

The task was divided into two sections; both sections required the completion of a sentence by selecting a determiner. The same sentence was used throughout the first section, where the articles required were in the definite context (*der, die, das*), and were assigned nominative Case, by virtue of being the subject of the sentence. A different sentence eliciting the indefinite context (*einen, eine, ein*) was used throughout the second section, and these nouns were assigned accusative Case, by virtue of being the direct object of a verb; for each context subjects had only three choices. Subjects were also asked to provide the plural form of the noun in question, but those results will not be discussed here. Examples of both contexts are shown in 6 and 7:

(6) Example of definite context:
   Der ☐ Die ☐ Das ☐ Mädchen ist hier.
   'The$_{MAS}$ The$_{FEM}$ The$_{NEUT}$ girl is here.'

(7) Example of indefinite context:
   Ich sehe einen ☐ eine ☐ ein ☐ Kleid.
   'I see a$_{MAS}$ a$_{FEM}$ a$_{NEUT}$ dress.'

Task 2 – gender and Case

This task was a written multiple choice task involving the selection of a determiner for 40 short dialogues from which a determiner was missing. Subjects were asked to select one answer from the 10 possibilities, which were listed beneath each dialogue; there was no zero option. The nouns for which the determiner was missing were all count singular nouns. The choice of articles allowed selection of the correct gender and Case, according to the context of the noun. Nouns in nominative Case were in subject position of the sentence or were complements of *sein* (to be) or *wie* (how – for example, how 'the object' looks). Nouns in accusative Case were all direct objects of various verbs. Nouns in dative Case were all indirect objects of prepositions that invariantly assign dative Case to their complements. The majority were introduced by the preposition *mit* 'with'.

This task was also used to elicit definiteness, but those results will not be presented here. A clear distinction should be drawn between the previous task (task 1 – detailed above) and this one. Task 1 tested the subjects' knowledge of gender and *only* gender, however, this task (task 2) required the selection of the correct article on the basis of gender *and* Case, creating a choice from 10 possibilities, due to the definite and indefinite options. Owing to the considerable overlap of the morphological forms in German, it is not possible to say whether non-target-like behavior is due to gender or Case, the consequence of which resulted in the grouping of these features for this task.

An example of an inanimate noun, requiring a neuter gender determiner in dative Case is shown in 8, with a gloss in 9:

(8) *Ein Telefongespräch*
Johann: Hallo Hans! Fährst du in die Arbeit heute? Wenn ja, kannst du mich bitte mitnehmen?
Hans: Nein, tut mir leid. Ich fahre mit <u>dem</u> Auto in die Werkstatt – gestern abend habe ich einen kleinen Unfall damit gehabt.
Antwort: der die das den dem einen eine ein einem einer

(9) *A telephone conversation*
John: Hi, Paul. Are you driving to work today? If so, can you give me a lift, please?
Paul: No, sorry. I am taking <u>the</u> car to the garage – I had a little accident with it yesterday evening.

Task 3 – adjective declension
This task was a written multiple choice gap-filling task set in the form of a short story, involving the selection of attributive adjective affixes for 72 different nouns, which were balanced for declension type (36 weak and 36 strong), gender, number and Case. This resulted in the following divisions; there were 54 singular nouns (18 of each gender; masculine, feminine and neuter) and 18 plural nouns; there were 24 nouns (six of each gender and six plural) of each of the following Cases, nominative, accusative and dative (genitive Case was not included in this study).

Subjects were asked to select one answer from the five possible endings shown along the top of each page. An extract from the text is shown 10, with a gloss in 11:

(10)   Bitte wählen Sie von den folgenden Endungen:
-e -en -em -er -es
Das BELIEBT_____ Lokal ist in einer BREIT_____ Allee. In dieser BEKANNT_____ Gegend findet man EXCLUSIV_____ Läden wie Gucci und Dior.

(11)   Please select from the following endings:
-e -en -em -er -es
The POPULAR eating place is in a WIDE avenue. In this WELL-KNOWN area, you can find EXCLUSIVE shops such as Gucci and Dior.

Proficiency groups

The 39 NNS were first divided according to their German proficiency. This was obtained via the 30 question multiple-choice Goethe proficiency test administered as part of the battery of tests. The Goethe test places subjects in one of the six Common European Framework (CEF) levels of proficiency, as shown in Table 6.6.

Table 6.6 CEF division of Goethe and OQPT proficiency scores

CEF level	Goethe score	OQPT score	Classification
A1	0 – 5	0 – 17	Beginners
A2	6 – 10	18 – 29	Elementary
B1	11 – 15	30 – 39	Lower intermediate
B2	16 – 20	40 – 47	Upper intermediate
C1	21 – 27	48 – 54	Advanced
C2	28 – 30	55 – 60	Very advanced

This classification resulted in four groups: advanced ($n = 16$), upper intermediate ($n = 12$), lower intermediate ($n = 9$) and elementary ($n = 2$). Due to the small number of participants in the elementary proficiency group, results from these subjects will not be discussed.

Secondly, a further division of participants, within their German proficiency, was made on the basis of the score obtained from the 60-question multiple-choice OQPT for English proficiency. Cut off points for these scores are also shown in Table 6.6. This resulted in the groups shown in Table 6.7.

Statistics showing the means of both proficiency test scores, the age tuition began, the length of tuition and the length of immersion in both English and German are shown in the appendix.

Table 6.7 Participants grouped by German and English proficiencies

L3 group number	L3 German proficiency	L2 English proficiency	N
1	Advanced	Upper intermediate	4
		Lower intermediate	7
		Elementary	5
2	Upper intermediate	Upper intermediate	4
		Lower intermediate	3
		Elementary	5
3	Lower intermediate	Upper intermediate	3
		Lower intermediate	3
		Elementary	3

Results

Before detailed statistical analyses were begun, reliability analyses were conducted; Cronbach's alpha scores for item analyses and subject analyses for all three tasks were a respectable > 0.8. Tests of normal distribution were performed individually for each task.

Performance on all three tasks, shown in Table 6.8, displayed predictable improvements as German proficiency increased. The following sections will provide, for each task, results on the basis of L2 proficiency groups (within the L3 proficiencies), followed by results on feature interactions.

Table 6.8 Non-target-like performance by task and German proficiency

	German proficiency groups	N	Mean/ s.d.	Task 1: Gender (D)		Task 2: Gender/Case (D)	Task 3: Adjective declension (A)
				Real nouns	Novel nouns		
1	Advanced	16	Mean	0.13	0.30	0.09	0.16
			s.d.	0.049	0.164	0.057	0.107
2	Upper Intermediate	12	Mean	0.26	0.40	0.23	0.34
			s.d.	0.146	0.181	0.181	0.160
3	Lower Intermediate	9	Mean	0.40	0.46	0.39	0.57
			s.d.	0.162	0.182	0.237	0.183
NS	Native Speakers	8	Mean	0.00	0.02	0.00	0.01
			s.d.	0.012	0.059	0.000	0.015

Task 1 – determiner gender

Proficiency effects

When the results were further divided by English proficiency (as per Table 6.7), a trend within the top two groups of L3 German proficiency was clearly evident; compare sub-groups upper intermediate with elementary L2 English for L3 German groups 1 and 2 (Table 6.9 and Table 6.10). It can be seen that the higher the L2 English proficiency the more target-like the performance on gender assignment, both for real and novel nouns. This trend is not as clearly evident in the lower intermediate L3 German proficiency group (group 3),[8] as although the upper intermediate L2 English group outperforms the elementary group, there is little or no difference between lower intermediate and elementary groups.

Table 6.9 Real nouns – non-target-like gender selection by German and English proficiency

Non-target-like gender selection – real nouns				
Proficiencies		N	Mean	s.d.
L3	L2			
1	Upper intermediate	4	0.11	0.017
	Lower intermediate	7	0.12	0.054
	Elementary	5	0.15	0.056
2	Upper intermediate	4	0.18	0.064
	Lower intermediate	3	0.27	0.145
	Elementary	5	0.31	0.191
3	Upper intermediate	3	0.50	0.233
	Lower intermediate	3	0.33	0.133
	Elementary	3	0.37	0.100
NS	Native speakers	8	0.00	0.012

Table 6.10 Novel nouns – non-target-like gender selection by German and English proficiency

Non-target-like gender selection – novel nouns				
Proficiencies		N	Mean	s.d.
L3	L2			
1	Upper intermediate	4	0.25	0.167
	Lower intermediate	7	0.31	0.150
	Elementary	5	0.33	0.204
2	Upper intermediate	4	0.33	0.192
	Lower intermediate	3	0.39	0.192
	Elementary	5	0.47	0.183
3	Upper intermediate	3	0.61	0.255
	Lower intermediate	3	0.39	0.096
	Elementary	3	0.39	0.096
NS	Native speakers	8	0.02	0.059

A one-way-between-subjects ANOVA was conducted on the real nouns, using the mean non-target-like selections as the dependent variable and the L3/L2 sub-groups as the grouping variable. This showed a significant effect for (L3/L2) group [$F(8,28) = 4.63$, $p = 0.001$], with a very strong partial eta squared effect size of 0.57; however, post-hoc tests on group comparisons (with Bonferroni adjustment) proved to be non-significant, perhaps due to small numbers in the respective sub-groups. A one-way between-subjects ANOVA, with a dependent variable of the mean non-target-like selections on the novel nouns and the L3/L2 sub-groups again as the grouping variable, showed no effect for group [$F(8,28) = 1.28$, $p = 0.292$]; however, an effect was observed for L3 (German proficiency only) grouping [$F(4,42) = 0.02$, $p < 0.001$].

Gender results by features

Comparisons were made on the gender selection for real nouns with regard to definite/nominative and indefinite/accusative contexts; a paired sample t-test showed that NNS performed significantly more target-like in gender assignments for definite/nominative context than for indefinite/accusative, ($t = -5.211$, $df = 38$, $p < 0.001$). This pattern was reflected at all levels of German proficiency (see Table 6.11) and also throughout the sub-groups of English proficiency.

A further comparison was made on the basis of target grammatical gender (see Table 6.12). A one-way-between-subjects ANOVA using the mean non-target-like selections for the real nouns as the dependent variable and target gender as the grouping variable showed a significant effect for target gender [$F(2,114) = 10.07$, $p < 0.001$], with a strong partial eta squared effect size of 0.15. Post-hoc tests, using Bonferroni adjustment, showed both feminine ($p < 0.001$) and neuter ($p = 0.001$) to be significantly more target-like than the masculine gender. The same pattern was present throughout all levels of German proficiency and all sub-groups of English proficiency.

Table 6.11 Non-target-like gender (determiner) by definite/Case context (real nouns)

German proficiency groups	*N*	*Definite/ Nominative*		*Indefinite/ Accusative*	
		Mean	*s.d.*	*Mean*	*s.d.*
Advanced	16	0.10	0.064	0.15	0.087
Upper intermediate	12	0.21	0.158	0.30	0.162
Lower intermediate	9	0.29	0.160	0.51	0.183

Table 6.12 Non-target-like gender (determiner) by target gender (real nouns)

Target gender	*N*	*Mean*	*s.d.*
Feminine	37	0.16	0.172
Masculine	37	0.37	0.211
Neuter	37	0.18	0.179

Table 6.13 Non-target-like gender (determiner) by gender assignment type (real nouns)

Gender assignment type	N	Mean	s.d.
Semantic	37	0.08	0.155
Rule-based	37	0.21	0.170
Neither	37	0.34	0.202

With regard to the novel nouns in this task, the same pattern of least target-like performance for indefinite/accusative context was evident, but t-test results proved non-significant (definite/nominative mean 0.33/s.d. 0.229, indefinite/accusative mean 0.42/s.d. 0.238; $t = 1.761$, $df = 38$, $p = 0.086$). Also patterning with real nouns was least target-like performance for target masculine gender on the novel nouns (mean 0.57/s.d. 0.411) and most target-like for feminine (mean 0.15/s.d. 0.260). A one-way-between-subjects ANOVA, using mean non-target-like selections for novel nouns as the dependent variable and target gender as the grouping variable, showed a significant main effect for target gender ($F(2,108) = 12.80$, $p < 0.001$) with a strong partial eta squared of 0.19.

Comparisons based on the gender assignment type (semantic, rule-based or neither) for the real nouns were also made (see Table 6.13). A one-way-between-subjects ANOVA was conducted, using gender assignment type as the grouping variable and non-target-like means (real nouns) as the dependent variable, which showed a significant effect for gender assignment type [$F(2,114) = 17.46$, $p < 0.001$], with a large partial eta squared effect of 0.23. Post-hoc tests, using Bonferroni adjustment, were all significant; showing the performance on the semantically assigned gender nouns to be significantly more target-like than both the rule-based gender nouns ($p = 0.005$) and the nouns assigned gender by neither semantics nor rules ($p < 0.001$). Furthermore, performance on the rule-based gender nouns was significantly more target-like than performance on the nouns assigned gender via neither semantics nor rules ($p = 0.026$).

Task 2 – gender and case on the determiner

Proficiency effects

The same trend is again evident in the top two groups, showing subjects with comparable L3 German proficiency but a higher L2 English proficiency outperforming those of lower English proficiency (compare subgroups upper intermediate with elementary L2 English for L3 German groups 1 and 2 in Table 6.14). Again this trend does not fully extend to the lower intermediate L3 German proficiency group (see endnote 8).

Table 6.14 Non-target-like gender/Case selection by German and English proficiency

Non-target-like gender/Case selection				
Proficiencies		N	Mean	s.d.
L3	L2			
1	Upper intermediate	4	0.04	0.024
	Lower intermediate	7	0.09	0.063
	Elementary	5	0.13	0.041
2	Upper intermediate	4	0.14	0.024
	Lower intermediate	3	0.18	0.043
	Elementary	5	0.32	0.262
3	Upper intermediate	3	0.43	0.296
	Lower intermediate	3	0.36	0.263
	Elementary	3	0.38	0.253
NS	Native speakers	8	0.01	0.015

A one-way-between-subjects ANOVA[9] was conducted, using non-target-like means as the dependent variable and the (L3/L2) sub-groups as the grouping variable, which produced a significant effect for (L3/L2) group [$F_{(8,28)} = 2.932$, $p = 0.016$], with a strong partial eta squared effect of 0.46; however, post-hoc tests, using Bonferroni adjustment, proved to be non-significant (again possibly due to small sub-groups).

Gender/Case results by features

Comparisons were again made on interacting features, firstly by target gender. The pattern here was similar to the first task (task 1), showing masculine to be the least target-like of the three genders – a pattern again reflected throughout all L3 German proficiency levels and the sub-groups of L2 English proficiency. In order to observe the effect of target gender, a one-way-between-subjects ANOVA was conducted on the non-target-like selections using a grouping variable of target gender. Although no significant effect was found [$F_{(2,114)} = 2.72$, $p = 0.071$], the pattern of higher non-target-like performance on determiners requiring masculine gender was shown throughout all L3 German proficiencies (see Table 6.15).

Table 6.15 Non-target-like gender/Case (determiner) selection by target grammatical gender

Target gender	N	Mean	s.d.
Feminine	37	0.15	0.192
Masculine	37	0.28	0.231
Neuter	37	0.19	0.201

Table 6.16 Non-target-like gender/Case (determiner) selection by target Case

Target Case	N	Mean	s.d.
Nominative	37	0.17	0.156
Accusative	37	0.24	0.199
Dative	37	0.20	0.271

Table 6.17 Non-target-like gender/Case (determiner) by gender assignment type

Gender assignment type	N	Mean	s.d.
Semantic	37	0.09	0.160
Rule-based	37	0.20	0.160
Neither	37	0.30	0.216

In order to determine if target Case could be responsible for differences in performance, data were compared on this basis (see Table 6.16). Accusative Case appeared to be causing the most problems, a fact that was again reflected throughout all German proficiency groups and, with the exception of L3 German group 3 with elementary L2 English (lowest German/lowest English), also throughout the English sub-groups. However, a one-way-between-subjects ANOVA using Case as the grouping variable, showed no significant effect for Case [$F(2,114) = 0.970$, $p = 0.382$].

The results were also analyzed by gender assignment type and again the semantically assigned nouns proved to cause the least problems (see Table 6.17), a pattern reflected throughout all German proficiency groups and their English sub-groups. A one-way-between-subjects ANOVA was conducted on the means of non-target-like selections, using gender assignment type as the grouping variable; however no effect for gender assignment type was found [$F(2,114) = 0.489$, $p = 0.615$].

Task 3 – adjective declension

Proficiency effects

Non-target-like behavior was particularly high on this task; however, the pattern of more target-like performance linked to English proficiency, which in the first two tasks was clearly evident only in the top two German proficiency groups, was this time present in all three German proficiency groups (see Table 6.18).

Table 6.18 Non-target-like adjective declension by German and English proficiency

Non-target-like adjective declension		N	Mean	s.d.
Proficiencies		*N*	*Mean*	*s.d.*
L3	*L2*			
1	Upper intermediate	4	0.14	0.040
	Lower intermediate	7	0.16	0.127
	Elementary	5	0.20	0.124
2	Upper intermediate	4	0.22	0.095
	Lower intermediate	3	0.38	0.129
	Elementary	5	0.41	0.180
3	Upper intermediate	3	0.49	0.287
	Lower intermediate	3	0.56	0.157
	Elementary	3	0.67	0.050
NS	Native speakers	8	0.01	0.015

A one-way between-subjects ANOVA was conducted, using mean non-target-like performance as the dependent variable and the (L3/L2) sub-groups as the grouping variable. This showed a highly significant effect for group [$F(8,28) = 6.77$, $p < 0.001$] with a very strong partial eta squared effect of 0.66. However, whilst post-hoc tests on the sub-groups (using Bonferroni adjustment) proved to be insignificant, the presence of a trend is unarguable.

Small group numbers were probably responsible for the fact that within group comparisons (for example, upper intermediate with elementary English for L3 German group 1) proved to be non-significant. In order to test this supposition and to ascertain the true effect that English proficiency has on the performance of these subjects in German adjective declension, a partial correlation was conducted. This analysis enabled the values for all L3 subjects to be incorporated into the calculation and shows the correlation between non-target-like performance and proficiency in English – with German proficiency partialed out or controlled for. In Table 6.19, the correlation is first calculated including German proficiency, the second calculation shows the correlation with the variable of German proficiency partialed out. Whilst these figures do not show a significant correlation, there is still a considerable change in both the correlation value and the p value, which perhaps with a larger sample of subjects could become significant.

Table 6.19 Partial correlation analysis on adjective declension

Non-target-like adjective declension	Including German proficiency	German proficiency partialed out
Correlation	−0.1862	−0.2738
df	(37)	(36)
p	0.256	0.096

Adjective declension results by features

Little difference was observed in the overall non-target-like perform-ance of weak (mean 0.35/s.d. 0.246) versus strong (mean 0.30/s.d. 0.207) declensions; however, further observation of the data with respect to the type of declension required (weak/strong) together with the gender/ number of the noun being modified, showed an interesting effect when the data were aggregated in this manner.

A one-way-between-subjects ANOVA was conducted, using the com-bined variables of declension type and gender/number as grouping factor and the dependent variable of non-target-like means (see Table 6.20). A significant effect was found for declension type + gender/number [$F(7,288)$ = 5.67, $p < 0.001$] with a moderate partial eta squared effect size of 0.12. Post-hoc tests using Bonferroni adjustment showed non-target-like per-formance on plural weak adjectives to be significantly higher than femi-nine weak ($p = 0.001$), masculine weak ($p = 0.006$), neuter weak ($p = 0.043$) and feminine strong ($p = 0.016$).

With respect to the feature of Case, nominative Case was the cause for most non-target-like performance (see Table 6.21). However, a one-way-between-subjects ANOVA, using Case as the grouping variable and mean

Table 6.20 Non-target-like adjective declension by gender/number and declension type

Gender/number and declension type	N	Mean	s.d.
Plural weak	37	0.45	0.216
Feminine weak	37	0.19	0.235
Masculine weak	37	0.22	0.266
Neuter weak	37	0.25	0.289
Plural strong	37	0.28	0.269
Feminine strong	37	0.23	0.244
Masculine strong	37	0.41	0.305
Neuter strong	37	0.43	0.294

Table 6.21 Non-target-like performance by Case

Non-target-like performance	*N*	*Mean*	*s.d.*
Nominative	37	0.38	0.229
Accusative	37	0.31	0.205
Dative	37	0.27	0.241

non-target-like selections as the dependent variable, showed there to be no significant effect of Case [$F(2,108) = 1.91$, $p = 0.153$].

Both patterns (least target-like performance for plural/weak declension and for nominative Case) were also found when the data were further divided into sub-groups by English proficiency.

Discussion and Conclusion

The aim of the current study was to answer the research questions posed earlier, repeated once again below:

(1) Will the adult L3 learners of equal German proficiency *but* a higher L2 English proficiency outperform those learners with a lower L2 English proficiency on the uninterpretable features (on the determiner and adjective) investigated?
(2) If so, does this occur at all levels of German proficiency or is there a level or threshold of proficiency in the L3 which subjects need to acquire before their L2 proficiency becomes relevant?

Grammatical gender is not marked on determiners in English; however, participants of comparable German proficiency, but higher English proficiency, displayed a more target-like behavior in their gender assignment of determiners in task 1. However, it should be noted that this trend was only clearly evident in the upper two proficiency levels; advanced and upper intermediate German (groups 1 and 2) – for both real and novel nouns. In task 2, which involved not only the uninterpretable feature of gender on the determiner but also Case, the results again showed a distinct trend of improved performance based on English proficiency, for groups 1 and 2. Results from task 3 (adjective declension) showed comparatively high rates of non-target-like performance, perhaps indicative of the complexity of concord in relation to adjective declension in German. However, although the morpho-syntactic spell-out of adjective declension is not present in L2 English, the results show that the positive trend, which appears to be related to the English proficiency of the participants, is present in all three groups of German proficiency observed in this study.

Therefore, in answer to the first research question, L3 learners from the advanced and upper intermediate German proficiency groups, with higher proficiency in L2 English, do outperform those of lower proficiency in English (although not always significantly) in all three tasks that investigate the uninterpretable features of gender and Case on the determiner and the attributive adjective in German.

In answer to the second research question, this beneficial effect of L2 proficiency was not evident at *all* levels of L3 proficiency for *all* features, as learners in the lower intermediate German proficiency group showed no effect of L2 proficiency in their performance on gender and Case on the determiner (task 1 and 2). However, the effect was evident in their performance using the same uninterpretable features but on attributive adjectives, where the same learners in the lower intermediate German proficiency group, with higher English proficiency, did outperform those of lower English proficiency. Quite possibly there is a threshold for the effect of L2 proficiency (as proposed in the second hypothesis) but presumably it is not the same for all features (or the realization of those features on specific properties).

Returning to the hypotheses that were proposed earlier, repeated here once more:

(1) L1 Japanese learners of advanced L3 German proficiency with a higher L2 English proficiency will outperform learners with a comparable L3 German proficiency but a lower L2 English proficiency on the forms that realize uninterpretable gender and Case values on the determiner and adjective. (The 'beneficial effect of bilingualism' hypothesis.)

(2) Proficiency in L2 English will have no effect on the L3 German performance (on the same forms) of L1 Japanese learners if those learners are of low German proficiency. (The 'threshold' hypothesis.)

The first hypothesis (the 'beneficial effect of bilingualism' hypothesis) is fully supported as advanced (and upper intermediate) L3 learners of German with a higher L2 English proficiency did outperform those learners of a comparable German proficiency but a lower L2 English proficiency on the uninterpretable features of gender and Case on the determiner and adjective.

The second hypothesis (the 'threshold' hypothesis) is only partially supported as although lower intermediate learners of German (group 3) did *not* show a clear and consistent effect of L2 English proficiency on uninterpretable features of gender and Case on the determiner – which could then be deemed a 'threshold' of L3 proficiency for these properties; they did, however, show an effect of L2 proficiency on the same features (gender and Case) on the attributive adjective.

Clearly, larger groups are needed to fully confirm the first hypothesis and also learners of even lower proficiencies, such as elementary German, to confirm or disprove the second hypothesis.

The low number of subjects per group is the probable reason for insignificant results when comparing English sub-groups within one group of German proficiency (for example, upper intermediate with elementary English within German group 1); however an additional criticism that could be levelled at this study is that such small groups cannot be generalized to represent larger groups of learners, and that perhaps these subjects are not representative of a specific group of individuals with the given levels of proficiency in German and English. This is of course a valid point; there were after all only three participants in each of the sub-groups of lower intermediate German proficiency. However, the analysis of the participants' behavior with regard to the interacting features (and not just the target structures) seems to indicate that they do behave in a uniform manner.

This study has found that the patterns of feature interaction that are present for this group of NNS, as a complete group ($n = 37$), are also present in the sub-groups by English proficiency. For example, in task 1 (gender) the mean for these 37 subjects showed more target-like performance for the definite/nominative context than for indefinite/accusative context – a fact that was reflected not only throughout the German proficiency groups but also throughout the English sub-groups. In tasks 1 and 2, more target-like behavior was found on semantically assigned nouns, and least target-like on the nouns for which gender assignment was neither semantic nor rule-based, a pattern present in the group of 37 and also throughout the sub-groups. In task 2 subjects were least target-like in contexts that involved the structural accusative Case – an unexpected result as a recent study from Eisenbeiss *et al.* (2006) found high accuracy scores for accusatives, both on direct objects and as complements of prepositions. Perhaps this is due to the morphological overlap of determiners in the two other Cases investigated, whereas determiners for accusative Case are more marked, for example, *den/einen* appear only for masculine singular accusative nouns, which perhaps also explains the least target-like behavior for masculine nouns. However, although this was an unexpected result, the pattern was once again mirrored throughout all sub-groups. Similarly in task 3 (adjectives), subjects were least target-like in their declension of adjectives modifying plural nouns requiring the weak declension – again this pattern was present throughout the German proficiency groups and their English sub-groups. The consistency of these results would seem to indicate that although the sub-groups are small, their behavior patterns with that of the larger groups – there are no unusual patterns that could be considered deviant or erratic – thus we could assume that given a considerably larger group of subjects the comparisons of sub-groups (within one German proficiency group) would be significant.

In summary, the combined results of these three tasks seem to imply that these sub-groups of upper English proficiency (within German proficiency groups 1 and 2) have generally established the gender of the relevant nouns in their grammars and furthermore they manage to value the relevant features of uninterpretable gender and Case on articles and adjectives (via the process of concord) far more accurately than their colleagues in lower English proficiency groups. In particular the results from task 3 (adjective declension), which involves an extra 'valuation' of features – gender, Case *and* context of preceding determiner, indicate a close correlation of performance on these L3 features with L2 English proficiency.

The presence of a trend in all three tasks is unarguable; furthermore, as these features are not present in the L1 or the L2, this effect cannot be due to transfer from either language. One possible explanation could be that the 'threshold hypothesis' as proposed by Cummins (1976) may be extended to adult language acquisition of uninterpretable features, at least with respect to the mode of written production data.

An alternative, perhaps more plausible, possibility is that learners of an L3 who have acquired an L2 to a relatively high level have become somehow more sensitive to new features in the third language, a similar assumption made by Klein (1995), discussed above. In other words, language learners who have already acquired one or more non-native languages exhibit heightened metalinguistic expertise, better lexical knowledge and more developed cognitive skills, which aid them in triggering the setting of UG parameters – this could be termed 'enhanced feature sensitivity'. Such an analysis, whilst making no claims as to the initial state of the (interlanguage) grammar of these learners, would also presume support for those theories that propose full access to UG, such as the Full Transfer Full Access proposal of Schwartz and Sprouse (1994, 1996) and also the Full Access proposal of Flynn and Martohardjono (1994), Flynn (1996) and Epstein *et al.* (1996, 1998). Further research, currently in progress, on the oral production data of the study detailed here, will hopefully provide a further complement to this interesting aspect of the L3 acquisition of the German DP.

Notes

1. None of the tasks in this study include any examples of genitive Case; therefore, a detailed linguistic account of this Case will not be provided here.
2. Demonstratives (when used as determiners) decline in the same manner as definite articles; similarly, possessives (again when used as determiners) decline as indefinite articles (see Durrell, 1996, Chapter 5 for more details). Further it should be noted that, neither plural determiners nor genitive Case are observed in the present study and as such are not shown. However, the article *(k)einer* '(n)one' would also specify the genitive Case for plural, and for

feminine and singular. Similarly *den* is specified for masculine and accusative, and also for plural and dative. By this definition the only uniquely marked article is *einen*, which assigns masculine gender and is marked for accusative Case in an indefinite singular context.

3. There has been much discussion as to the (non-)existence of the functional category D in Japanese, particularly with reference to Case markers. In line with Tsujimura (1996), the assumption here is made that Case markers combine directly with the NP and further, that adjectives are part of an extended NP.

4. Case markers may be omitted in casual speech where nouns are lexically governed (Kanno, 1996).

5. In Japanese, there exists a grammatical category of adjectival nouns (Tsujimura, 1996) that share some functions of both adjectives and nouns. For some speakers (personal communication, A. Okamoto) these are often used to denote color, as in (i), which would give a literal translation of 'dog of brownness', whereas (ii) simply contains the adjectival marker -*i*.

    (i)   *cyairo-no inu-o*   as opposed to   (ii)   *cyairo-i inu-o*
         brown$_{GEN}$ dog$_{ACC}$ brown dog$_{ACC}$

6. There are some regional and/or register variations with regard to the grammatical gender of a small number of nouns in German. To ensure that all of the nouns used in this task could be deemed of stable gender and to counteract any effect of regional variance, NS were included from all areas of Germany.

7. German nouns that denote a female profession are often marked by the suffix -*in*, for example, *Lehrer/Lehrerin* (male teacher/female teacher), *Fahrer/Fahrerin* (male driver/female driver). Furthermore, neuter gender is generally assigned to young persons and (animal) offspring; *das Junge* (young/offspring), *das Mädchen* (girl), *das Baby* (baby), *das Kalb* (calf).

8. A reviewer has suggested that one participant may be skewing the means in the low intermediate German group, and that perhaps the L2 does still have a beneficial effect at this level. This is, however, only partially true. Subject number J17 showed higher non-target-like performance in all tasks discussed here. However, removal of this subject from the means for task 1 (real and novel nouns) would still leave results that suggest that at this level the L2 has little or no effect on the subjects' performance (see below). Task 3 showed a trend related to the L2 even with this subject included; if removed the means on this task simply improve somewhat (0.49 to 0.35). Task 2 is the only task where the removal of this subject would produce the L2 proficiency trend. The means and s.d.s for all sub-groups of group 3 are provided below as comparison with group 3 upper intermediate English, shown here without subject J17:

    Task 1: Real nouns: without J17 – Group 3/Upper intermediate English, mean 0.37/SD 0.047 – Group 3/Low intermediate English, mean 0.33/SD 0.133 – Group 3/Elementary English, mean 0.37/SD 0.100
            Novel nouns: without J17 – Group 3/Upper intermediate English, mean 0.50/SD 0.236 – Group 3/Low intermediate English, mean 0.39/SD 0.096 – Group 3/Elementary English, mean 0.39/SD 0.096

    Task 2: Without J17 – Group 3/Upper intermediate English, mean 0.26/SD 0.018 – Group 3/Low intermediate English, mean 0.36/SD 0.262 – Group 3/Elementary English, mean 0.38/SD 0.253

    Task 3: Without J17 – Group 3/Upper intermediate English, mean 0.35/SD 0.245 – Group 3/Low intermediate English, mean 0.56/SD 0.157 – Group 3/Elementary English, mean 0.67/SD 0.050

9. The alpha level of significance was set at $p = 0.017$, as Levene's test of equality of variance was significant for this ANOVA.

References

Ben-Zeev, S. (1977) The influence of bilingualism on cognitive development and cognitive strategy. PhD thesis, University of Chicago.

Cenoz, J. and Valencia, J.F. (1994) Additive trilingualism: Evidence from the Basque country. *Applied Psycholinguistics* 15, 195–207.

Chomsky, N. (1995) *The Minimalist Program.* Cambridge, MA: MIT.

Cummins, J. (1976) The influence of bilingualism on cognitive growth: A synthesis of research findings and explanatory hypotheses. *Working Papers on Bilingualism* 9, 1–43.

Durrell, M. (1996) *Hammer's German Grammar and Usage.* London: Arnold.

Eisenbeiss, S., Bartke, S. and Clahsen, H. (2006) Structural and lexical Case in child German: Evidence from language-impaired and typically developing children. *Language Acquisition* 13 (1), 3–32.

Epstein, S., Flynn, S. and Martohardjono, G. (1996) Second language acquisition: Theoretical and experimental issues in contemporary research. *Brain and Behavioural Sciences* 19, 677–758.

Epstein, S., Flynn, S. and Martohardjono, G. (1998) The strong continuity hypothesis: Some evidence concerning functional categories in adult L2 acquisition. In S. Flynn, G. Martohardjono and W. O'Neil (eds) *The Generative Study of Second Language Acquisition* (pp. 61–77). Mahwah, NJ: Lawrence Erlbaum.

Flynn, S. (1996) *A Parameter-setting Model of L2 Acquisition.* Dordrecht: Reidel.

Flynn, S. and Martohardjono, G. (1994) Mapping from the initial state to the final state: The separation of universal principles and language-specific principles. In B. Lust, M. Suñer and J. Whitman (eds) *Syntactic Theory and First Language Acquisition: Crosslinguistics Perspectives. Volume 2: Binding, Dependencies and Learnability* (pp. 429–451). Hillsdale, NJ: Lawrence Erlbaum.

Flynn, S., Foley, C. and Vinnitskaya, I. (2004) The cumulative-enhancement model for language acquisition: Comparing adults' and children's patterns of development in first, second and third language acquisition of relative clauses. *International Journal of Multilingualism* 1, 1–14.

Groseva, M. (1998) Dient das L2-System als ein Fremdsprachen-lernmodell? In B. Hufeisen and B. Lindemann (eds) *Tertiärsprachen. Theorien. Modelle. Methoden* (pp. 21–30). Tübingen: Stauffenburg.

Hufeisen, B. and Lindemann, B. (eds) (1998) *Tertiärsprachen. Theorien. Modelle. Methoden.* Tübingen: Stauffenburg.

Ianco-Worrall, A. (1972) Bilingualism and cognitive development. *Child Development* 43, 1390–1400.

Kanno, K. (1996) The status of a non-parameterized principle in the L2 initial state. *Language Acquisition* 5, 317–355.

Kessler, C. and Quinn, M.E. (1987) Language minority children's linguistic and cognitive creativity. *Journal of Multilingual and Multicultural Development* 8, 173–186.

Klein, E.C. (1995) Second versus third language acquisition: Is there a difference? *Language Learning* 45, 419–465.

Lasagabaster, D. (2000) The effects of three bilingual education models on linguistic creativity. *International Review of Applied Linguistics* 38, 213–228.

Leung, Y-k.I. (2005) L2 vs L3 initial state: A comparative study of the acquisition of French DPs by Vietnamese monolinguals and Chinese-English bilinguals. *Bilingualism: Language and Cognition* 8, 39–61.

Oxford Quick Placement Test (2001) Oxford: Oxford University Press.

Peal, E. and Lambert, W.E. (1962) The relation of bilingualism to intelligence. *Psychological Monographs* 76, 1–23.

Ricciardelli, L. (1992) Bilingualism and cognitive development in relation to threshold theory. *Journal of Psycholinguistic Research* 21, 301–316.

Sanz, C. (2000) Bilingual education enhances third language acquisition: Evidence from Catalonia. *Psycholinguistics* 21, 23–44.

Schwartz, B.D. and Sprouse, R. (1994) Word order and nominative case in nonnative language acquisition: A longitudinal study of (L1 Turkish) German interlanguage. In T. Hoekstra and B.D. Schwartz (eds) *Language Acquisition Studies in Generative Grammar* (pp. 317–368). Amsterdam: Benjamins.

Schwartz, B.D. and Sprouse, R. (1996) L2 cognitive states and the full transfer/full access model. *Second Language Research* 12, 40–72.

Tsujimura, N. (1996) *An Introduction to Japanese Linguistics*. Cambridge: Blackwell.

Tsushima, W.T. and Hogan, T.P. (1975) Verbal ability and school achievement of bilingual and monolingual children of different ages. *Journal of Educational Research* 68, 349–353.

Whitaker, J., Rueda, R. and Prieto, A. (1985) Cognitive performance as a function of bilingualism in students with mental retardation. *Mental Retardation* 23 (6), 302–307.

Appendix: Mean ages/proficiency scores/LoI/LoT for English and German

Proficiencies		Male/Female		Age	English				German			
L3 German	L2 English	M	F		OQPT score /60	Age tuition begun	LoT yrs	LoI yrs	Goethe score /30	Age tuition begun	LoT yrs	LoI yrs
1 Adv.	Elem.	4	1	27.60	24.40	13.00	6.0	0.2	22.60	19.60	4.1	4.5
	L.Int.	3	4	28.71	34.00	12.43	7.9	0.1	24.43	19.00	3.7	4.6
	U.Int.	1	3	33.70	41.50	12.75	8.5	0.1	23.75	21.50	5.3	7.5
2 U.Int.	Elem.	3	2	34.26	25.60	12.80	6.4	0.1	18.00	23.40	3.9	8.1
	L.Int.	2	1	22.23	37.67	13.00	7.7	0.3	18.33	19.33	2.2	0.5
	U.Int.	1	3	32.35	45.00	11.00	7.0	5.6	18.25	28.00	2.6	1.2
3 L.Int.	Elem.	2	1	26.50	24.67	13.00	6.0	0.2	12.00	24.33	1.6	2.3
	L.Int.	0	3	18.67	35.33	13.00	5.5	0.0	12.00	15.33	3.2	3.2
	U.Int.	1	2	24.67	43.67	11.67	10.7	3.0	13.67	22.67	1.2	1.2
TOTALS		17	20	28.43	33.82	12.49	7.2	0.9	18.62	21.74	3.2	4.0
s.d.					9.12	7.963	1.45	1.86	2.26	5.393	5.95	2.32	6.28
Min.					18.00	20.00	5.00	3.0	0.0	6.00	13.00	0.0	.04
Max.					63.00	53.00	13.00	12.0	11.0	29.00	38.00	10.0	29.0

Notes: LoI = length of immersion
LoT = length of tuition

Chapter 7

Third Language Acquisition of Norwegian Objects: Interlanguage Transfer or L1 Influence?

Fufen Jin

Introduction

The study of third language acquisition (henceforth L3A) from a generative perspective is a quite recent trend. Yet it has provided important insights into the language learning process, particularly the roles of first language (L1) and second language (L2) in the acquisition of a third language (L3). Although nearly all L3 studies in the existing literature (e.g. Bohnacker, 2006; Leung, 1998, 2003, 2006; Lozano, 2002a, 2002b; Vinnitskaya *et al.*, 2003) point towards full access to Universal Grammar (UG) and crosslinguistic transfer, the findings differ as to the source of crosslinguistic transfer in L3A. Leung (1998) proposes the interlanguage transfer hypothesis, according to which transfer from interlanguages may occur when L2 and L3 are typologically close. In her later work, Leung (2003) further claims that the L3 initial state is the steady state of a previously acquired language that is typologically closest to L3. In the similar vein, Vinnitskaya *et al.* (2003) contend that language acquisition is cumulative, and that all prior language experience can be either neutral or enhancing in subsequent language acquisition. Lozano (2002a, 2002b), on the other hand, argues that L1 can cause persistent fossilization if L1 features do not match L2/L3. In a more recent study, Bohnacker (2006) looks at L1 Swedish, L2 English and L3 German learners in the acquisition of the verb second (V2) property. Both Swedish and German are V2 languages; English is non-V2. Bohnacker (2006) finds evidence for L2 transfer alongside L1 transfer in the L3A of V2 property.

In order to further attest the role of L1 and L2 in L3A, the present study sets out to investigate the acquisition of objects of L3 Norwegian by Chinese-speaking learners who have been advanced learners of L2 English. The issue under investigation falls into the area of L3 syntax, where relatively little research has been conducted (see Leung, 2007, for a review). Norwegian is a closer kin to English than Chinese in that Norwegian belongs to the same language family as English (i.e. Germanic for both languages), but a different one from Chinese (i.e. Sino-Tibetan). Typologically, Chinese is known as a topic-prominent language, whereas Norwegian and English are referred as subject-prominent languages. As for the syntactic property under investigation, objects may be dropped in Chinese, but usually cannot be in English or Norwegian, in which languages a referential pronoun/noun phrase is necessary to fill in the object position. This contrast between Chinese and Norwegian/English with respect to the object-drop property is illustrated in (1) below:[1]

(1)   (a)   ni kan wan zhe ben shu, jizhu yao huan *e* gei wo
          you read finish this CL book, remember must return to me
  (b)   When you finish reading this book, please remember to give *(it) back to me.
  (c)   Når du er ferdig med å lese boken, husk å gi *(den) tilbake til meg.
          when you are ready with to read book-the, remember to give back to me

This crosslinguistic difference between L1 and L2/L3 provides a good opportunity to identify the source of crosslinguistic transfer. The research question to be addressed therefore is whether the crosslinguistic transfer comes from L1 (Chinese) syntax or from the typologically closer L2 (English) interlanguage syntax, when the Chinese-speaking learners begin to acquire Norwegian as a L3.

The rest of this chapter is organized as follows. The second section gives a descriptive overview of null objects in Norwegian and in Chinese. Null objects in English are not discussed, because object drop in English is generally believed to be a lexically controlled phenomenon (see, for example, Levin, 1993). In the third section, I present syntactic analyses of the languages under investigation, assuming the proposal by Zushi (2003), who gives a new account of the null-object property in minimalist terms. In the fourth section, I present a brief review of studies on null objects in second language acquisition. This is followed by predictions in the fifth section that are based on the interlanguage transfer hypothesis (Leung, 1998) and the L3 initial state hypothesis (Leung, 2003). In the sixth section, I report on my own experiment, and present results from the experiment. The final section contains a brief discussion and concluding remarks.

Descriptions of Norwegian and Chinese Null Objects

Norwegian

The canonical Norwegian word order is Subject Verb Object (SVO), as illustrated in (2a). Norwegian is also known as a V2 language, that is, the finite verb occurs in the second position in root clauses. This means that one and only one constituent is allowed to appear before the finite verb.

The standard analysis of V2 involves leftward movement of the finite verb to the head Complementizer (C), and movement of a constituent into the Spec of Complementizer Phrase (CP) (cf. Vikner, 1995). When the constituent is a non-subject, for example an object, inversion of the subject and the verb is required in order to satisfy the V2 requirement (cf. *2b*):

(2) (a) Jeg så denne filmen i går.
          I saw that film   yesterday
     (b) Denne filmen så jeg i går
          that film   saw I yesterday

What is less well known is that there are situations where Norwegian allows null object sentences. In the following, I outline three such situations: i.e. in colloquial Norwegian, when null objects have an arbitrary reference, and in coordinate verb phrases. First, colloquial Norwegian allows topic-linked null objects (Kristin Eide, personal communication; also cf. Sigurdsson & Maling, 2007). This is illustrated in (3). The utterance in (3b) actually involves a topicalized null object (i.e. 'the film'), whose reference can be identified in the previous discourse. The alleged existence of a null object in the sentence-initial position is manifested by word order, i.e. an inversion of the subject and the verb, which is typical of a V2 construction:

(3) (a) Har du sett *Titanic*?
          have you seen *Titanic*
          'Have you seen *Titanic*?'
     (b) Så jeg i går.
          saw I   yesterday
          'I saw (it) yesterday.'

It should be noted that topic-linked null objects have a very restricted distribution in Norwegian. An object can drop only if it is in the sentence initial position in V2 configuration (cf. Rizzi, 2000). Thus object drop is prohibited in embedded clauses, as shown in (4):

(4) Han sa at han har sett *(denne filmen).
     He said that he has seen that film.

The second type of null objects is referred to as arbitrary null objects, because the null objects have arbitrary references, corresponding to *one* in English, as shown in (5a) below. Sigurdsson and Maling (2007) point out that these null arguments are not topic-linked, and that their antecedents must be indefinite. But in Norwegian at least, the antecedents of the arbitrary null arguments are not necessarily indefinite. For example, in judging a Norwegian null object sentence such as (5b), where there is a definite antecedent, six out of 14 native speakers of Norwegian readily accept it. When the six native speakers of Norwegian were asked to interpret the sentence, they unanimously interpret the null argument as having an arbitrary reference. Sentence (5b) is used as a test sentence (S8) in the Norwegian task of the experiment. As we will see, it is the only experiment sentence that receives varied judgment by native speakers.

(5a) (i) Har noen en korketrekker? (example adapted from Sigurdsson & Maling, 2007)
Has anybody a corkscrew
'Does anybody have a corkscrew?'

    (ii) Ja, Christer har
Yes, Christer has
'Yes, Christer has one.'

(5b) % Mari sa at hun ønsker å kjøpe det nye huset. Men jeg er sikker
Mari said that she wish to buy the new house. But I am sure
på at hun ikke vil kjøpe i år. (6/14)
of that she not will buy this year
'Mari said that she wish to buy the new house. But I am sure that she will not buy (it) this year'

The third type of null objects is referred to as conjunct object drop (see Åfarli & Creider, 1987; Sigurdsson & Maling, 2007). Åfarli and Creider (1987) observe that an object can drop from the second conjunct of a coordinate verb phrase, as illustrated in (6):

(6)   Jens hugg ved og stablet op...
Jens chopped firewood and piled (it) up
(Åfarli & Creider, 1987: 339)

But importantly, not all Norwegian dialects allow conjunct object drop. According to Åfarli and Creider (1987), the local dialect of Trondheim, where the experiment was carried out, is one of the spoken Norwegian varieties that accepts conjunct object drop. But it is important to point out that it is very unlikely for low-proficiency Chinese-speaking learners to have any exposure to null object Norwegian sentences, for the following reasons. Firstly, such structures are not introduced into the Norwegian language textbooks. Secondly, there is no 'standard' spoken Norwegian in Norway. Each Norwegian speaks his or her own dialect. Learners of Norwegian are taught a variety of written Norwegian called Bokmål 'book language',[2] which is quite distinct from the local dialect of Trondheim in diction and pronunciation. Due to this language situation in Norway, learners typically cannot understand the local dialect until they reach an advanced proficiency level.

Chinese

The canonical word order of Chinese is generally believed to be SVO (see for example, Li & Thompson, 1981), as illustrated in (7a). For obvious reasons (e.g. Chinese lacks finite–non-finite distinction on its verbs), Chinese is not a V2 language. Compared with Norwegian, Chinese allows null objects rather freely, both in written and spoken forms, both in main and embedded clauses, as shown in (7b–c):

(7) (a) wo zuotian kan le yi ge dianying
    I yesterday see Asp one CL film
    'I saw a film yesterday.'

 (b) wo zuotian kan le
    I yesterday see Asp
    'I saw (it) yesterday.'

 (c) Ta shuo ta zuotian kan le
    he say he yesterday see Asp
    'He said he saw (it) yesterday.'

Chinese also allows referential pronouns in object positions. In that case, animate vs. inanimate distinction is made: overt pronouns in object position are possible only when they refer to animate entities; they are obligatorily dropped when referring to inanimate entities.

Linguistic Assumptions

There have been many attempts to account for null object phenomena (see for example, Huang, 1984, 1989, 1991; Park, 2004; Sigurdsson & Maling, 2007; Zushi, 2003). The present study assumes the proposal of Zushi (2003), as it offers a nice account of object-drop phenomena cross linguistically and assumes Minimalist concepts. Much of his analysis, however, is based on the pioneering work of Huang (1984, 1989, 1991) on null objects in Chinese. So we begin with Huang's analysis. Huang (1984) observes that null objects in Chinese can be A'-bound, but cannot be A-bound, as illustrated in (8):

(8) Zhangsan $_i$ shuo Lisi bu renshi e$_{j/*i}$
    Zhangsan say Lisi not know
    'Zhangsan said that Lisi did not know (him).' (Huang, 1984: 537)

In (8), the null object cannot be coreferential with the matrix subject (i.e. *Zhangsan*); it must refer to some other person whose reference is determined in the discourse. Based on this observation, Huang proposes that null object sentences involve a discourse-identified zero topic which shares a referential index with the null object. As to the nature of null objects, Huang proposes two different analyses. Under one analysis (cf. Huang, 1984, 1989), null objects are variables resulting from operator (OP) movement. Thus null object sentences such as (8) have the kind of structure illustrated in (9):

(9)   [OP$_i$ [Zhangsan shuo] [Lisi bu renshi e$_i$]]

An alternative analysis, on the other hand, sees null objects as null epithets. Huang (1991) observes that null objects in Chinese share important properties with anaphoric epithets in that both may be A'- bound, but not A'-bound, as shown in (10):

(10)   (a)   *John$_i$ thinks that I admire the idiot$_i$.
       (b)   John$_i$, I think the idiot$_i$ should be fired.

Based on this observation, Huang argues that null objects can be taken as the null counterparts of epithets, and that a zero topic (TOP) is base-generated in the A' position from where it binds the null object. Under this analysis, null object sentences such as (8) have a representation such as (11):

(11)   [TOP e$_i$ [Zhangsan shuo] [Lisi bu renshi e$_i$]]

Whichever analysis is adopted, null object phenomena are believed to be related to a zero topic parameter. That is to say, whether an object can drop or not in a given language depends on a parameter concerning the occurrence of zero topics. Huang derives this distinction from a more fundamental parameter, i.e. discourse-oriented vs. sentence-oriented, and concludes that discourse-oriented languages license zero topics, whereas sentence-oriented languages do not.

As syntactic theories develop from the Government and Binding framework to the Minimalist Program (MP), a question arises as to how Huang's account fits into the MP, which assumes that all parameters are morphological in nature (cf. Chomsky, 2001). Zushi (2003) maintains the spirit of Huang's second analysis, i.e. a zero topic is base-generated in situ, from where it binds a null argument. Meanwhile he proposes a new approach to zero topics, assuming the basic concepts of the MP. Zushi derives the presence or absence of zero topics from different properties of the projection of Tense (T). He assumes that in English-type languages, T has an EPP feature, which must be eliminated either by a Determiner Phrase (DP) moved to Specific Tense Phrase (SpecTP) or by an expletive inserted by Merge. The operation that checks off the EPP feature has two consequences. First, it makes the projection of T closed, and second, T has the property of an argument. In Chinese-type languages, on the other hand, T has no feature to be checked off, and therefore no element is required to enter into a checking relation with T. Hence T in Chinese-type languages has no nominal feature, and its projection can be regarded as predicative. Zushi (2003) further argues that a topic phrase, including a zero topic, is licensed by predication, in the sense that it serves as a subject of the projection of T which is predicative. Accordingly, zero topics are licensed (through predication) in Chinese-type languages, but not in English-type languages. Based on the above analysis, the structures of Chinese-type languages and English-type languages can be represented as (12a and b), respectively:

(12) (a) Structure of Chinese-type   (b) English-type languages
          languages

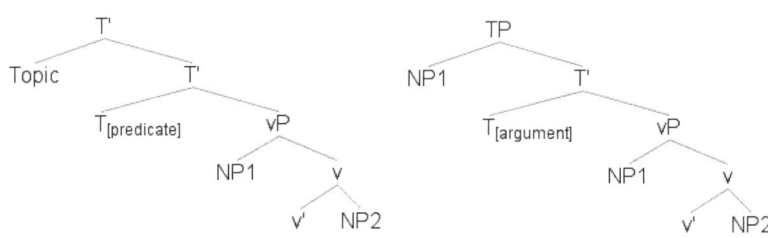

In the clause structure for Chinese-type languages in (12a), the topic phrase is adjoined to T′ by a pure merge, rather than movement into that position. Although the topic phrase is not related to any position within vP, it can be licensed by predication in the sense that it serves as a subject of the projection of T (which has the property of predicate). Since no checking off of the EPP feature is involved, T in Chinese-type languages is not closed, so that the domain where the null argument seeks its identifier to receive its reference value can be extended. In the clause structure for English-type languages in (12b), on the other hand, T has an EPP feature, so NP1 moves to SpecTP in order to check the EPP feature of T. After checking off the EPP feature, the projection of T is closed; T has the property of argument, which, according to Zushi (2003), cannot license a zero topic.

At this conjuncture, a question arises as to how this approach accounts for topic-linked null object sentences in colloquial Norwegian, such as (5a), repeated here as (13a). Zushi regards V2 verb movement to C as a process that turns the structure into a predicate, requiring a 'subject' to be predicated of. Then (13a) has a representation like (13b):

(13) (a) Så jeg i går.
          Saw I yesterday
          'I saw (it) yesterday.'
     (b) [$_{CP}$ [$_{TOP}$ e$_i$] så [$_{TP}$ jeg pro$_i$ i går]

Null Objects in Second Language Acquisition

To my knowledge, there are four studies on null objects (along with null subjects) in the L2 literature (namely, Park, 2004; Wakabayashi & Negishi, 2003; Yuan, 1997; Zobl, 1994). These four studies all involve L2 learners of

English whose L1s have null subject/object properties. Park (2004) investigates Korean-speaking children's production of null object/subject sentences in their acquisition of L2 English. Wakabayashi and Negishi (2003) examine the status of null subjects and null objects in adult Japanese-speaking learners' L2 English. Both Zobl (1994) and Yuan (1997) study adult Chinese-speaking learners' acquisition of L2 English subjects and objects. Though the four studies vary in methods of data collection, the findings all point to an asymmetry between null subjects and null objects, that is, learners have more difficulty unlearning the null object property than the null subject property. In Yuan's (1997) study, for example, it is found that Chinese-speaking learners have persistent difficulties detecting the ungrammaticality of L2 English sentences with null objects. Yuan (1997) argues that the difficulty lies in a lack of positive evidence in L2 English input data that can help Chinese-speaking learners abandon the [+ zero topic] setting. Note, however, that Yuan's (1997) data on the control sentences (i.e. non-null object English sentences) show that the Chinese learners consistently accept English sentences with overt objects, which can be interpreted as acquisition of the linguistic competence at issue (see White, 2003). In addition, it is important to look at learners' performance at the individual level, as group results in Yuan's (1997) study indicate that the status of null objects is quite indeterminate in Chinese learners' interlanguage grammars of English. It would be interesting to find out whether the English interlanguage (EIL) system and the Norwegian interlanguage (NIL) system of an individual subject are congruent with respect to zero topic parameter resetting.

Predictions

In light of the interlanguage transfer hypothesis (Leung, 1998) and the L3 initial state hypothesis (Leung, 2003), the L3 initial state is the steady state of a previously acquired language that is typologically closest to L3. If this proves to be true, L2 English interlanguage will constitute the initial state of L3 Norwegian, because Norwegian is conceived as a typologically closer language to English than to Chinese. L2 English parameter values, then, are predicted to serve as part of the initial state of L3A. To put it on a more concrete footing, the following predictions can be made:

(1) The group results are expected to show strong correspondence between EIL and NIL in terms of zero topic parameter resetting. That is to say, learners' performance on resetting zero topic parameter is consistent in both languages.
(2) For an individual learner, the percentage of his correct rejections to null object sentences in English and in Norwegian should be very close.

The Current Study

Participants

The participants in this study include 40 L1 Chinese–L2 English–L3 Norwegian learners and 14 native Norwegian speakers as a control group. The learners were (or had been) mostly graduate students at the Norwegian University of Science and Technology (NTNU), located in the city of Trondheim in the central part of Norway. Their average age at the time of testing was 30.7, ranging from 27 to 45. Their mother tongue was Mandarin Chinese. They started learning English as an L2 after puberty (about 13 years old), and had reached a high level of proficiency, as indicated by their Test of English as a Foreign Language (TOEFL) scores (615.6 on average, ranging from 590 to 642).

None of the learners had studied Norwegian prior to coming to Norway. Their age range of first exposure to Norwegian was 18 to 35. They started to take Norwegian language courses after they enrolled at NTNU. Exposure to Norwegian was therefore a mixture of formal instruction as well as naturalistic settings. Thus the measure of proficiency was based on two factors: the length of formal instruction and the length of stay in Norway after they started to take the language courses. Accordingly, the learners were broken into three proficiency levels, i.e. beginner, low-intermediate and upper-intermediate. Detailed information of the learners is presented in Table 7.1.

The learners were also asked to fill in a questionnaire concerning their language learning experiences. According to the questionnaire they filled out, all the learners were non-English majors, and they had not studied any languages other than English and Norwegian. English remained as the dominant language in their social life long after they started their Norwegian language courses. All learners from the beginner and the lower-intermediate groups and most of the learners from the upper-intermediate group reported that they found it difficult to understand the local dialect. When asked whether English or Chinese was closer to Norwegian, they unanimously answered that English, rather than Chinese, was closer to Norwegian.

Table 7.1 Information about the learners

No. of participants	TOEFL score	Norwegian proficiency levels	Average length of Norwegian classes	Average length of residence in Norway
14	611.2	Beginner	56 hours	9 months
12	620.4	Low-intermediate	124 hours	1.6 years
14	615.1	Upper-intermediate	265 hours	4.5 years

Experiment tasks

The participants were asked to do a grammaticality judgment and sentence correction task in both English and in Norwegian. Both the English and the Norwegian tasks contained a list of 20 randomized written sentences, including 5 null object sentences and 15 distracters (see Appendix 1 for a whole set of materials). All the null object sentences are topic-linked. The null objects were distributed in both root clauses and embedded clauses, three in root clauses, two in embedded clauses (see (15) for illustrations in English). Animate and inanimate distinctions were also made. For the null objects in root clauses, two were inanimate, and one was animate. For the null objects in embedded clauses, one was inanimate and the other was animate. The test sentence structures in the English and Norwegian tasks were the same, but the Norwegian sentences were not direct translations of the corresponding English sentences. Vocabulary in the Norwegian task was kept to the range of beginner level to ensure that no participants had lexical problems. The two tasks were carried out with a seven-day interval, with the Norwegian task before the English one.

(15) (a)   Null objects in root clauses
            I immediately recognized the students, and later Mary also recognized (S4).
            When you finish using the computer, please let me use for a while. (S10)
            Mary's bike had gone wrong. I am going to repair for her tomorrow. (S17)
       (b)   Null objects in embedded clauses
            Mary lost her bike last week, but John said the police had found for her. (S8)
            John said those students were in the library, but I told him I didn't find there. (S20)

Results

The participants are scored 1.0 if they identified the ungrammaticality of null argument in the two languages, and filled the null position with an overt pronoun. They get 0 if they failed to reject the sentences with null objects. They get 0.5 if they identified the ungrammaticality of null object sentences, but failed to correct them. The maximum score one can receive is 5.0 (total rejection and correction of null object sentences); the minimum score one can receive is 0 (total acceptance of null object sentences). Interestingly, for the participants in this experiment, those who had identified the source of error had no problem supplying the relevant corrections. This means that a learner's judgment score equals his sentence correction score (hereafter only the learners' judgment scores will be presented; sentence correction scores will not be provided separately).

Table 7.2 Participants' rejections rates in the (L2) English and the (L3) Norwegian tasks

Sentence no.	L2 English (n = 40)	L3 beginner (n = 14)	L3 low-inter. (n = 12)	L3 up-inter. (n = 14)	Control (n = 14)
4	19 (47.5%)	4 (28.6%)	4 (33.3%)	9 (64.3%)	14 (100%)
8	28 (70%)	2 (14.3%)	1 (8.3%)	5 (35.7%)	8 (57.1%)
10	25 (62.5%)	3 (21.4%)	5 (41.7%)	8 (57.1%)	13 (92.8%)
17	34 (85%)	3 (21.4%)	3 (25%)	11 (78.6%)	14 (100%)
20	38 (95%)	4 (28.6%)	2 (16.7%)	7 (50%)	14 (100%)
Mean percentage	72%	21.4%	25%	57.1%	90%

Rejection rates of English and Norwegian null object sentences in learner and control groups are presented in Table 7.2 (also see Appendix 2 for individual learners' judgment scores).

As we see from Table 7.2, native speakers of Norwegian readily rejected all null object Norwegian sentences, except for S8, which received a varied judgment (6 out of 14 speakers accepted it; see pp. 146–147 for a discussion about this sentence). In contrast with the native speakers, Chinese learners do seem to have some difficulty rejecting null objects both in their L2 English and L3 Norwegian. The learners rejected English null object sentences at a mean rate of 72%; the most advanced group rejected Norwegian null sentences at a mean rate of 57.1%, a little over a chance level. This finding is consistent with the previous studies on null objects in second language acquisition (e.g. Yuan, 1997; Zobl, 1994). Following Eubank and Grace (1998), who employ 70% as a criterion for reaching native-like provision levels, I interpret the learners' 72% rejection rate to English null object sentences as an indication that they have reset the zero topic parameter to the English setting, though there may be individual variability, which will be uncovered when we come to the individual results.

Another striking result that can be observed from Table 7.2 is that the learners are more accurate in L2 English than in L3 Norwegian in rejecting the null object sentences. This is reflected in the overall higher L2 accuracy rate than that of L3. This observation is confirmed by the *t*-test results. Significant differences were found between learners' judgments on English null object sentences and Norwegian null object sentences across proficiency levels [paired *t*-tests: $t_{beginner}(13) = 5.211$ $p = 0.000$; $t_{low-inter.}(11) = 6.425$ $p = 0.000$; $t_{upper-inter.}(13) = 2.188$ $p = 0.047$]. Therefore prediction (1), which predicts strong correspondence between EIL and NIL in terms of zero-topic parameter resetting, is not borne out. Among the three different L3 proficiency groups, significant differences were found between the L3 beginner group and the upper-intermediate group [independent samples *t*-tests: $t(26) = 2.996$ $p = 0.006$], and between the low-intermediate group and the upper-intermediate group [$t(24) = 3.273$ p = 0.003]; there is no significant difference between beginner and low-intermediate groups [$t(24) = 0.174$ p = 0.864]. This indicates that learners do not make great improvement in their ability to recognize the ungrammaticality of null object structures until they reach the upper-intermediate proficiency level.

Furthermore, we can observe that within each proficiency level group, the learners' rejection rates on individual Norwegian sentences are quite comparable, suggesting that the learners did not make any distinction between animate and inanimate objects, nor did they distinguish objects in main clauses from objects in embedded clauses. So all types of null objects will be treated the same; no further analysis is made between animate and inanimate objects, and null objects in main clauses and embedded clauses.[3]

Now we take a look at individual results. As we are primarily interested in L1 transfer effects in the initial state of L3A, we only focus on L3 beginners. Since there are no significant differences between the beginner and the low-intermediate groups, we treat them as one group. Individual judgment scores in Table 7.3 demonstrate that half of the learners (13 out of 26) scored 0 in judging Norwegian null object sentences. In other words, half of the L3 beginners readily accepted all the ungrammatical null object sentences in Norwegian. Only a small number (2 out of 26) of learners consistently rejected them. In judging the null object sentences in English, by contrast, over half of the learners (14 out of 26) consistently rejected sentences with null objects; only one out of 26 accepted all the English null object sentences. This contrastive performance between L2 and L3 is a strong indication of L1 influence instead of transfer from English interlanguage. Thus, prediction (2), which predicts a high level of congruence for a learner's correct rejections to null object sentences in Norwegian and in English, is not supported. Note, however, that there is the same number of learners (11 out of 26) who score within the range of 1–3 in the Norwegian task and the English task, indicating variability in these learners' intuition

Table 7.3 Individual judgment scores for L3 beginners and low-intermediates

Score range	Norwegian (L3)	English (L2)
0	13/26 (50%)	1/26 (3.8%)
1–3	11/26 (42.3%)	11/26 (42.3%)
4–5	2/26 (7.7%)	14/26 (53.8%)

Table 7.4 The 11 learners who scored 1–3 in the Norwegian task

Id.	B6	B7	B12	I3	I4	I5	I6	I7	I9	I11	I12	Mean
Eng.	5	4	3	5	3	5	5	5	3	4	4	4.18
Nor.	3	3	1	2	2	1	2	2	3	1	1	1.91

about null objects in English/Norwegian. In order to find out whether the variability in these learners' intuition about null objects in L3 Norwegian is due to transfer from their English interlanguage, it is important to show whether the 11 learners whose scores are within the range of 1–3 in the Norwegian task, are the same as those 11 learners in the English task. The 11 learners, along with their scores in the Norwegian and the English tasks, are presented in Table 7.4.

The *t*-test result revealed a significant difference between the learners' judgment scores on the null object sentences in English and in Norwegian [$t(20) = 6.250$ $p = 0.000$], suggesting that there is little trace of transfer from the English interlanguage. Nevertheless, we cannot rule out the possibility that interlanguage transfer may occur in some individual learners, as we can observe from Table 7.4 that certain individual learners' (e.g. B7, I9) scores in the two tasks are very close.

Discussion and Conclusion

This chapter has reported on an empirical study investigating L3A of Norwegian objects by L1 Chinese-speaking learners, who have achieved advanced proficiency of English as an L2. It was assumed that Chinese and English/Norwegian are parameterized with respect to a [zero topic] parameter, which, according to Zushi (2003), is derived from different properties of T: T in Chinese is predicative, whereas in English/Norwegian it is argumentative. This parametric variation gives rise to structural differences between Chinese and English/Norwegian. The predicative property of T in Chinese licenses zero topics, which can directly merge with SpecT; the argumentative property of T in English/Norwegian, on the other hand, bars direct merge of a Topic with SpecT, though Verb to Complementizer (V-to-C) movement in Norwegian can be regarded a process that turns the structure into a predicate, and thereby a zero topic is licensed. Due to these parametric variations between Chinese and English/Norwegian, Chinese-speaking learners have to learn that, in contrast to direct merge of a Topic with SpecT in their L1, T in English and Norwegian has an EPP feature, which requires movement of the subject Noun Phrase (NP) to SpecTP. In the meanwhile, they have to learn that after checking off of the EPP feature, T has the property of argument, which no longer can license a zero topic. Furthermore, learners have to acquire the V2 property before they can master topic-linked null objects in Norwegian. Given this complexity involved in unlearning null object property, it takes time for Chinese learners to reset the [zero topic] parameter and the related properties of T, leading to a prolonged duration of indeterminate status of null objects in their L2 and L3 interlanguages.

Group results from the experiments show that the Chinese learners rejected English null object sentences at the rate of 72%. Individual results indicate that over half of the learners performed native-like in judging and correcting English null object sentences. These results were interpreted as indicative of parameter resetting, though a number of individual learners were found to show variability in their intuition about null objects in English/Norwegian. Clear evidence has been found pointing to little transfer from L2 English interlanguage in the L3A of Norwegian objects. There were significant differences between L2 and L3 responses to null object sentences both at the group level and at the individual level. And it was found that there was great improvement in the learners' ability to recognize the ungrammaticality of null object structures in Norwegian as their proficiency level increased to upper-intermediate. The predictions based on the interlanguage transfer hypothesis and the L3 initial state hypothesis proposed by Leung (1998, 2003) were largely not supported, though some traces of L2 interlangauge transfer were spotted in certain individual learners.

At this point, one may argue that the fact that Norwegian allows null objects in certain conditions may serve as positive evidence indicating Norwegian has the same parameter setting as Chinese, thus preventing learners from resetting the [zero topic] parameter in the L3 initial stage. I shall contend that it is very unlikely for low-proficiency learners of Norwegian to encounter such 'positive evidence'. As I have pointed out before, Norwegian beginners have literally no exposure to Norwegian null object sentences at all, for the reasons that (1) the null object sentence structures are not introduced into the Norwegian language textbooks; and (2) Chinese-speaking learners of Norwegian often find it difficult to understand the local dialect, even after they have a lot of exposure to the language. The Chinese learners' difficulty in rejecting null object sentences in L3, then, can largely be attributed to L1 influence.

To sum up, results from this study provide evidence pointing to a strong L1 effect and little trace of L2 English interlanguage transfer in Chinese-speaking learners' L3 acquisition of Norwegian objects. This strongly suggests that Chinese-speaking learners assume the L1 parameter setting when they begin to acquire L3 Norwegian. In general, the finding from the present study is more in line with Lozano's (2002a, 2002b) argument that L1 can cause persistent fossilization if L1 features do not match L2/L3. It largely disconfirms the interlanguage transfer hypothesis (Leung, 1998) and the L3 initial state hypothesis (Leung, 2003), though we cannot rule out the possibility that interlanguage transfer may occur in some individual learners. In any case, an important conclusion we can draw from the present study is that L1 influence cannot be eliminated as a direct source of transfer in L3A, even after learners have previously acquired a typologically closer L2.

Notes

1. The abbreviations used in the examples are: Asp = aspect marker; CL = classifier; Top = topic.
2. The other variety of written Norwegian is called Nynorsk 'Neo-Norwegian'. The two varieties behave similarly with regard to null object property.
3. One of the anonymous reviewers asked whether the same results would be obtained if more test items were added. I acknowledge that this is a limitation of the experiment. After all, the tests contained only five test sentences, with only one–two tokens for each condition (i.e. embedded vs. root clause, animate vs. inanimate objects). A larger scale experiment with more tokens for each condition will provide more reliable results.

References

Åfarli, T. and Creider, C. (1987) Nonsubject pro-drop in Norwegian. *Linguistic Inquiry* 15, 339–345.

Bohnacker, U. (2006) When Swedes begin to learn German: From V2 to V2. *Second Language Research* 22, 443–486.

Chomsky, N. (2001) Derivation by phase. In M. Kenstowicz (ed.) *Ken Hale: A Life in Language* (pp. 1–52). Cambridge, MA: MIT Press.

Eubank, L. and Grace, S.T. (1998) V-to-I and inflection in non-native grammars. In M-L. Beck (ed.) *Morphology and its Interface in L2 Knowledge* (pp. 69–88). Amsterdam: John Benjamins.

Huang, C-T.J. (1984) On the distribution and reference of empty pronouns. *Linguistic Inquiry* 15, 531–574.

Huang, C-T.J. (1989) Pro-drop in Chinese: A generalized control theory. In O. Jaeggli and K. Safir (eds) *The Null Subject Parameter* (pp. 185–214). Dordrecht: Kluwer.

Huang, C-T.J. (1991) Remarks on the status of the null object. In R. Freidin (ed.) *Principles and Parameters in Comparative Grammar* (pp. 56–76). Cambridge, MA: MIT Press.

Leung, Y-k.I. (1998) Transfer between interlanguages. In A. Greenhill, M. Hughes, H. Littlefield and H. Walsh (eds) *Proceedings of the 22nd Boston University Conference on Language Development* (pp. 477–487). Somerville, MA: Cascadilla Press.

Leung, Y-k.I. (2003) Failed features versus full transfer full access in the acquisition of a third language: Evidence from tense and agreement. In H. Zobl and H. Goodluck (eds) *Proceedings of the 6th Generative Approaches to Second Language Acquisition Conference (GASLA 2002): L2 Links* (pp. 199–207). Somerville, MA: Cascadilla Press.

Leung, Y-k.I. (2006) Full transfer versus partial transfer in L2 and L3 acquistion. In R. Slabakova, S. Montrul and P. Prévost (eds) *Inquiries in Linguistic Development: In Honor of Lydia White* (pp. 157–187). Amsterdam: John Benjamins.

Leung, Y-k.I. (2007) Third language acquisition: Why it is interesting to generative linguists. *Second Language Research* 23, 91–110.

Levin, B. (1993) *English Verb Classes and Alternations: A Preliminary Investigation.* Chicago: Chicago University Press.

Li, C. and Thompson, S. (1981) *Mandarin Chinese: A Functional Reference Grammar.* Berkeley: University of California Press.

Lozano, C. (2002a) Focus, pronouns and word order in the acquisition of L2 and L3 Spanish. Ph.D. thesis, University of Essex, UK.

Lozano, C. (2002b) The interpretation of overt and null pronouns in non-native Spanish. *Duham Working Papers in Linguistics* 8, 53–66.

Park, H. (2004) A minimalist approach to null subjects and objects in second language acquisition. *Second Language Research* 20, 1–32.

Rizzi, L. (2000) *Comparative Syntax and Language Acquisition.* London: Routledge.

Sigurdsson, H-A. and Maling, J. (2007) Argument drop and the empty left edge condition. On WWW at: http://ling.auf.net/lingBuzz/. Accessed 09.02.2007.

Vikner, S. (1995) *Verb Movement and the Licensing of NP-positions in the Germanic Languages.* Oxford: Oxford University Press.

Vinnitskaya, I., Flynn, S. and Foley, C. (2003) The acquisition of relative clause in a third language: Comparing adults and children. In H. Zobl and H. Goodluck (eds) *Proceedings of the 6th Generative Approaches to Second Language Acquisition Conference (GASLA 2002): L2 Links* (pp. 340–345). Somerville, MA: Cascadilla Press.

Wakabayashi, S. and Negishi, R. (2003) Asymmetry of subjects and objects in Japanese speakers' L2 English. *Second Language* 2, 53–73.

White, L. (2003) *Universal Grammar and Second Language Acquisition.* Cambridge: Cambridge University Press.

Yuan, B. (1997) Asymmetry of null subjects and null objects in Chinese speakers' L2 English. *Studies in Second Language Acquisition* 19, 467–97.

Zobl, H. (1994) Prior linguistic knowledge and the conservatism of the learning procedure: Grammaticality judgments of unilingual and multilingual learners. In S. Gass and L. Selinker (eds) *Language Transfer in Language Learning* (pp. 176–196). Amsterdam: Benjamins.

Zushi, M. (2003) Null arguments: The case of Japanese and Romance. *Lingua* 113, 559–604.

Appendix 1: Materials for the Experiment

English grammaticality judgment and sentence correction task

Instruction: Judge whether the following sentences are well-formed or not. Correct the sentences that you believe are not well-formed.

Null object sentences in English

4. I immediately recognized the students, and later Mary also recognized.

8. Mary lost her bike last week, but John said the police had found for her.

10. When you finish using the computer, please let me use for a while.

17. Mary's bike has gone wrong. I am going to repair for her tomorrow.

20. John said those students were in the library, but I told him I didn't find there.

Distracters in the test
1. Recently has been very cold here.
2. Soon will there be a large number of tourists, and the place will become noisy.
3. There will not be many opportunities await us in the rest of our days.
5. Foreigners are easy to be misunderstood.
6. In China town can buy Chinese noodle.
7. I wonder who that has knitted the sweater.
9. This is the job which John applied last week.
11. The experiment has been started. I hope will be successful.
12. What the policeman who found Cathy get?
13. Near the beautiful house is an ancient tree.
14. Which exam is the student worrying?
15. I once met John's girlfriend. Was very beautiful.
16. The contracts have signed already, haven't they?
18. They wanted to build a tower which its top would reach the heaven.
19. Who did you believe that the man saw?

Norwegian grammaticality judgment and sentence correction task

Null object sentences in Norwegian
4. John liker den jenta, men jeg liker ikke.
8. Mary sa at hun ønsker å kjøpe det nye huset. Men jeg er sikker på at hun ikke vil kjøpe i år.
10. Når du er ferdig med å lese boken, husk å returnere til meg.
17. Jeg inviterte henne å se filmen i dag. Men hun så allerede i går.
20. Jeg spurte om han har truffet mora mi. Han fortalte meg at han ikke har sett.

Distracters in the test
1. Regnet i går?
2. Farfar kan ikke være ute fordi han ikke er frisk.
3. De alltid spiser hjemme og ofte inviterer gjester hjem.
5. Det er mye som må gjøres i dag.
6. I kiosken selger aviser og bøker.
7. Hvis man er sulten igjen senere, tar man kanskje litt kveldsmat.
9. Jeg er vanskelig å lære norsk, for grammatikken er så komplisert.
11. Jeg var på norskkurset i går. Jeg synes 0 var dårlig.
13. Mellom postkontoret og bokhandelen er en minibank.
12. Anders spør om de skal reise til Oslo.

14. Etter frokost jeg vil ha en kopp te eller kaffe.
15. Tom har en 3 år gammel datter. Er så pen!
16. Du skal bare høre på hva jeg sier.
18. Det er mange mennesker håper å bli rike.
19. Har dere en god bok at jeg kan lese?

Appendix 2: Individual learners' judgment scores in the English and the Norwegian task

L3 beginner (n = 14)			L3 low-intermediate (n = 12)			L3 upper-intermediate (n = 14)		
Id.	Eng.	Nor.	Id.	Eng.	Nor.	Id.	Eng.	Nor.
B1	4	0	I1	5	0	A1	5	1
B2	2	0	I2	3	0	A2	5	4
B3	2	0	I3	5	2	A3	5	3
B4	2	0	I4	3	2	A4	4	4
B5	3	0	I5	5	1	A5	4	0
B6	5	3	I6	5	2	A6	3	3
B7	4	3	I7	5	2	A7	3	1
B8	5	0	I8	1	0	A8	4	3
B9	1	0	I9	3	3	A9	2	4
B10	2	0	I10	5	0	A10	3	3
B11	0	0	I11	4	1	A11	4	4
B12	3	1	I12	4	1	A12	3	1
B13	5	4				A13	5	4
B14	4	4				A14	4	5
Mean	3.00	1.07		4.00	1.17		3.86	2.86

Key: B = L3 beginner; I = L3 low-intermediate; A = L3 upper-intermediate.

Chapter 8

Null Objects in L1 Thai–L2 English–L3 Chinese: An Empiricist Take on a Theoretical Problem

Sirirat Na Ranong and Yan-kit Ingrid Leung

Introduction

The study of crosslinguistic influence or language transfer[1] has generated much intense interest in the field of Second Language Acquisition L2A) for a few decades (see Andersen, 1983; Gass & Selinker, 1983, 1992; Kellerman, 1979, 1983; Odlin, 1989, 2003, amongst others). The last couple of years have seen the line of inquiry branching out into the young field of third language acquisition (L3A). Researchers working on L3A seriously attempt to find out the source of transfer in cases of additional non-native / non-primary or multilingual language acquisition by investigating various potential (confounding) factors, such as second language (L2)/third language (L3) proficiency (Dewaele, 2001; Hammarberg, 2001; Williams & Hammarberg, 1998), the privileged status of the first language (L1) (De Angelis & Selinker, 2001), age effects (Cenoz, 2001), typological proximity between languages (Cenoz, 2001; De Angelis & Selinker, 2001; Ecke, 2001; Hammarberg, 2001; Ringbom, 2001; Williams & Hammarberg, 1998), psychotypology (Bouvy, 2000; Kellerman, 1979, 1983), as well as recency effect (Hammarberg, 2001; Williams & Hammarberg, 1998). However, most of the L3 studies focused primarily on lexical transfer (see Cenoz & Jessner, 2000; see also studies in Cenoz *et al.*, 2001, 2003, amongst others); indeed most research in the field of L3A is descriptive in nature and seldom extends beyond the domain of the lexicon (see Leung, 2007 for a review).

Contrary to common misconceptions, despite embracing universalist assumptions questing for 'sameness', L2A researchers working from the Universal Grammar (UG) perspective have not ignored the relevance of language transfer in the study of L2 acquisition (cf. review in Odlin, 2003). In fact the importance of the issue has been maintained or indeed revived (through more rigid theorizing on the explanatory level) within the generative/UG-based L2A framework, in the earlier days through the study of parameter resetting (see White, 1989) and more recently as a result of a few prominent works that have made explicit claims about the role of L1 at the initial stages of L2 acquisition on the abstract (morpho)syntactic level. The debate in the 1990s and the various proposals on L1 transfer in the L2 initial state that grew out of it (i.e. the Full Transfer Full Access model (Schwartz & Sprouse, 1994, 1996), the Minimal Trees hypothesis (Vanikka & Young-Scholten, 1994, 1996), the Valueless Features hypothesis (Eubank, 1993, 1994)) are clear exemplifications. In addition, theories about the L2 steady state/end state such as the Failed Functional Feature hypothesis (Hawkins & Chan, 1997) have also tried to resolve the question of L2 failure in the light of L1 effects. In spite of the conflicting results on ultimate attainment and the continued heated debate in this area, evidence from a large number of studies has pointed to (at least some degree of) L1 transfer at the early stages of the L2 (morpho)syntactic development (see the initial state studies cited above; see also for example Haznedar, 1997; Snape *et al.*, 2006; White, 1985, 1986).

A similar line of inquiry on the status of (morpho)syntax in non-native grammars in relation to transfer effects has been extended to the field of L3A (e.g. Flynn *et al.*, 2004; García Mayo *et al.*, 2005; Klein, 1995; Leung, 2005, 2006; Lozano, 2003). Admittedly, the picture is more complex in L3 than in L2 because of the involvement of at least two or more previously learnt languages and the intriguing interplay between the above-mentioned confounding factors such as typology, proficiency, recency, etc. The literature on L3 (morpho)syntax to date suggests that both L1 and L2 can potentially pose influence on L3; typological proximity[2] is a key determinant of the exact source of transfer (Flynn *et al.*, 2004; Leung, 2005, 2006).

Following this, this chapter sets out to further investigate the issue of transfer on the abstract syntactic level and the role of typological proximity in L3A. Leung (2005, 2006) has made a strong claim of full transfer of the typologically most similar language to the L3 initial state (in her case of L3 French, it was L2 English rather than L1 Chinese that was claimed to transfer fully). Do we have evidence that properties other than verbal and nominal morphosyntax transfer as well to the L3 initial state? Does full transfer hold in other language combinations? And what exactly is meant by 'typological similarity' when we talk about syntax and not vocabulary/cognates (cf. endnote 2)? In this study we aim to refine the claim about full transfer; we also aim to explore what 'typology' means in the domain of syntax. We shall focus on the status of (Mandarin) Chinese[3] null objects in L3 non-native grammars. The target population consists of native speakers of Thai who are L2 high-intermediate/advanced users of English and L3 beginners of Chinese. As far as this chapter is concerned, at least on the surface level, Thai and Chinese (as opposed to English) could be considered to be typologically close to each other because both belong to the discourse-oriented type of languages that license the occurrence of surface null objects. However, whether underlyingly the status of null objects in syntax is the same for the two languages or not is controversial (see below).

Therefore, apart from our goals in advancing research on language acquisition, in particular, L3 acquisition, in this study we also seek to contribute some modest knowledge to theoretical syntax by providing empirical data from native speakers (other than intuitions of the syntacticians themselves) to shed some light on the status of Thai and Chinese null objects in both the source and the target grammars.[4] As mentioned above, although null objects are allowed in both Thai and Chinese on the surface level, syntacticians disagree as to whether null objects in abstract syntax have the same status in both languages (see Hoonchamlong, 1991; Huang, 1984, 1989; Pingkarawat, 1989). The debate largely stems from the different intuitions different researchers have concerning the pronominal status of null objects in pure syntactic contexts without discourse. This is of theoretical interest; it has implications for the construction of a (uniform) theory of parameter(s) with respect to null arguments not only linking Chinese and Thai but also Chinese-type and Spanish-type languages in general. As will be made clear later in this chapter, the move from the Principles-and-Parameters approach to Minimalist Syntax in linguistic theory does not necessarily nullify the relevance of our data, which certainly also have consequences for making claims about typology and transfer in L3 (and L2). Owing to space limitation we shall restrict ourselves to one specific aspect of null objects to address the issue at hand – by testing the possibility of co-indexation (and co-reference) between embedded null objects and overt matrix subjects in both Thai and Chinese.

Theoretical and Acquisition Contexts

The status of (null) objects in Chinese, Thai and English

Consider the following examples:

Thai[5]
(1) (a) *e* hen Bill laeo
          e see Bill already
          '(He) saw Bill'.
     (b) John hen *e* laeo
          John see *e* already
          'John saw (him).'
     (c) *e* hen *e* laeo
          e see *e* already
          '(He) saw (him).'
     (d) John bok wa *e* hen Bill laeo
          John say that *e* see Bill already
          'John said that (he) saw Bill.'

> (e)   John bok wa Bill hen *e* laeo
>   John say that Bill see *e* already
>   'John said that Bill saw (him).'
>
> (f)   John bok wa *e* hen *e* laeo
>   John say that *e* see *e* already
>   'John said that (he) saw (him).'

English

(2)   (a)   **e* saw Bill
      (b)   *John saw *e*
      (c)   **e* saw *e*
      (d)   *John said that *e* saw Bill
      (e)   *John said that Bill saw *e*
      (f)   *John said that *e* saw *e*

Chinese

(3)   (a)   *e* kanjian Bill le.
            e see Bill already
            '(He) saw Bill.'
      (b)   John kanjian *e* le.
            John see *e* already
            'John saw (him).'
      (c)   *e* kanjian *e* le.
            e saw   *e* already
            '(He) saw (him).'
      (d)   John shuo *e* kanjian Bill le.
            John said *e* see Bill already
            'John said that (he) saw Bill.'
      (e)   John shuo Bill kanjian *e* le.
            John said Bill see (him) already
            'John said that Bill saw (him).'
      (f)   John shuo *e* kanjian *e* le.
            John said (he) see (him) already
            'John said that (he) saw (him).'

Both Chinese and Thai are null argument languages in that they allow dropping of both subjects and objects in sentential contexts as the examples in (1) and (3) illustrate. Specifically as far as null objects that form the focus of the present chapter are concerned,[6] the examples above (see the *e* in boldface) show that the object position can be empty in both languages in both the matrix clause (see (1b)–(1c) for Thai and (3b)–(3c) for Chinese) and the embedded clause (see (1e)–(1f) for Thai and (3e)–(3f) for Chinese). In English, both types of object drop are generally not possible as indicated in (2b)–(2c) and (2e)–(2f) but Haegeman (1987) discussed some exceptional cases of null objects in English in certain genres and registers (e.g. recipes).[7] In this chapter, we deal with sentences that would fall under the formal register in English and thus it will be assumed that English is a language that does not license object drop.

The study of null objects especially its occurrence in discourse-oriented languages such as Chinese and Thai has attracted quite a lot of attention in the field of theoretical syntax (e.g. Cole, 1987; Hoonchamlong, 1991; Huang, 1984, 1989, 1991; Y. Huang, 1995; Pingkarawat, 1989; Rizzi, 1997; Speas, 1995; Xu, 1986; Xu & Langendoen, 1985).[8] Most of these studies are concerned with the licensing and the identification of null objects, as well as the asymmetry between null objects and null subjects in terms of their syntactic status.

Huang (1984) is a seminal work on Chinese null objects (and null subjects). He argued that the syntactic status of null subjects and that of null objects in Chinese are not the same: the former is a genuine pronominal or genuine *pro* and the latter is a variable. A *pro* is an empty category that can be A-bound and a variable is one that is A'-bound. For illustrative purposes, let us consider the following examples from Huang (1984: examples 22–23) in (4)–(5):

(4) (a) Zhangsan$_i$ xiwang [e$_i$ keyi kanjian Lisi].
        Zhangsan hope   can   see   Lisi
        'Zhangsan$_i$ hopes that [he$_i$] can see Lisi.'
    (b) *Zhangsan$_i$ xiwang [Lisi keyi kanjian e$_i$].
        Zhangsan hope   Lisi can see
        'Zhangsan$_i$ hopes that Lisi can see [him$_i$].'
(5) (a) Zhangsan$_i$ zhidao [e*i* mei banfa shuifu Lisi].
        Zhangsan know   no method persuade Lisi
        'Zhangsan$_i$ knows [he$_i$] cannot persuade Lisi.'
    (b) *Zhangsan$_i$ zhidao [Lisi mei banfa shuifu e$_i$].
        Zhangsan know   Lisi no method persuade
        'Zhangsan$_i$ knows that Lisi cannot persuade [him*i*].'

Examples (4)–(5) are single bi-clausal sentences each containing a matrix clause and an embedded clause. In (4a) and (5a), according to Huang (1984: 538-539), the embedded null subject may refer either to the matrix subject *Zhangsan* or to someone whose reference is fixed outside the sentence. In contrast, in (4b) and (5b) the embedded null object may refer only to someone whose reference is fixed outside the entire sentence, but not to the matrix subject *Zhangsan*. In other words, the embedded subject in (4a) and (5a) may be locally bound by the matrix subject *Zhangsan* whereas the embedded object in the examples (4b) and (5b) cannot. One syntactic diagnostic for a genuine *pro* is therefore to test whether co-indexation (and co-reference) between a null element in the embedded clause and the overt subject in the matrix clause is possible.

Based on his observations on the asymmetry between null subjects and null objects such as (4)–(5) above, Huang (1984) argued that Chinese null objects cannot be *pro*. He further generalized his claim and contended that null objects in natural languages cannot be a genuine *pro* except those with rich object agreement such as in Pashto (see Huang, 1984: 543 for discussion). He postulated a new theory using a number of UG principles to predict the occurrences of a genuine zero pronoun and to derive the crosslinguistic null argument facts the *pro*-drop parameter previously captured (or failed to capture).[9] As far as null objects in Chinese-type languages are concerned, since they are not *pro*, they would fall outside of the *pro*-drop parameter. Huang (1984, 1989) analyzed them as a variable bound by a null operator (null topic) in a higher clause (Huang treated both representations below as identical):[10]

(6) (a) [$_{\text{Top}}$ e_i], [Zhangsan shuo [Lisi bu renshi e_i.]] (Huang, 1984, example 34)
   (b) [OP$_i$] [Zhangsan shuo [Lisi bu renshi e_i.]] (adapted from Huang, 1989, example 3b)

Huang (1984) therefore motivated an additional parameter, the topic-drop parameter, itself derived from a more general parameter related to topic prominence (and possibility of topic-deletion) and subject prominence (and availability of agreement features) (i.e. the discourse-oriented vs. sentence-oriented parameter) and separate from the *pro*-drop parameter to account for the phenomenon of null objects.

Contrary to Huang (1984), some other theoretical syntacticians such as Cole (1987), Pingkarawat (1989) and Hoonchamlong (1991) have shown that null objects in languages such as Thai and Korean exhibit a symmetrical status to null subjects in that both can be a genuine *pro*. The following example (7) in Thai is originally from Cole (1987: example 19, cited in Pingkarawat, 1989):

(7) Chart$_i$ khitwaa Nuan hen e_i
   Chart think say Nuan see e
   'Chart$_i$ thinks that Nuan saw e_i.'

Pingkarawat (1989) observed that the e in (7) can refer to either *Chart* or someone else in the discourse but there is no syntactic restriction that disallows e to co-index with Chart; thus it can obtain a genuine *pro* status. Hoonchamlong (1991) had the same intuition as Pingkarawat (1989) and argued that null objects in Thai can co-index with the subject in the matrix clause and are a genuine *pro*.[11] Apart from the observations on the possibility of co-indexation, which were against Huang's intuitions on Chinese, on a conceptual level Pingkarawat (1989) and Hoonchamlong (1991) also questioned Huang's (1984) Generalized Control Rule (GCR) (see endnote 9). They both viewed Huang's (1984) GCR as an ad-hoc rule and there seems to be no theoretical ground on which to justify its use in determining a genuine zero pronoun (see a similar view expressed in Y. Huang, 1995 and Kong, 2001). Pingkarawat (1989) and Hoonchamlong (1991) therefore rejected the adoption of GCR as a criterion for analysis of a genuine *pro*.

We situate our study within this debate. In this chapter we test the empirical foundation that has driven Huang's (1984) formulation of his theory of null arguments, i.e. impossibility of co-indexation between embedded null objects and overt matrix subjects in Chinese (and by extension, in all of the 'cool' languages in Huang's typology) by eliciting intuitions from Chinese and Thai native speakers. We try to see if we can solve the controversy empirically and unify Chinese and Thai on a micro level and de-motivate the need to postulate two separate parameters on a macro level to account for the phenomenon of null arguments in natural languages. We are also interested in finding out what consequences our native speaker data have for interlanguage analysis when we apply the syntactic theory to non-native language acquisition. One might query that the issue at hand is simply outdated since Huang's analysis is more than 20 years old and linguistic theory has evolved a long way from Principles-and-Parameters to the Minimalist Program. Note that Zushi (2003) has extended Huang's zero topic analysis and re-formulated the topic-drop parameter with reference to Japanese and Romance languages in Minimalist terms. Park (2004) also adopted Minimalism in the analysis of Korean (and English interlanguage) which has maintained the spirit of Huang's emphasis on the notion of (null) topics in discourse-oriented languages. It thus appears that even though the field of theoretical syntax has moved two decades forward, the relevance of our humble challenge against an important aspect of Huang's theory still holds and the puzzle still needs to be solved.

Previous studies on the acquisition of (null) objects

In the field of language acquisition, be it native or non-native, researchers are interested in examining whether learners from a null argument language background are able to unlearn the L1 native setting when they acquire an L2 that prohibits null arguments and vice versa; they are also interested in the potential asymmetry in the acquisition or unlearning pattern of null subjects and null objects for languages that allow both null subjects and null objects. Studies to date that concern a Chinese-type null argument language either as the source or the target language include Wang *et al.* (1992) for L1A; Yip and Matthews (2005) for bilingual L1A; Zobl (1994), Yuan (1997), Kong (2001), Wakabayashi and Negishi (2003), Park (2004) and Jiang (2006) for L2A; Jin (2005, and also Chapter 7 this volume) for L3A. For reasons of space we shall only briefly review a subset of these studies below.

Wang *et al.* (1992) investigated the asymmetrical status between null subjects and null objects in child L1 English and child L1 Chinese grammars. Wang *et al.* looked at whether both groups of children used the same mechanism in producing null subjects and null objects in their respective languages and whether these children have diverging patterns of production from adult native speakers of English and Chinese. Their results showed that the L1 English children performed differently in null objects than in null subjects, thus confirming the null subject–null object asymmetry in terms of the frequency of their occurrence as well as the differing mechanisms licensing null subjects and null objects respectively. In contrast, Chinese children showed systematic use of both null subjects and null objects and did not display any such asymmetry between two types of null pronouns.

Yuan (1997) provided evidence that native speakers of Chinese had more difficulty unlearning null objects than null subjects in L2 English. He looked at a group of L1 Chinese–L2 English participants with seven different proficiency levels in English (beginners to very advanced) who were studying or teaching English in China. The participants had to do a grammaticality judgment task in English that contained various types of null argument contexts. The overall results showed that learners were more accurate in their performance on test items involving null subjects than null objects, suggesting that null subjects are indeed easier to unlearn. Subscribing to the view that both the *pro*-drop parameter and the topic-drop parameter are responsible for the phenomenon of null arguments in natural languages, Yuan (1997) suggested that the null subject option can be reset by Chinese speakers on the basis of positive evidence from English impoverished agreement. Morphological evidence tells them that English is a [+Agr] language (unlike Chinese), but the features of agreement are not rich enough to license null subjects of the kind found in Spanish. By contrast, there is no positive evidence to tell Chinese speakers that English does not allow null topics, and since these license null objects, Chinese speakers continue to allow null objects.

Turning to L3A, Jin (2005, Chapter 7 this volume) studies the acquisition of Norwegian subjects and objects by Chinese–English bilingual speakers. Unlike Chinese, Norwegian is typologically close to English in that the dropping of subjects and objects is generally not allowed. The purpose of her study is to investigate whether Chinese learners of Norwegian have difficulty rejecting null subjects and null objects in the target language and whether an asymmetry of performance exists. Jin's findings on learners' performance in a grammaticality judgment task demonstrate that the asymmetry between null subjects and null objects is maintained in L3A. Her Chinese native speakers rejected sentences with null subjects but not those with null objects in Norwegian. Jin (2005) argues that this asymmetry occurs because the mechanisms licensing null subjects and null objects are different. In Chinese, topics and sentential subjects occur in the same position and so Chinese learners tend to equate the use of topic to the obligatory sentential subjects in English and Norwegian, but such a clue is missing in the case of objects; the unlearning of null subjects is therefore easier compared to null objects. Jin (Chapter 7 this volume) also reports evidence against L2 English transfer in the case of null objects: a significantly higher accuracy rate is obtained for English null object items than the Norwegian counterparts. Jin dismisses the possibility that colloquial/dialectal null object use of Norwegian serves as positive evidence for her L3 beginners. She argues that the high rate of null object use in Norwegian amongst her beginning learners is attributable to L1 Chinese transfer.

Our own previous research on L1 Thai–L2 English–L3 Chinese null arguments (both subjects and objects) using an online preference task in Chinese and Thai (Na Ranong & Leung, 2005) suggested that on the surface level there is a strong parallelism between L1 Thai and L3 Chinese grammars in terms of learners' significantly higher preference for object drop than subject drop. Our results (see Na Ranong, in progress) based on an adapted version of Yuan's (1997) offline English grammaticality judgment task indicate an asymmetry in performance between null subjects and null objects in learners' L2 English, in line with Yuan (1997) and Jin (2005); this asymmetry could be interpreted as some support for L2 influence in L3A. However, recall from the above review that Jin (Chapter 7 this volume) has found evidence against L2 English transfer (and thus typology as well) in her L3 Norwegian case as far as null objects are concerned. Given these conflicting findings, it would therefore be interesting to turn to a more abstract level of syntax and examine L1–L3 and L2–L3 relationships and the issue of typology further. It is against this backdrop that the acquisition aspect of our study on the abstract syntax of null objects was set up.

Research Questions

Recall from the first section of this chapter that the aims of the present study are threefold: (1) to refine the claim about full transfer in L3A; (2) to explore what 'typology' means in the domain of syntax; and (3) to contribute some modest knowledge to theoretical syntax/linguistic theory by providing empirical data from native speakers to shed some light on the status of null objects in native Chinese and native Thai grammars. Following the line of inquiry in theoretical syntax and generative L2A that we reviewed in the second section of this chapter and applying it to L3A, we seek to answer the following research questions:

(1) Do native speakers of Chinese (our L1 Chinese group) allow co-index-ation between null objects in embedded clauses and subjects in matrix clauses in Chinese bi-clausal situations? Or do they have the same intuitions as Huang (1984)?

(2) Do native speakers of Thai (our L1 Thai group) allow co-indexation between null objects in embedded clauses and subjects in matrix clauses in Thai? Do they have the same intuitions as, for example, Pingkarawat (1989) and Hoonchamlong (1991)?

(3) Do these same native Thai speakers (our Thai L1 group) who are learning Chinese as an L3 allow such a co-indexation in their Chinese interlanguage grammars and do they pattern with native speakers of Chinese? Does their performance in Chinese pattern with their per-formance in Thai?

(4) Do native speakers of English who are also learning Chinese as an L2 but who do not have any knowledge of Thai (our L1 English group) allow such a co-indexation in their Chinese interlanguage grammars and do they pattern with native speakers of Chinese and the L1 Thai group?

Methodology

Participants

In this study, we report data collected from three groups of participants. The first group (L1 Thai group) consists of 20 native speakers of Thai. All were Chinese-major students at Thammasat University, Bangkok, Thailand and had been studying Chinese for 1.5 years at the time of testing. They had learned English prior to learning Chinese, ranging from 8–12 years. The participants' mean age at the time of testing was 19.2 (range 19–21, s.d. 0.681). Based on the *Oxford Quick Placement Test* (2002) and the *Hànyǔ Shuǐpíng Kǎoshì* (HSK – (2002) Chinese proficiency test), partici-pants were classified as high-intermediate/advanced L2 English users and beginner/pre-intermediate L3 Chinese learners. The second group of participants (L1 English group) consists of seven native speakers of British English who were Chinese-major students at School of Oriental and African Studies (SOAS), University of London, UK. They had been study-ing Chinese for one year at the time of testing.[12] Participants' mean age was 21.29 (range 20–24, s.d. 1.380). The third group (L1 Chinese group) was a control group that comprised 20 native speakers of Mandarin Chinese who were studying at the postgraduate level at the University of Essex, UK. They were all from mainland China. The participants' mean age was 25.8 (range 22–32, s.d. 2.441).

All participants had to complete a bio-data questionnaire to elicit data on their basic personal information. The two experimental groups (L1 Thai and L1 English) had to answer additional questions on their foreign language learning experience, one of the key questions of which was on psychotypology, i.e. their perceived distance between the languages learnt. Participants were asked to rate their perception of closeness between English and Chinese (for both experimental groups) and that between Thai and Chinese (for the L1 Thai group only) on a 10-point rating scale (1 the least close and 10 the closest). The results show that the L1 Thai group viewed Chinese and Thai to be typologically more similar than Chinese and English: participants' average rating of typological closeness between Chinese and Thai was 7.15 (range 5–8, s.d. 0.875) and that between English and Chinese was 4.05 (range 1–7, s.d. 1.669. For the L1 English participants, their average rating was 3 (range 2–5, s.d. 1.155).

Materials

Two versions of the same experimental task were designed (one in Chinese, the other in Thai). It was an offline written interpretation task that consisted of single bi-clausal sentences without context involving embedded null or overt objects in the respective language followed by a question in English asking about possible referent(s) and five options (all animate).[13] In each version, there were a total of 34 items (24 target items and 10 distractors). The 24 target items were divided into two types (embedded null object or embedded overt object) with 12 tokens each (each test sentence thus appeared twice in each version of the task: once with embedded null object, another with embedded overt subject, but they were spread out). In the Chinese version all the sentences were presented in both simplified Chinese characters and in pinyin. In the Thai version all the sentences were presented in the Thai script. The sentences in the Thai version were translated from those in the Chinese version and modified lexically.

Participants were asked to read the sentences and to judge who the null or overt object in each sentence could possibly refer to. They had then to choose the possible answers, which could be more than one. The L1 Chinese and the L1 English groups only completed the Chinese version of the task. The L1 Thai group was asked to complete the Chinese version of the task first and then the Thai version two days later.

A sample of the test items in each language are shown below (English transliteration and translations did not appear in the original tasks):

Chinese version – null object

张三说李四不认识 Ø。

Zhāngsān shuō Lìsì bù rèn shi Ø
Zhangsan say Lisi *not know* Ø
'Zhangsan said that Lisi does not know (him).'

Who can Ø possibly refer to?

(1)	我的爸爸	wǒ de bà ba
		my linker father
		my father
(2)	张三	Zhāngsān
(3)	圆圆	Yuányuán
(4)	李四	Lǐsì
(5)	None of the above	

Answer:_____

Chinese version – overt object

张三说李四不认识他。

Zhāngsān shuō Lǐsì bù rèn shi tā.
Zhangsan say Lisi not know him
'Zhangsan said that Lisi does not know him.'

Who can *tā* possibly refer to?

(1)	我的爸爸	wǒ de bà ba
		my linker father
		my father
(2)	张三	Zhāngsān
(3)	圆圆	Yuányuán
(4)	李四	Lǐsì
(5)	None of the above	

Answer:_____

Thai version – null object

ศักดิ์สิทธิ์บอกว่าธีรเดชไม่รู้จัก Ø

Saksit bok wa Theeradej mai ru chak Ø
Saksit say that Theeradej no know Ø
'Saksit said that Theeradej does not know (him).'

Who can Ø possibly refer to?

(1)	พ่อของฉัน	por khong chan
		my linker father
		my father
(2)	ศักดิ์สิทธิ์	Saksit
(3)	พิยดา	Piyada
(4)	ธีรเดช	Theeradej
(5)	ไม่มีข้อใดถูก	None of the above

Answer:_____

Thai version – overt object

ศักดิ์สิทธิ์บอกว่าธีรเดชไม่รู้จักเขา.

Saksit bok wa Theeradej mai ru chak khao
Saksit told that Theeradej not know him
'Saksit said that Theeradej does not know him.'

Who can เขา possibly refer to?

(1)	พ่อของฉัน	por khong chan
		my linker father
		my father
(2)	ศักดิ์สิทธิ์	Saksit
(3)	พิยดา	Piyada
(4)	ธีรเดช	Theeradej
(5)	ไม่มีข้อใดถูก	None of the above

Answer:_____

Results

Group results

The main focus of our analysis is on participants' acceptance rate of the co-indexation between null objects in the embedded clause and the subjects in the matrix clause. We also provide results on co-indexation in the overt object condition to compare with the null object condition. Contra the case of embedded null objects, Huang (1984) observed that the co-indexation between embedded overt objects and subjects in the matrix clause is possible and it is used to avoid ambiguity of reference. One could thus expect that native speakers of Chinese would draw a rather sharp contrast in their acceptance rates of co-indexation between embedded objects and matrix subjects in the two experimental conditions. On the other hand, Hoonchamlong (1991) stated that the overt and null embedded object pronouns in Thai are equally free to seek an appropriate antecedent as long as this does not conflict with Principle B, especially the DJR condition (see endnote 9); embedded object pronouns (null and overt) can refer either to the subject in the matrix clause or someone else in the discourse. If we follow Hoonchamlong (1991), we would expect participants' acceptance rates of co-indexation in the null and overt object conditions to be quite similar, at least for the Thai native speakers' performance in Thai.

Table 8.1 Group rates of acceptance of co-indexation between embedded objects (null or overt) and matrix subjects

Participant group	Chinese version: null objects	Chinese version: overt objects	Thai version: null objects	Thai version: overt objects
L1 Chinese	62.08%	78.75%	n/a	n/a
L1 Thai	61.25%	83.33%	70%	81.25%
L1 English	64.28%	76.19%	n/a	n/a

Table 8.1 presents the mean acceptance rates of co-indexation (and co-reference) between objects in the embedded clause (null or overt) and subjects in the matrix clause in both versions of the experimental tasks by the three groups of participants. Findings demonstrate a similar trend of performance for all groups in the Chinese version of the task: around 60% of participants in each group accepted the possibility of co-indexation between null objects in the embedded clause and overt subjects in the matrix clause; as for overt objects in the embedded clause, the acceptance rates of co-indexation were in the higher range of 76%–83% for all groups.

In the Thai version of the task, the L1 Thai group's performance shows a similar trend as that in the Chinese version: they accepted the possibility of co-indexation with matrix subjects more in the embedded overt object condition (81.25%) than the embedded null object condition (70%). Their percentages of accepting co-indexation with matrix subjects in the embedded overt object condition in the Chinese and Thai tasks were approximately the same (83.33% vs. 81.25% respectively). However, the extent of their acceptance of co-indexation between matrix subjects and embedded null objects was higher in the Thai version than the Chinese version (70% vs. 61.25%).

Inferential statistical analyses were conducted to see whether there is any significant difference between groups in the Chinese task. A one-way ANOVA indicated no significant difference in the null object condition ($F(3,63) = 0.344$, $p > 0.05$). Similarly, no significant difference was found in overt object condition ($F(3,63) = 0.226$, $p > 0.05$).

With regard to the Thai native speakers' judgments in Thai and in Chinese, paired-sample t-tests were conducted. No significant difference was found either in the acceptance of co-indexation in the null object condition $t(19) = -1.074$, $p = 0.290$, two-tailed or in overt object condition $t(19) = -0.386$, $p = 0.702$, two-tailed).

Intra-group comparisons within the same version of the experimental task on null vs. overt object conditions were also computed using paired-sample t-tests. In the Chinese version of the task, a significant difference was found in the Thai group ($t(19) = -3.803$, $p = 0.001$, two-tailed) and in the Chinese group ($t(19) = -2.743$, $p = 0.013$, two-tailed) but not in the L1 English group ($t(19) = -1.198$, $p = 0.276$, two-tailed). Similarly, in the Thai version, results from the L1 Thai group also showed a significant difference ($t(19) = -3.226$, $p = 0.004$, two-tailed) between the two experimental conditions (null vs. overt object).

Individual results

L1 Chinese group – Chinese version

First, let us consider the Chinese native speaker participants' judgment in the null object condition. Computing the numbers in the second column of Table 8.2, there were eight out of 20 participants who allowed co-indexation in 10–12 items (out of a total 12 items) while three participants did not allow such a possibility in any of the test items. In contrast, in the embed-

Table 8.2 Individual results (L1 Chinese group – Chinese version)

Participant number	Number of items in the null object condition (12 tokens total) participant accepted co-indexation with matrix subjects	Number of items in the overt object condition (12 tokens total) participant accepted co-indexation with matrix subjects	Number of divergent responses in null object vs. overt object conditions of the same test sentence
1	8	10	2
2	10	9	1
3	0	1	1
4	11	12	1
5	0	4	4
6	1	2	1
7	11	9	1
8	12	12	0
9	11	11	0
10	11	10	1
11	11	11	0
12	9	10	1
13	11	12	1
14	9	12	3
15	7	11	4
16	4	12	8
17	0	12	12
18	7	11	4
19	9	10	1
20	7	8	1

ded overt object condition, 14 participants uniformly allowed co-indexation with matrix subjects for 10–12 items while two participants (nos. 3 and 6) rarely allowed co-indexation in any test item (they allowed co-indexation in only one – two items). It should be noted in passing that participants who did not or rarely allowed co-indexation in the null object condition also rarely allowed co-indexation in the overt object condition (i.e. participant nos. 3, 5, 6). Another interesting observation is that participant 17 did not allow co-indexation in any test items in the null object condition but allowed co-indexation in 12 test items in the overt object condition.

The number of divergent responses in the null object vs. overt object conditions for each participant was also calculated and is shown in the last column of Table 8.2. With the criterion that 'zero–four' divergent responses counts as 'consistent performance', 18 of the 20 participants' judgments were consistent between the two conditions. This could mean that participants treated overt and null objects in the same way in terms of what counts as an antecedent.

L1 English group – Chinese version

Table 8.3 presents the individual results of the L1 English group in the Chinese version of the experimental task. Amongst the seven participants, four allowed co-indexation in almost every test item and their judgments were equal in both the null object and the overt object conditions. Another two participants (nos. 1 and 2) allowed co-indexation in only four test items in the null object condition but their acceptance rate was significantly higher in the overt object condition. The remaining participant (no. 4) disallowed co-indexation with matrix subjects in both the null object and overt object condition.

Table 8.3 Individual results (L1 English group – Chinese version)

Participant number	Number of items in the null object condition (12 tokens total) participant accepted co-indexation with matrix subjects	Number of items in the overt object condition (12 tokens total) participant accepted co-indexation with matrix subjects	Number of divergent responses in null object vs. overt object conditions of the same test sentence
1	4	12	8
2	4	7	3
3	12	12	0
4	1	0	1
5	10	10	0
6	11	11	0
7	12	12	0

L1 Thai group – Chinese version

Table 8.4 Individual results (L1 Thai group – Chinese version)

Participant number	Number of items in the null object condition (12 tokens total) participant accepted co-indexation with matrix subjects	Number of items in the overt object condition (12 tokens total) participant accepted co-indexation with matrix subjects	Number of divergent responses in null object vs. overt object conditions of the same test sentence
1	11	10	1
2	9	10	1
3	9	12	3
4	12	10	2
5	6	11	5
6	10	12	2
7	4	8	4
8	1	10	9
9	6	11	5
10	3	9	6
11	7	9	2
12	11	11	0
13	7	12	5
14	10	12	2
15	9	7	2
16	12	11	1
17	5	7	2
18	6	10	4
19	7	8	1
20	2	10	8

Turning now to the L1 Thai group, we shall first look at individual participants' performance in the Chinese version of the experimental task. Taking the null object condition as the starting point, Table 8.4 demonstrates that six participants allowed co-indexation between the embedded null objects and the matrix subjects for most of the test items (10–12 out of a total of 12) while four participants allowed such a co-referential reading for zero–four test items. In contrast, in the overt object condition, 14 participants uniformly accepted co-indexation between the matrix subjects and the embedded overt objects consistently (in 10–12 items). The rest of the participants allowed such a co-indexation for more than half of the test items.

Comparing the number of divergent responses between the two conditions (see criterion above), 14 participants' judgments were consistent between the two conditions with only two participants (nos. 8 and 20) showing a very high degree of divergence.

L1 Thai group – Thai version

We now examine the Thai native speakers' performance in the Thai version of the interpretation task. From Table 8.5, we observe that in the null object condition, eight participants allowed co-indexation between the embedded null objects and the matrix subjects for 10–12 items; most of the rest of the participants allowed co-indexation more than half of the test items. Regarding the co-indexation possibility in the overt object condition,

Table 8.5 Individual results (L1 Thai group – Thai version)

Participant number	Number of items in the null object condition (12 tokens total) participant accepted co-indexation with matrix subjects	Number of items in the overt object condition (12 tokens total) participant accepted co-indexation with matrix subjects	Number of divergent responses in null object vs. overt object conditions of the same test sentence
1	10	11	1
2	7	9	2
3	12	12	0
4	12	12	0
5	8	12	4
6	12	11	1
7	10	11	1
8	5	11	6
9	6	9	3
10	7	10	3
11	8	12	4
12	12	11	1
13	11	11	0
14	9	9	0
15	10	10	0
16	9	9	0
17	8	9	1
18	3	3	0
19	7	9	2
20	2	4	2

12 participants uniformly opted for the co-referential reading between the embedded overt object and the matrix subject for 10–12 items while six other participants allowed co-indexation for nine test items. The other two participants allowed co-indexation in only three–four test items.

With regards to the number of divergent test items between the two conditions, 19 participants showed consistency in response; only one participant (no. 8) showed a divergence of accepting co-indexation between the two conditions for 6 items.

L1 Thai group – comparison between null object and overt object conditions in Chinese and Thai versions

Table 8.6 L1 Thai group – comparison between Thai and Chinese versions of task in terms of acceptance of co-indexation with matrix subjects in null object and overt object conditions

Participant number	Null objects in Thai version (12 tokens)	Null objects in Chinese (12 tokens)	Overt object in Thai version (12 tokens)	Overt object in Chinese (12 tokens)
1	10	11	11	10
2	7	9	9	10
3	12	9	12	12
4	12	12	12	10
5	8	6	12	11
6	12	10	11	12
7	10	4	11	8
8	5	1	11	10
9	6	6	9	11
10	7	3	10	9
11	8	7	12	9
12	12	11	11	11
13	11	7	11	12
14	9	10	9	12
15	10	9	10	7
16	9	12	9	11
17	8	5	9	7
18	3	6	3	10
19	7	7	9	8
20	2	2	4	10

Finally we investigate the parallelism between the Thai speakers' native Thai grammars and their L3 Chinese interlanguage grammars with respect to the null object property. As indicated in Table 8.6 above, as far as the embedded null object condition is concerned (this is the crucial part for the purpose of this chapter), most participants (a total of 19) judged the co-indexation possibility consistently between the two languages. Only participant no. 7 showed six divergent responses in his acceptance of co-indexation in null objects conditions in both versions of the task. For the overt object condition, again most participants (a total of 18) judged the co-indexation in both languages consistently; the remaining two participants had a divergence of six items between both versions of the task.

L1 Thai group – relationship between participants' proficiency scores, perceived distance between languages and judgment of co-indexation in each condition

The individual results presented in Table 8.7 suggest that the proficiency score attained by a participant in the HSK test is not linked in any systematic way to his or her judgment in the Chinese task. Similarly, the rating of his or her perception of closeness (psychotypology) between Thai and Chinese for the Thai native speakers does not seem to correlate with the degree of divergence observed in their performance in the two versions of the task. In addition psychotypology ratings do not seem to have any effect on English native speakers' performance in the Chinese task.

Discussion

Native speaker data and theoretical syntax

As reported in the previous section, findings of the present study suggest that the majority of the Chinese native speakers we tested allowed co-indexation between a null object in the embedded clause and the subject in the matrix clause in a single bi-clausal sentence without discourse. Recall that our group results demonstrated that the Chinese native speakers tested in this study as a group accepted matrix subject-embedded null object co-indexation more than 60% of the time. In addition, according to the individual results, eight participants allowed matrix subject-embedded null object co-indexation most of the time (i.e. 10 to 12 items out of a total of 12 items) and only three out of the 20 participants did not allow such co-indexation at all. Comparing the null object vs. overt object conditions, statistically there is a significant difference, but individual results confirmed that the majority of the Chinese native speakers are consistent with their judgment in the two conditions.

Therefore, considering the co-indexation issue alone, evidence from the present study lends some support to the claim that in purely syntactic

Table 8.7 L1 Thai group – relationship between participants' proficiency scores, perceived distance between languages and judgment of co-indexation in each condition

Participant (N = 20)	Age	HSK Chinese proficiency test scores (total = 120)	Perception of closeness Thai–Chinese (10 points)	Perception of closeness English–Chinese (10 points)	No. of test items co-indexation allowed – Chinese null object condition (total = 12)	No. of test items co-indexation allowed – Chinese overt object condition (total = 12)	No. of test items co-indexation allowed – Thai null object condition (total = 12)	No. of test items co-indexation allowed – Thai overt object condition (total = 12)
1	21	59	5	4	11	10	10	11
2	19	38	6	1	9	10	7	9
3	20	47	7	4	9	12	12	12
4	20	37	8	5	12	10	12	12
5	19	30	6	5	6	11	8	12
6	19	35	8	5	10	12	12	11
7	19	25	6	3	4	8	10	11
8	20	51	8	7	1	10	5	11
9	20	53	8	3	6	11	6	9
10	20	50	7	5	3	9	7	10
11	19	40	8	1	7	9	8	12
12	20	52	7	4	11	11	12	11
13	20	46	8	1	7	12	11	11
14	19	33	8	6	10	12	9	9
15	20	55	7	5	9	7	10	10
16	19	41	7	4	12	11	9	9
17	19	41	7	3	5	7	8	9
18	19	52	7	6	6	10	3	3
19	19	56	8	4	7	8	7	9
20	21	40	7	5	2	10	2	4

terms, Chinese null objects could have the status of a genuine *pro*. This led us to cast doubt on Huang's (1984) observation about the status of null objects and his proposal concerning the topic-drop parameter.[14]

Turning to the Thai native speakers, as we saw in the results section the participants as a group had a strong tendency to accept matrix subject-embedded null object co-indexation (a group mean acceptance rate of 70% was observed as per Table 8.1). The individual data in Table 8.5 also pointed to the fact that eight native speakers of Thai tested in our study allowed co-indexation above 80% of the time and four of these speakers actually had acceptance responses 100% of the time. Comparing participants' performance in the null vs. overt object conditions, again significant statistical difference was found but individual results are largely consistent across both conditions.

In a nutshell, the present data gathered from Chinese native speakers and Thai native speakers implies that the status of the null object in Thai and in Chinese native grammars may not be dissimilar. It could be the case that null objects in both languages are indeed a genuine *pro*. Therefore Chinese and Thai may indeed fall within the same parameter, if not the same setting, so far as the *pro*-drop phenomenon is concerned. The empirical motivation behind Huang's (1984) postulation of the separate topic-drop parameter is called into question; this problem applies to whatever version of linguistic theory is adopted to accommodate this parameter.

Typology, transfer and the privileged role of L1

Recall from the findings reported in the results section that a strong parallelism exists between the L1 Thai group's performance in the Chinese and Thai versions of the experimental task. Considering the group results, the acceptance rates of co-indexation between the embedded object and the matrix subject in both languages were similar and no statistically significant difference was found in either condition (null or overt object). Taking into account the individual participant analysis of the L1 Thai group, all participants tended to have similar judgments in both their native language and their L3 interlanguage. All these could be taken to support the idea of typology (and psychotypology – recall that our bio-data questionnaire results point to the convergence of typology and psychotypology) as a key determinant of the source of transfer in our L3 case. Equally, however, the same data could reflect the privileged role of L1 in L3A (see the same problem facing Singleton & O'Laoire, 2004, 2005 in the lexical domain, and their solution). We return to the issue below.

Considering the L1 English group next, at first glance, it is surprising to notice that these participants who have not acquired a null argument language previously demonstrated a similar performance pattern as the L1 Thai participants (and the Chinese native controls). Group results indicated that the L1 English participants did not differ from the L1 Thai speakers or the Chinese natives statistically. On the individual level four out of the seven participants tested allowed co-indexation in both null object (and overt object) conditions, this again suggesting that the judgment of the L1 English group was highly comparable to the L1 Thai group (and the L1 Chinese group). If the assumption that the L1 English participants' native grammars did not permit null objects is correct, then one might expect these speakers to face a difficulty in acquiring the opposite setting of the parameter concerned in L2 Chinese. However, contrary to this expectation, our findings suggest that the L1 English speakers were rather successful in their performance in the experiment, in that they were no different than the Chinese native controls. This implied two things: that these English speakers knew that null objects are licensed in Chinese and that they also knew that co-indexation is possible between the embedded null object and the matrix subject in Chinese. The next thing to ask is what has contributed to their success?

In this case, the L1 English participants' apparent success in resetting the parametric value may arise from the fact that they treated null object pronouns in Chinese as syntactically equivalent but phonetically variant to English overt object pronouns. Based on the observations by Kong (2001: 74), English embedded overt object pronouns behave in some similar ways to Chinese embedded null object pronouns with regard to co-indexation possibilities. The English examples below could illustrate this (Kong, 2001: examples 26a–b):

(8) (a) John$_i$ thinks that Mary likes him$_i$.
    (b) As for Bill$_{i'}$ John thinks that Mary likes him$_i$.

Kong (2001) argued (against Huang, 1984) that like the embedded null object in Chinese, the embedded overt object pronoun in English can co-index both with *John*, which is in an A-position (as shown in (8a)) and with *Bill*, which is in an A′ position (as shown in (8b)). Recall also that the embedded overt object in Chinese can be A-bound as well. Thus it is not inconceivable that our L1 English participants perceived the embedded object pronouns in both languages to have a similar status probably based on a hypothesis driven by the surface position of constituents that says something like 'treat the pronominal element right after the verb in the embedded clause in both languages as essentially the same, whether I see it or not':

(9) (a) Johni thinks that Bill saw himi.
    (b) Johni shuo Bill kanjian tai le.
    (c) Johni shuo Bill kanjian Øi le.

As our results showed, as a group the English speakers did not differ in their judgments in the null object and overt object conditions in the Chinese task statistically. In addition, four out of seven of the English participants accepted co-indexation in the null object and overt object conditions in exactly equal rates. Based on this, we would like to argue that the L1 English group perceived some 'surface' similarity between null object pronouns (and overt object pronouns) in Chinese as well as the overt object pronouns in English and adopted an explicit strategy that helped them to perform in a native-like manner in the Chinese task. We interpret this strategy to have a root in the participants' English native grammars on the underlying syntactic level in terms of binding principles. This view of L1 transfer and of the nature of L2 interlanguage captures the same spirit as Hawkins and Chan's (1997) Failed Functional Features hypothesis, although unlike them, we are dealing with beginning L2 learners here.

Since L1 Thai and L1 English speakers performed similarly in the Chinese task, one is tempted to ask if in fact this similar performance was attributable to some universal learning mechanism instead of transfer. Our data on the overt object condition argued against this idea. While the English participants indeed patterned with the Chinese and the Thai native speakers on the null object condition, the latter two groups seemed to be more sensitive to the subtle distinction between null objects and overt objects than the English group (we speculated this to be due to pragmatics which plays a crucial role in discourse-type languages in that it helps native speakers to decide which pronoun they should use in a particular context – see Pingkarawat, 1989, Hoonchamlong, 1991 and Y. Huang, 1995 for further discussion). If it were a universal mechanism that underlay the Thai and the English learners' acquisition of Chinese, we would expect no difference at all in the performance on the Chinese task between the two groups of learners. As reported on p. 000, we have some evidence suggesting the contrary.

Therefore, although typology and L1 are confounded in our L3 case in the sense that Thai is both the language that is typologically closest to the target language Chinese and it is also our L3 learners' mother tongue, together with the L2 English results, overall our data could be taken to support the interpretation that L1 plays a privileged role in both L2 and L3 acquisition of syntax as least as far as the subtle property of Chinese null objects is concerned. Interestingly, this is consistent with Jin (Chapter 7 this volume), who also looks at the status of objects in L3 coincidentally, but contra Flynn *et al.* (2004) and Leung (2005, 2006). Needless to say, given the language combination of our case, the small scale of our study as well as the limitation with our methodology (i.e. only one single experimental task was used which was very explicit in nature), more research is required before a definitive conclusion on the 'typology vs. L1' debate can be reached in L3 syntax.

Acknowledgements

This chapter forms part of the first author's PhD dissertation supervised by the second author while both authors were at the Department of Language and Linguistics, University of Essex, UK. An earlier version of the chapter was presented at SLRF-2006, University of Washington, Seattle, USA. The first author's study at Essex was funded by the Royal Thai Government. Both authors are grateful to Roger Hawkins and a reviewer for very useful comments and suggestions.

Notes

1. The words 'interference', 'transfer' and 'crosslinguistic influence' have been widely used in the field, sometimes interchangeably. We are aware that there are subtle distinctions of the use of the terms as defined by Weinrich (1953) for 'interference', Odlin (1989) for 'transfer' and Sharwood Smith and Kellerman (1986) for the distinction between 'transfer' and 'crosslinguistic influence'. In this chapter, we shall be treating the terms largely as equivalents and following the L2 syntax literature, we shall be mostly using the term 'transfer'.
2. Typological proximity between languages in terms of syntax may be defined as languages sharing the same parametric setting, however a 'parameter' is defined. But, see the case reported in Tsang (Chapter 9 this volume), which involves L1 Tagalog–L2 English–L3 Cantonese. Tsang notes that although Tagalog and Cantonese share similar binding patterns for reflexives (or the same 'parameter setting' so to speak), in terms of genetic typology Tagalog and Cantonese belong to two totally distinct language families. Tsang speculates that such typological distinctions between the two languages may undermine potential transfer effects from one to another on the (abstract) syntactic level.
3. Unless otherwise specified, Mandarin is the variety of Chinese that we refer to throughout this chapter.
4. Almost every experimental study in the field of generative L2A that involves testing instruments other than spontaneous oral production has included native speakers of the target L2 as control subjects, presumably to verify the validity of the experimental tasks concerned (e.g. Kanno, 1997 amongst many others) and to serve as a yardstick to judge if L2 learners have a similar *pattern* of performance as natives in order to shed light on the role of UG in L2A. Very few of these studies have used native speaker data to explicitly attest or even challenge the version of linguistic theory assumed in previous research (cf. Gürel, 2006 and Yamada, 2005). Moreover, none of these studies to our knowledge has tested the native L1 grammars of the L2 learners with reference to the target property (when the property under investigation is relevant in both L1 and L2).
5. Romanization of Thai words follows the Thai Romanization program version 1.10 by Wirote Aroonmanakul (2000).
6. See Na Ranong and Leung (2005) and Na Ranong (in progress) for data and analysis concerning null subjects in the same acquisition case.
7. An example of object drop in English recipes is below: 'Skin and bone chicken, and cut *ec* into thin slices. Place *ec* in bowl with mushrooms. Puree remaining ingredients in blender, and pour *ec* over chicken. Combine *ec* and chill *ec* well before serving' (Haegeman, 1987: example 18).

8. Some of these syntacticians (Cole, 1987; Hoonchamlong, 1991; Huang, 1984, 1989, 1991; Pingkarawat, 1989) adopted the Principles-and-Parameters approach for their analyses. Others like Rizzi (1997) and Speas (1995) used the Minimalist Program, while Y. Huang (1995) adopted the Neo-Gricean pragmatic framework, and Xu and Langendoen (1985) and Xu (1986) used Lexical Function Grammar (LFG) for their analysis. For different viewpoints on the possibility of co-indexation, Xu and Langendoen (1985), Y. Huang (1995) and Kong (2001) argued against Huang (1984); they claimed that embedded null objects in Chinese can co-index with the subjects in the matrix clause in Chinese.

9. The five 'independently motivated and generalized principles of UG' that Huang (1984: 552) used to determine a genuine *pro* are:
   (1) Principle of recoverability.
   (2) The assumption that a zero pronoun is a pronoun.
   (3) The assumption that the agreement-marking Agr on a verb qualifies as a potential 'antecedent' of a zero pronoun.
   (4) The binding theory of Chomsky (1981), in particular the condition of disjoint reference (DJR) or condition (B).
   (5) The Generalized Control Rule (GCR).
   In particular, DJR states that 'a pronoun must be free in its governing category' and GCR says 'co-index an empty pronominal with the closes nominal element'. In Huang (1989), he reformulated GCR as follows: 'An empty pronominal is controlled in its control domain (if it has one)'. GCR, even its reformulated version, is subject to criticism from other syntacticians. See our discussion on Thai.

10. See also Huang (1991) in which he offers an alternative analysis of null objects as null epithets.

11. Hoonchamlong has used various syntactic analyses (i.e. Subjacency, Strong Crossover and Left Branch Condition) to disprove the variable status of embedded objects in Thai. She argued strongly that Thai null objects are genuine *pro*.

12. The HSK Chinese proficiency test results were not available for this group of participants. However, from what we gathered from the number of language contact hours that they had received and from our discussion with the instructor, these learners were also at the beginner/pre-intermediate stage.

13. A reviewer asked about the issue of 'biased' verbs that favor particular responses in the case of reflexives (e.g. Yuan, 1998). According to the reviewer, verbs such as 'complain' will favor the distant link while those such as 'introduce' will favor the local link. We have checked the verbs used in our task against the verbs in Yuan (1998) – there was no verb used in our task that was the same as Yuan's. However, like Yuan (1998: 329), when designing the experimental task we did have included test items in which the context itself would bias the participants to choose the long-distance antecedent, but our results showed that even under these pragmatically-favored circumstances co-indexation with the matrix subject was not necessarily allowed by the participants. Therefore 'biased' verbs or contexts do not seem to play a role here.

14. An alternative interpretation might be that Chinese speakers may have different grammars. Some have grammars where null objects are *pro*, but some have grammars like Huang's where null objects are variables. We feel that the plausibility of this interpretation is low given that only very few (i.e. three out of 20) of the Chinese native speakers tested in our study would fall into the second group.

References

Andersen, R. (1983) Transfer to somewhere. In S. Gass and L. Selinker (eds) *Language Transfer in Language Learning* (pp. 177–201). Rowley, MA: Newbury House.

Bouvy, C. (2000) Towards the construction of a theory of crosslinguistic transfer. In J. Cenoz and U. Jessner (eds) *English in Europe: The Acquisition of a Third Language* (pp. 143–156). Clevedon: Multilingual Matters.

Cenoz, J. (2001) The effect of linguistic distance, L2 status and age on cross-linguistic influence in third language acquisition. In J. Cenoz, B. Hufeisen and U. Jessner (eds) *Cross-linguistic Influence in Third Language Acquisition: Psycholinguistic Perspectives* (pp. 8–20). Clevedon: Multilingual Matters.

Cenoz, J. and Jessner, U. (eds) (2000) *English in Europe: The Acquisition of a Third Language.* Clevedon: Multilingual Matters.

Cenoz, J., Hufeisen, B. and Jessner, U. (eds) (2001) *Cross-linguistic Influence in Third Language Acquisition: Psycholinguistic Perspectives.* Clevedon: Multilingual Matters.

Cenoz, J., Hufeisen, B. and Jessner, U. (eds) (2003) *The Multilingual Lexicon.* Dordrecht: Kluwer.

Chomsky, N. (1981) *Lectures on Government and Binding.* Dordrecht: Foris.

Cole, P. (1987) Null objects in Universal Grammar. *Linguistic Inquiry* 18, 597–612.

De Angelis, O. and Selinker, L. (2001) Interlanguage transfer and competing linguistic systems in the multilingual mind. In J. Cenoz, B. Hufeisen and U. Jessner (eds) *Cross-linguistic Influence in Third Language Acquisition: Psycholinguistic Perspectives* (pp. 42–58). Clevedon: Multilingual Matters.

Dewaele, J. (2001) Activation or inhibition? The interaction of L1, L2 and L3 on the language mode continuum. In J. Cenoz, B. Hufeisen and U. Jessner (eds) *Cross-linguistic Influence in Third Language Acquisition: Psycholinguistic Perspectives* (pp. 69–89). Clevedon: Multilingual Matters.

Ecke, P. (2001) Lexical retrieval in a third language: Evidence from errors and tip-of-the tongue states. In J. Cenoz, B. Hufeisen and U. Jessner (eds) *Cross-linguistic Influence in Third Language Acquisition: Psycholinguistic Perspectives* (pp. 90–114). Clevedon: Multilingual Matters.

Eubank, L. (1993) On transfer of parametric values in L2 development. *Language Acquisition* 3, 183–208.

Eubank, L. (1994) Optionality and the initial state in L2 development. In T. Hoekstra and B.D. Schwartz (eds) *Language Acquisition Studies in Generative Grammar* (pp. 369–388). Amsterdam: John Benjamins.

Flynn, S., Foley, C. and Vinnitskaya, I. (2004) The Cumulative-Enhancement Model for language acquisition: Comparing adults' and children's patterns of development in first, second and third language acquisition of relative clauses. *International Journal of Multilingualism* 1, 3–16.

García Mayo, M.P., Lázaro Ibarola, A. and Liceras, J.M. (2005) Placeholders in the English interlanguage of bilingual (Basque/Spanish) children. *Language Learning* 55, 445–489.

Gass, S. and Selinker, L. (eds) (1983) *Language Transfer in Language Learning.* Rowley, MA: Newbury House.

Gass, S. and Selinker, L. (eds) (1992) *Language Transfer in Language Learning* (2nd edn). Amsterdam: John Benjamins.

Gürel, A. (2006) L2 acquisition of pragmatic and syntactic constraints in the use of overt and null subject pronouns. In R. Slabakova, S. Montrul and P. Prévost (eds) *Inquiries in Linguistic Development: In Honor of Lydia White* (pp. 259–282). Amsterdam: John Benjamins.

Haegeman, L. (1987) Register variation in English: Some theoretical observations. *Journal of English Linguistics* 20, 230–248.

Hammarberg, B. (2001) Roles of L1 and L2 in L3 production and acquisition. In J. Cenoz, B. Hufeisen and U. Jessner (eds) *Cross-linguistic Influence in Third Language Acquisition: Psycholinguistic Perspectives* (pp. 21–41). Clevedon: Multilingual Matters.

Hawkins, R. and Chan, C.Y-h. (1997) The partial availability of universal grammar in second language acquisition: The 'failed functional features hypothesis'. *Second Language Research* 13, 187–226.

Haznedar, B. (1997) L2 acquisition by a Turkish-speaking child: Evidence for L1 influence. In E. Hughes, M. Hughes and A. Greenhill (eds) *Proceedings of the 21st Annual Boston University Conference on Language Development* (pp. 257–268). Somerville, MA: Cascadilla Press.

Hoonchamlong, Y. (1991) Some issues in Thai anaphora: A government and binding approach. PhD Dissertation, University of Wisconsin-Madison.

Hànyǔ Shuǐpíng Kǎoshì (HSK) (2002) Beijing Language and Culture University Press.

Huang, C-T.J. (1984) On the distribution and reference of empty pronouns. *Linguistic Inquiry* 16, 531–574.

Huang, C-T.J. (1989) Pro-drop in Chinese: A generalized control theory. In O. Jaeggli and K. Safir (eds) *The Null Subject Parameter* (pp. 185–214). Dordrecht: Kluwer.

Huang, C-T.J. (1991) Remarks on the status of the null object. In K. Freidin (ed.) *Principles and Parameters in Comparative Grammar* (pp. 56–76). Cambridge, MA: MIT Press.

Huang, Y. (1995) *The Syntax and Pragmatics of Anaphora: A Study with Special Reference to Chinese.* Cambridge: Cambridge University Press.

Jiang, L. (2006) Second language acquisition of English 'pronominality' by advanced proficiency Chinese-speaking learners. PhD thesis, University of Essex.

Jin, F. (2005) The role of L1 and L2 in L3A. Paper presented at the 21SCL/21st Scandinavian Conference of Linguistics, NTNU, Trondheim, Norway.

Kanno, K. (1997) The acquisition of null and overt pronominals in Japanese by English speakers. *Second Language Research* 13, 265–287.

Kellerman, E. (1979) Transfer and non-transfer: Where we are now. *Studies in Second Language Acquisition* 2, 37–57.

Kellerman, E. (1983) Now you see it, now you don't. In S. Gass and L. Selinker (eds) *Language Transfer in Language Learning* (pp. 112–134). Amsterdam: John Benjamins.

Klein, E. (1995) Second vs. third language acquisition: Is there a difference? *Language Learning* 45 (3), 419–465.

Kong, S. (2001) The acquisition of obligatory English subjects by speakers of discourse-orientated Chinese. PhD thesis, University of Essex.

Leung, Y-k.I. (2005) L2 vs. L3 initial state: A comparative study of the acquisition of French DPs by Vietnamese monolinguals and Cantonese–English bilinguals. *Bilingualism: Language and Cognition* 8 (1), 39–61.

Leung, Y-k.I. (2006) Full transfer vs. partial transfer in L2 and L3 acquisition. In R. Slabakova, S. Montrul and P. Prévost (eds) *Inquiries in Linguistic Development: In Honor of Lydia White* (pp. 157–187). Amsterdam: John Benjamins.

Leung, Y-k.I. (2007) L3 acquisition: Why it is interesting to generative linguists. Invited review article. *Second Language Research* 23 (1), 95–114.

Lozano, C. (2003) Universal Grammar and focus constraints: The acquisition of pronouns and word order in non-native Spanish. PhD thesis, University of Essex.

Na Ranong, S. (in progress) Investigating lexical and syntactic transfer in L3 acquisition: The case of L1 Thai–L2 English–L3 Chinese. PhD thesis, University of Essex, UK.

Na Ranong, S. and Leung, Y-k.I. (2005) The status of null subjects and null objects in L1 Thai–L2 English–L3 Chinese interlanguage grammars. Paper presented at the 11th International Conference on Processing Chinese and Other East Asian Languages (PCOEAL), Chinese University of Hong Kong, Hong Kong.

Odlin, T. (1989) *Language Transfer: Crosslinguistics Influence in Language Learning.* Cambridge: Cambridge University Press.

Odlin, T. (2003) Crosslinguistic influence. In C. Doughty and M. Long (eds) *The Handbook of Second Language Acquisition* (pp. 436–486). Malden, MA: Blackwell.

Oxford Quick Placement Test (2002) Oxford: Oxford University Press.

Park, H. (2004) A minimalist approach to null subjects and objects in second language acquisition. *Second Language Research* 20, 1–32.

Pingkarawat, N. (1989) Empty noun phrases and the theory of Control, with special reference to Thai. PhD Dissertation, University of Illinois at Urbana-Champaign.

Ringbom, H. (2001) Lexical transfer in L3 production. In J. Cenoz, B. Hufeisen and U. Jessner (eds) *Cross-linguistic Influence in Third Language Acquisition: Psycholinguistic Perspectives* (pp. 59–68). Clevedon: Multilingual Matters.

Rizzi, L. (1997) A parametric approach to comparative syntax: Properties of the pronominal system. In L. Haegeman (ed.) *Elements of Grammar: Handbook in Generative Syntax* (pp. 281–337). Dordrecht: Kluwer.

Schwartz, B.D. and Sprouse R. (1994) Word order and nominative case in non-native language acquisition: A longtitudinal study of (L1 Turkish) German interlanguage. In T. Hoekstra and B.D. Schwartz (eds) *Language Acquisition Studies in Generative Grammar* (pp. 317–368). Amsterdam: John Benjamins.

Schwartz, B.D. and Sprouse R. (1996) L2 cognitive states and the Full Transfer/Full Access model. *Second Language Research* 12, 40–72.

Sharwood Smith, M. and Kellerman, E. (1986) Crosslinguistic influence in second language acquisition: An introduction. In E. Kellerman and M. Sharwood Smith (eds) *Crosslinguistic Influence in Second Language Acquisition* (pp. 1–9). Oxford: Pergamon.

Singleton, D. and O'Laoire, M. (2004) Psychotypology and the 'L2 factor' in cross-lexical interaction: An analysis of English and Irish influence in learner French. Paper presented at EUROSLA-2004, Edinburgh, UK.

Singleton, D. and O'Laoire, M. (2005) Cross-lexical interaction in Irish–English bilinguals' French: Further exploration of the psychotypology factor. Paper presented at EUROSLA-2005, Dubrovnik, Croatia.

Snape, N., Leung, Y-k.I. and Ting, H-C. (2006) Comparing Chinese, Japanese and Spanish speakers in L2 English article acquisition: Evidence against the Fluctuation Hypothesis? In M.G. O'Brien, C. Shea and J. Archibald (eds) *Proceedings of the 8th Generative Approaches to Second Language Acquisition Conference (GASLA 2006): The Banff Conference* (pp. 132–139). Somerville, MA: Cascadilla Proceedings Project.

Speas, M. (1995) Economy, agreement and the representation of null arguments. On WWW.at: http://www-unix.oit.umass.edu/~pspeas/prodrop.pdf. Accessed 08.08.2008.

Vanikka, A. and Young-Scholten, M. (1994) Direct access to X'-theory: Evidence from Korean and Turkish adults learning German. In T. Hoekstra and B.D. Schwartz (eds) *Language Acquisition Studies in Generative Grammar* (pp. 265–316). Amsterdam: John Benjamins.

Vainikka, A. and Young-Scholten, M. (1996) Gradual development of L2 phrase structure. *Second Language Research* 12, 7–39.

Wang, Q., Lillo-Martin, D., Best, C. and Levitt, A. (1992) Null subject vs. null object: Some evidence from the acquisition of Chinese and English. *Language Acquisition* 2, 221–254.

Wakabayashi, S. and Negishi, R. (2003) Asymmetry of subjects and objects in Japanese speakers' L2 English. *Second Language* 2, 53–73.

Weinrich, U. (1953) *Languages in Contact*. The Hague: Morton.

White, L. (1985) The pro-drop parameter in adult second language acquisition. *Language Learning* 35, 47–62.

White, L. (1986) Implications of parametric variation for adult second language acquisition: An investigation of the 'pro-drop' parameter. In V. Cook (ed.) *Experimental Approaches to Second Language Acquisition* (pp. 55–72). Oxford: Pergamon Press.

White, L. (1989) *Universal Grammar and Second Language Acquisition*. Amsterdam: Benjamins.

Williams, S. and Hammarberg, B. (1998) Language switches in L3 production: Implications for a polyglot speaking model. *Applied Linguistics* 19 (3), 295–333.

Xu, L.J. (1986) Free empty category. *Linguistic Inquiry* 17, 75–93.

Xu, L.J. and Langendoen, D.T. (1985) Topic structures in Chinese. *Language* 61, 1–27.

Yamada, K. (2005) The status of the Overt Pronoun Constraint in grammatical theory and SLA of Japanese. In N. Snape (ed.) *Essex Graduate Student Papers in Language and Linguistics* 7, 180–201.

Yip, V. and Matthews, S. (2005) Dual input and learnability: Null objects in Cantonese–English bilingual children. In J. Cohen, K.T. McAlister, K. Rolstad and J. MacSwan (eds) *Proceedings of the 4th International Symposium on Bilingualism* (pp. 2421–2431). Somerville, MA: Cascadilla Press.

Yuan, B. (1997) Asymmetry of null subjects and null objects in Chinese speakers L2 English. *Studies in Second Language Acquisition* 19, 467–497.

Yuan, B. (1998) Interpretation of binding and orientation of the Chinese reflexives *ziji* by English and Japanese speakers. *Second Language Research* 14, 324–340.

Zobl, H. (1994) Prior linguistic knowledge and the conservatism of the learning procedure: Grammaticality judgments of unilingual and multilingual learners. In S. Gass and L. Selinker (eds) *Language Transfer in Language Learning* (pp. 176–196). Amsterdam: Benjamins.

Zushi, M. (2003) Null arguments: The case of Japanese and Romance. *Lingua* 113, 559–604.

Chapter 9

The L3 Acquisition of Cantonese Reflexives

Wai Ian Tsang

Introduction

Among all the Chinese dialects, Cantonese is the second most spoken in the world (Grimes, 2000; Matthews & Yip, 1994). It is being learnt by many non-Chinese inhabitants as their second (L2) or third language (L3) in Hong Kong, where Cantonese is the main Chinese dialect spoken by the majority of people (HKSAR, 2007; Matthews & Yip, 1994). This inspires research on the acquisition of this dialect as a non-native language.

This chapter thereby examines the acquisition of Cantonese as an L3 by learners whose native language is Tagalog, the lingua franca of the Philippines. The investigation focuses on the acquisition of Cantonese reflexives by these L3 learners, aiming at discerning their interpretation of the monomorphemic and polymorphemic reflexives in two contexts: finite and non-finite. The interaction between the two contexts and the two types of reflexive has been much discussed in the scenario of second language acquisition (L2A). It would be interesting to examine if the L2A findings would be replicated in the acquisition of a third language (L3A).

The organisation of the chapter is as follows. A review of L2 acquisitional studies on reflexives and general L3 acquisitional studies is first presented. It is followed by the binding patterns and the finite/non-finite distinction of the three languages concerned: English, Cantonese and Tagalog. With the theoretical and acquisitional background, we turn our attention to the experimental study proper, with the test results analyzed and discussed in the subsequent sections.

Acquisition of L2 Reflexives

L2 acquisition of reflexives in general

In most generative research on the L2 acquisition of reflexives, one of the foci is on the binding of reflexives in both finite and non-finite structures (Eckman, 1994; Finer, 1991; Finer & Broselow, 1986; Hirakawa, 1990; Yip & Tang, 1998). The predominant view is that L2ers were more accurate in judging finite sentences than non-finite ones.

Finer and Broselow (1986) probe into the acquisition of English reflexive binding by Korean learners of English.[1] Korean differs from English in that it can have the 'farthest' governor for the reflexive, as in (1):

(1)　(a)　Mr A_i says that Mr B_j thinks that Mr C_k will paint himself$_{i/j/k}$.
　　(b)　Mr A_i says that Mr B_j wants Mr C_k to paint himself$_{i/j/k}$.

Furthermore, there is no morphological finite/non-finite distinction in the language. Three possibilities were thus postulated for the acquisition of English reflexives: (1) L1 transfer; (2) adopting the most conservative option (i.e. L2); or (3) neither (1) nor (2). Results gathered from a picture identification task displayed an interesting outcome: Korean subjects responded differently to finite and non-finite embedded clauses. They took Mr C as the antecedent of 'himself' in (1a) and Mr B in (1b). Neither L1 knowledge nor L2 input can account for that. As reviewed in Hirakawa (1990), Finer and Broselow offer two explanations. First the [± tense] nature has an effect on the judgments. Second, the learners analyzed the sentences according to the surface order and treated the subject of the infinitival clause as the object. To conclude, Finer and Broselow conjecture that an Universal Grammar (UG) option (which is legitimate in languages other than English and Korean) was adopted.

Extending his earlier study with Broselow, Finer (1991) maintains the UG-bound status of grammars of L2ers for reflexive binding and further notes that finiteness does matter in the L2ers' accuracy. By probing into the acquisition of English reflexive binding by Korean, Japanese and Hindi L2 learners, he observes the pattern in the 1986 study being replicated for the Korean and Japanese learners in the latter research:[2]

As shown in Table 9.1, although the responses of the subjects were mostly local binding, Korean and Japanese tend to have many more non-local antecedents in the non-finite contexts (23 and 28 instances). In contrast, the speakers of Hindi opted for local antecedents (LOCs) in both finite and non-finite contexts.

Analogous to Finer, Hirakawa (1990) looks into the acquisition of English binding by L2ers. Unlike Finer, who endorses a UG-constrained

Table 9.1 Binding patterns by Korean, Japanese and Hindi L2 learners
Source: Adapted from Finer (1991: 360)

	[+F]		[–F]	
	Local	*Non-local*	*Local*	*Non-local*
Korean	251	4	305	23
Japanese	164	9	173	28
Hindi	269	1	315	8

explanation for the Korean choices, Hirakawa points out the possibility of first language (L1) transfer among the Japanese subjects. The subjects were asked to make their judgments in a multiple-choice grammaticality judgment test with five types of structure tested, two of which are of relevance here:

Type A: John said that Peter hit himself.
Type C: Mary asked Theresa to introduce herself.

The data collected revealed a pattern that was similar to the one in Finer (1991). The Japanese subjects were found to be more accurate in finite items (76.95%) than non-finite ones (55.14%). In particular, a higher percentage of non-local binding was observed in the non-finite context ([+F]: 17.13%, [−F]: 36.45%). Unlike Finer and Broselow, who consider the possible influence of surface order, Hirakawa discards this possibility. This is because the Japanese subjects in the study opted for object-antecedent in the monoclausal sentences (e.g. Mary shows Betty a picture of herself.). Nevertheless, no explanation is offered for the difference in terms of finiteness.

Just as Finer and Hirakawa, Eckman (1994) tests whether the L2 grammar is amenable to UG constraints. The two languages concerned are Japanese and English. The learners of Japanese were English native speakers whereas the learners of English came from L1 speakers of Arabic, Japanese, Mandarin and Spanish. A picture-identification task was conducted with the focus on consistent individual data. The first striking result is that the majority of the L2ers of English systematically preferred local binding and subject-orientation at the same time. Both the English natives and the L2ers in the experiment also allowed only locally bound reflexives. The preference, unlike the patterns observed by Finer and Hirakawa, prevailed in both finite and non-finite contexts, which implies no significant differences between the two types of clause.

A finding similar to Eckman's regarding the finite/non-finite distinction was observed in Yip and Tang (1998). The study looks into the acquisition of English reflexive binding by Cantonese learners and focuses on the issue of transfer effects. Here 268 Cantonese learners of English participated in a sentence-judgment task. The task was in the form of written-stimulus sentences with some Yes/No questions about possible/impossible antecedents. Three structures were tested: finite clauses (e.g. Mary thought that Theresa often painted herself.), non-finite clauses (e.g. Mary asked Theresa to paint herself) and dative clauses (e.g. Mary gave Theresa a photo of herself.). One of the observations revealed in the experimental task is that judgments on finite clauses were not significantly different from those on non-finite ones. Yip and Tang also submit that L1 transfer occurred among the less proficient learners. The learners might regard the English reflexives as morphologically simple ones and thus allow non-local binding. Reanalysis takes place later, leading to target-like interpretations.

As shown in the above studies, the possible significance of finiteness in reflexive binding among L2ers appears to be just a tendency (see Finer) or is left unexplained (see Hirakawa). Therefore, it is not surprising to find analyses that show the reverse: the subjects' judgments being independent of finiteness, as in Eckman (1994) and Yip and Tang (1998).[3]

L2 acquisition of Chinese reflexives

Unlike the above studies that examine the L2 acquisition of English reflexives, Yuan (1998) explores the opposite path: the English/Japanese acquisition of Chinese reflexives within the generative framework. The investigation is motivated by the respective binding properties in the three languages (see Table 9.2).

In the light of these characteristics, Yuan poses three main questions:

- Do the similarities between two languages (e.g. Japanese and Mandarin) give the learners some 'advantageous position'?
- Is there a connection between long distance (LD) binding and subject orientation in the learners' grammar?
- Is the L2 grammar UG-bound?

Through a multiple-choice comprehension test, the following observations were gathered:

- Japanese learners performed much better than English learners.
- There existed an asymmetry in English learners' judgment: they allowed more LD binding in the non-finite context.
- Cases allowing LD binding and co-indexing *ziji* with local objects were found.

Yuan interprets the above patterns as evidence for supporting the possibility of L1 transfer/interference. First, LD binding in Japanese makes it easier for Japanese learners to acquire Mandarin binding in their grammar, but without any experience of LD binding, English learners have to transfer their L1 local setting. As to the finite/ non-finite distinction among English learners, Yuan conjectures that they interpreted Chinese AGR as having the same properties as the English counterpart (i.e. morphologi-

Table 9.2 Binding patterns of English, Mandarin and Japanese

	Nature of the antecedent	
English	Local	Subject/object
Mandarin	Local/LD	Subject
Japanese	Local/LD	Subject

cally null for a [–F] AGR but not for a [+F] AGR). The morphologically empty [–F] AGR can co-index with the AGR in the higher clause, enabling LD binding. By contrast, the morphologically filled [+F] AGR does not allow the co-indexation, thereby allowing only local binding. Yuan further points out that the acceptance of both LD binding of *ziji* and local object orientation is only 'a violation of Chinese grammar' (1998: 334). Languages such as Icelandic and Serbo-Croatian allow this pattern. Thus, the learners' grammar can still be UG-constrained.[4]

L3 Acquisition in General

Attention has been paid in order to identify the different sources and factors that influence L3 acquisition, some of which are inherited from L2A. One main concern is the nature of transfer. With transfer in place, the possible source languages and their respective roles are examined (as in Cenoz, 2001; De Angelis & Selinker, 2001; Flynn *et al.*, 2004; Hammarberg, 2001; Williams & Hammarberg, 1998). Apart from the source languages, variables such as performance-oriented judgments are also considered (as in Bouvy, 2000).

De Angelis and Selinker (2001) examine the nature of transfer with particular focus on two subtypes of transfer: 'lexical interlanguage transfer' and 'morphological interlanguage transfer'. 'Lexical transfer' means the use of non-target lexical forms while 'morphological transfer' refers to the use of non-target morphological forms (such as bound morphemes). Studying the interlanguage production of two L3 Italian learners, De Angelis and Selinker observed both types of transfer, which are restricted to the transfer of form. The transfer, as they explain, is due to the activation of the learners' L2 Spanish, which is made possible largely by the similarities between Spanish and Italian as perceived by the learners. Such perception in turn undermines the possible role of the L1 in the acquisition of an L3.

Cenoz (2001) also acknowledges the possible influence of L2 in her study of a group of L3 learners of English who live in the Basque country in Spain and whose mother tongue is Basque and/or Spanish. In a storytelling task, the older learners were found to produce more crosslinguistic transfer instances, which is not in line with other studies. Such performance, as she explains, is largely due to their rather low language proficiency of the target language; a higher proficiency will thus alleviate the transfer effect. Cenoz further observes that Spanish, rather than Basque, was used as the source of function words in the interlanguage, which can be accounted for by 'linguistic distance': Spanish is 'closer' to English than Basque, confirming the role of typological proximity. She remarks that the use of Spanish even among the Basque L1 subjects indicates the influence of psychotypology, i.e. their awareness and perception of the typological similarities between the target language (i.e. English) and other languages in their minds (i.e. Spanish in this case).

Williams and Hammarberg (1998) and Hammarberg (2001) further highlight the different roles of L1 and L2 in the acquisition of an L3. While acknowledging different 'conditioning factors' such as typology and recency, they explore the longitudinal data from an L3 learner of Swedish. In both studies, which are based on the examination of language switches, word search and word construction, morphology, phonology and phonetic settings, the distinctive roles played by L1 and L2 in the production of the L3 learner are advanced. L1 serves as 'an external instrumental language' that facilitates the production and acquisition in a pragmatic manner. L2, on the other hand, operates as a 'supplier language' in the production and acquisition of new words and phonological patterns in L3. Such division of labor between L1 and L2, as Hammarberg (2001) maintains, hinges on the scores of L2 for those conditioning factors: L2, which is a foreign language to the learner and scores high for factors such as typology, recency and status of the language, tends to be activated more often than L1 in the early stage of acquiring L3.

Not only the nature of the source language(s) but also the sequence of acquiring the source language(s) as well as the target language seems to have played a role, as shown in Flynn *et al.* (2004). They put forward a 'Cumulative-Enhancement Model for Language Acquisition' after examining Kazakh adults and children, whose L2 is Russian, and their acquisition of English Restricted Relative Clauses (RRCs) as an L3. Three types of RRCs were tested: lexically headed with semantic content; lexically headed without any semantic content; and free relative. Performance across these RRCs among the L3 subjects in an elicited imitation task revealed two contrastive but interesting patterns. While adult subjects produced more lexically headed relative clauses, children subjects responded with far more free relatives. This leads Flynn *et al.* to make two claims about their acquisitional path: first, free relatives are not 'developmentally primary', as in L1 acquisition, and their L2, Russian, could have facilitated their acquisition of the English RRCs; second, the simultaneous or near-simultaneous acquisition of Russian (L2) and English (L3) among the children subjects helps account for their difference from their adult counterparts. This in turn implies that experience in languages other than L1 (L2 in this case) and the sequence of learning an L2 or L3 can play a role in L3 acquisition, thereby supporting the cumulative effect of different linguistic experience in language acquisition.

Unlike the above studies, which are concerned with the source language(s) and their respective roles in L3A, Bouvy (2000) focuses on the learners' performance in the target language. She emphasises that L2/L3 transfer is 'performance-induced' in that it is related to the use of the target language by the learners, as indicated in her error corpus of the oral production of L2/L3 learners of Dutch/German. Such transfer basically results from psychotypology, with the errors that ensued reducing in number as a matter of course.

Holding the assumption that the performance of a learner as proposed by Bouvy can in turn be induced by his/her competence of the language, the present chapter would take the stance of the other studies as reviewed and apply a number of factors governing L3A to the structure concerned: typological proximity, psychotypology, recency, proficiency and status of a language.

Finiteness and Binding in English, Cantonese and Tagalog

Finiteness and reflexive binding in English

From a descriptive point of view, English finiteness is realized morpho-logically in an obligatory manner. In traditional accounts (such as Greenbaum, 1996; Quirk *et al.*, 1985), finiteness in English is syntactically viewed as a composite of tense, person and number:

(2) (a) Amy likes tiramisu.
    (b) Amy liked tiramisu.
(3) (a) John is clever.
    (b) You are clever.
(4) (a) John likes taking pictures.
    (b) The boys like taking pictures.

The state of 'liking' in (2) shows a contrast in tense. The verb form in (2a) expresses a present state relative to the speech time whereas (2b) is a past one. By definition, the verb 'like' in the example is finite in that its change in the form can indicate a 'distinction between present and past' (Greenbaum, 1996: 251). Example (3) is about the contrast in person. With the change in the subject (from the third-person-singular 'John' to the second-person-singular/plural 'you'), the verb form of 'be' changes as well. This implies that 'be', in the form of 'is' and 'are', is the finite verb in the two sentences. The link between number and finiteness is shown in example (4). The subject in (4a) is 'John', a third-person-singular nominal, while in (4b) it is 'the boys', a third-person-plural nominal. This results in the corresponding difference in the verb form, meaning that 'like' is the finite verb in these sentences.[5]

Finiteness in English does not interact with the binding of the reflexive in the language. A polymorphemic reflexive (e.g. himself, themselves), which is the only type of reflexive available in the language, always co-indexes an LOC:

(5) (a) *John likes self.
    (b) John$_i$ likes himself$_i$.

    (c)   John$_i$ wants Peter$_j$ to like himself$_{*i/j}$.

    (d)   John$_i$ knows that Peter$_j$ likes himself$_{*i/j}$.

In (5), 'himself' refers to the subject of the matrix sentence 'John'. In (5c) and (5d), 'himself' only refers to the subject of the embedded clause (i.e. 'Peter') but not the one of the matrix clause (i.e. 'John'). In other words, English reflexives are bound locally (they are not able to cross over to another finite or non-finite clause).

Finiteness and reflexive binding in Cantonese

While English finiteness is defined mainly in terms of tense and agreement, it is acknowledged that there is neither tense marking nor subject–verb agreement in Mandarin/Cantonese (Cheung, 1972; Kwok, 1972; Li & Thompson, 1981; Matthews & Yip, 1994; Yip & Rimmington, 1997). Nevertheless, two major attempts, Huang (1989) and Ernst (1994), have been made in the pre-Minimalist stage to track down finiteness in Mandarin (which is also applicable to Cantonese).

Huang (1989) defines finiteness in Mandarin in terms of an 'AUX' category, which covers aspect markers and modals. By definition, a finite clause has AUX whereas a non-finite one has not. As to the syntactic properties associated with finiteness, Huang notes that control infinitivals must not contain any overt subject (as in: *wo bi Zhangsan* [*PRO zuo yundong*] 'I force Zhangsan [to do exercise].' vs. **wo bi Zhangsan$_i$* [*ta$_j$ zuo yundong*] 'I force Zhangsan [he do exercise].').

While Huang links finiteness to some overt representations in Mandarin, Ernst (1994) puts forward the existence of a phonologically null INFL where [± Finite] is located. In other words, [± Finite] is not expressed by any overt lexical items in the language. While Ernst's analysis is not implausible, the proposal of having a phonologically null projection for finiteness might be too strong. Without any 'overt' element for finiteness, one might also argue for the absence of the notion in Chinese (cf. Hu *et al.* (2001), which is a theory-neutral account). With the belief that it is more fruitful, in terms of learnability, to have some overt item that can serve as the indicator of finiteness in the language, the present chapter would subscribe to Huang's analysis as the starting point of our discussion of reflexive binding.

As for reflexive patterns, just like English, Cantonese has the polymorphemic reflexive (e.g. *keoi5zi6gei2* 'himself/herself/itself'). In addition to this compound reflexive, there is a monomorphemic reflexive in Cantonese — *zi6gei2* 'self'. Unlike 'self' in English, *zi6gei2* can stand on its own (see example (6)) as well as function as an emphatic reflexive (see example (7)):[6]

(6)   (a)   keoi5   gok3dak1   zi6gei2   hou2   ceon2
                 (s)he   feel   self   very   stupid

'(S)he feels that she is really stupid.'
(b)   aa3 Ming4 zung1ji3 zi6gei2
Ming   like   self
'Ming likes himself (*self).'
(7)   (a)   Ming4zai2 zi6gei2 zou6 gung1fo3
Little Ming self   do   homework
'Little Ming does homework by himself.'
(b)   keoi5 zi6gei2 zou6 gung1fo3
(s)he   self   do   homework
'(S)he does homework by himself/herself.'

As shown in (6), *zi6gei2* can follow a nominal (6a) or pronominal (6b) to express the emphatic meaning. Note that the form in (7b) is the same as the polymorphemic one.[7]

As to the binding condition of the reflexives, the monomorphemic reflexive in Cantonese can be bound locally or have an LD antecedent:

(8)   (a)   aa3 John$_i$ zung1ji3 zi6gei2$_i$
John   like   self
'John likes himself.'
(b)   aa3 John$_i$ soeng2 Peter$_j$ zung1ji3 zi6gei2$_{i/j}$
John   want   Peter   like   self
'John wants Peter to like him/himself.'

On the other hand, the polymorphemic one tends to be co-referential with the LOC, but LD binding is not completely ruled out:

(9)   (a)   aa3 John$_i$ zung1ji3 keoi5zi6gei2$_i$
John   like   him-self
'John likes himself.'
(b)   aa3 John$_i$ soeng2 Peter$_j$ zung1ji3 keoi5zi6gei2$_{i/j}$
John   want   Peter   like   him-self
'John wants Peter to like him/himself.'

In other words, the Cantonese polymorphemic form can be a local reflexive (just like the English one). Likewise, it can have an LD reading.[8] This implies that the monomorphemic and polymorphemic reflexives are not in complementary distribution, and the context should play a key role in fixing the antecedent of a reflexive.

Finiteness and reflexive binding in Tagalog

As a language in the Austronesian family, Tagalog has aVerb Subject Order (VSO) order:[9]

(10)   Gusto ni Juan na   i-ligtas ni   Peter siya
want ERG John INF INF-save ERG Peter him[10]
'John wants Peter to save him.'

The example above also illustrates how finiteness is realized in Tagalog. Similar to its English counterpart, Tagalog finiteness is expressed by affixes, such as *i-ligtas* 'to save'.[11]

As far as reflexive binding is concerned, Tagalog has only the polymorphemic reflexive:

(11) Gusto ko ang sarili ko
      like   I   NOM self-NOM[12]
      'I like myself.'
(12) * Gusto ko ang sarili John
      like   I NOM self

Just as in Cantonese, both local and LD binding are available in Tagalog, as shown in an example from Andrews (1985: 143):

(13) T[um]angap ang Rosa$_i$ ng sulat para sa bata$_j$ sa   kaniya-ng sarili$_{i/j}$
      [AF]-receive TOP Rosa OBJ letter BEN DIR child DIR her-REL self
      'Rosa received a letter for the child from herself/himself.'

In the above example, the polymorphemic reflexive *kaniya-ng sarili* can be co-indexed with the nearer antecedent (i.e. 'the child') or the farther one (i.e. 'Rosa'). Similarly, such possibility of either the local or LD reading is also noted when sentences with finite and non-finite clauses are examined:

(14) Gusto ni Juan$_i$ na   si Pedro$_j$ ang mag alaga sa kaniya-ng sarili$_{i/j}$
      want ERG John INF ABS Peter TOP take care DIR him-REL self[13]
      'John wants Peter to take care of himself.'
(15) Alam ni John$_i$ na kinakausap ni Peter$_j$ sa kaniya-ng sarili$_{i/j}$
      know ERG John that talk to   ERG Peter NOM him-REL   self
      'John knows that Peter talks to himself.'

In (14), where the reflexive is located within a non-finite clause 'Peter to take care of himself', either the farther noun phrase 'John' or the local one 'Peter' can be the referent. The same binding pattern is also observed in (15), in which the reflexive is in the finite clause 'that Peter talks to himself'.

Table 9.3 recapitulates the differences among the English, Cantonese and Tagalog reflexives mentioned previously:

Table 9.3 Binding properties of English, Cantonese and Tagalog

	Reflexive	*Binding Domain*
English	Polymorphemic	LC
Cantonese	Monomorphemic/polymorphemic	LC/LD
Tagalog	Polymorphemic	LC/LD

Methodology

Test structure

To test the acquisitional patterns of the Tagalog learners, the following structures of anaphoric binding in Cantonese were canvassed:

Test type (1): Monomorphemic reflexive *zi6gei2* in finite clauses
(a)　aa3daai2 gok3dak1 aa3sei3 zung1ji3 zi6gei2
　　　　Big　　feel　　Four　like　　self
　　　'Ah Big feels that Ah Four likes himself/herself (*self).'

Test type (2): Monomorphemic reflexive *zi6gei2* in non-finite clauses
(b)　aa3ji2 giu3 aa3sei3 tiu1zin3 zi6gei2
　　　　Two　ask　Four challenge　　self
　　　'Ah Two asks Ah Four to challenge himself/herself (*self).'

Test type (3): Polymorphemic reflexive *keoi5zi6gei2* in finite clauses
(c)　lou5daai2　zi1　lou5ji2 naau6 keoi5zi6gei2
　　　Old　Big know Old Two scold　him-self
　　　'Old Big knows that Old Two scolds himself/herself.'

Test type (4): Polymorphemic reflexive *keoi5zi6gei2* in non-finite clauses
(d)　aa3saam1 soeng2 aa3sei3 jyun4loeng6 keoi5zi6gei2
　　　　Three　want　Four　　forgive　　him-self
　　　'Ah Three wants Ah Four to forgive himself/herself.'

As listed above, the first two patterns involved the use of the monomorphemic reflexive '-self' in finite and non-finite structures. The other two concerned the polymorphemic reflexive 'himself/herself' in the same contexts. The key comparison was related to the interpretations of monomorphemic and polymorphemic reflexives in the two different contexts – finite and non-finite.

Materials and procedure

To examine the participants' interpretation of Cantonese reflexives, a timed offline co-reference-judgment task was administered in a classroom setting. The task was conducted in one session of around 30 minutes, with the actual testing time being about 15 minutes. Subjects received both aural and written presentations of 28 Cantonese sentences (20 test structures, five for each test type, and eight filler sentences) at eight-second intervals and were asked to choose the antecedent for the reflexive concerned (see Appendices 1 and 2).[14] To ensure that the subjects understood what was expected of them, the experimenter went through all the written instructions with the subjects and completed four experimental trials with them.

After the offline task, the subjects were asked to complete a questionnaire where background information concerning their age, length of residence and English study in Hong Kong, and other second language(s) spoken was solicited (see Appendix 3).[15]

Subjects

A total of 35 subjects participated in the study, 15 of whom formed the experimental group. Aged between 12 and 18, these L1 speakers of Tagalog were learning English and Cantonese in an international school at the time of the experiment. While they attended English lessons every day, they had Cantonese input in the classroom context twice a week. Their responses in the questionnaire revealed that they acquired English earlier, preferred English to Cantonese, and had more confidence in using English than using Cantonese, thereby suggesting the language repertoire of L1 Tagalog–L2 English–L3 Cantonese.[16]

The remaining 20 subjects were L1 speakers of Cantonese who were recruited as controls. At the time of testing, they were taking a postgraduate diploma course in teaching English as a second language. They were also requested to complete the questionnaire about their background information. Table 9.4 shows the main background details of the participants.

Table 9.4 Background details of participants

	Number of subjects	Average duration of learning English	Average duration of learning Cantonese
Cantonese learners	14	11.2 years	7.5 years
Native speakers	20	–	–

Data manipulation

An ANOVA was used to discern any significant differences in the following comparisons:

(1) three binding patterns (i.e. LD vs. LOC vs. LD/LOC) in each structure;
(2) test types 1 and 2 (i.e. *-self* in finite clauses vs. *-self* in non-finite clauses);
(3) test types 3 and 4 (i.e. *oneself* in finite clauses vs. *oneself* in non-finite clauses);
(4) test types 1 and 3 (i.e. *-self* in finite clauses vs. *oneself* in finite clauses);
(5) test types 2 and 4 (i.e. *-self* in non-finite clauses vs. *oneself* in non-finite clauses);
(6) L3 learners and controls in each of the four structures.

Results and Analysis

Table 9.5 reports the responses from the two groups of subjects on the four test types. The responses for the three binding patterns in each test type, namely LD, LOC and LD/LOC, are presented first, followed by comparisons across test types.

Table 9.5 Responses patterns for reflexive binding from L3 learners and controls

	L3 subjects	Controls
Type 1 (-self in [+F])		
Aa3daai2 gok3dak1 aa3sei3 zung1ji3 zi6gei2		
LD (non-local)	31%	72%
LOC (local)	40%	18%
LD/LOC	29%	10%
Type 2 (-self in [–F])		
Aa3ji2 giu3 aa3sei3 tiu1zin3 zi6gei2		
LD (non-local)	23%	19%
LOC (local)	50%	61%
LD/LOC	27%	20%
Type 3 (oneself in [+F])		
Lou5daai2 zi1 lou5ji2 naau6 keoi5zi6gei2		
LD (non-local)	23%	61%
LOC (local)	39%	26%
LD/LOC	39%	13%
Type 4 (oneself in [-F])		
Aa3saam1 soeng2 aa3sei3 jyun4loeng6 keoi5zi6gei2		
LD (non-local)	20%	20%
LOC (local)	54%	64%
LD/LOC	26%	16%

Intra-type comparison

Type 1

Type 1 sentences concern the monomorphemic reflexive in the finite context. Responses from the L3 group did not display any statistical difference among the three choices, although they seemed to favor local binding a bit more. In sharp contrast was the preference for LD antecedent among the control group (72%), as supported by ANOVA ($F(2, 297)$ = 76.91, $p < 0.001$). There were also statistical differences between the two groups of subjects on their response patterns. In other words, the control group was found to LD bind the reflexive more than the L3 learners ($F(1, 168) = 32.31$, $p < 0.001$) whereas the learners chose to bind the reflexive locally or ambiguously more than their native counterparts (LOC: $F(1, 168) = 10.61$, $p = 0.001$; LOC/LD: $F(1, 168) = 10.25$, $p < 0.025$).

Type 2

For Type 2, where the monomorphemic reflexive is situated in the non-finite clause, L3 learners chose the local Noun Phrase (NP) (LOC) as the antecedent at a higher level (50%) than the LD option or the ambiguous LOC/LD one and their choices displayed statistical significance ($F(2, 207)$ = 7.062, $p = 0.001$). Similarly, the control group locally bound the reflexive (61%), which also reached statistical significance ($F(2, 297) = 30.91$, $p < 0.001$). The difference between the L3 learners and the control group did not reveal any statistical significance.

Type 3

Just as the case in Type 1, the learners' responses did not indicate any significant pattern for the polymorphemic reflexive in the finite context. On the contrary, the control group opted for the LD antecedent for the reflexive at a much higher level (61%) than the local or ambiguous one ($F(2, 297) = 33.69$, $p = 0.001$). There were also some highly statistical differences between the two groups of subjects on their response patterns. The control group was found to LD bind the reflexive more frequently than the L3 learners ($F(1, 168) = 32.31$, $p = 0.001$) whereas the learners chose to bind the reflexive ambiguously more than the native counterparts (LOC/LD: $F(1, 168) = 16.22$, $p = .001$).

Type 4

For Type 4 test items with the polymorphemic reflexive in the non-finite clause, the L3 experimental group exhibited a higher rate of local binding (LOC) (54%) than LD or ambiguous LOC/LD binding; their choices displayed statistical significance ($F(2, 207) = 11.66$, $p < 0.001$). Their responses patterned with those from the control group (64%), which also reached statistical significance ($F(2, 297) = 40.14$, $p < 0.001$). No significant group effect was observed.

Inter-type comparison

Two kinds of comparison were made among four test types: (1) mono/polymorphemic reflexive in two different contexts (finite vs. non-finite);

and (2) monomorphemic reflexive vs. polymorphemic reflexive in the finite/non-finite contexts.

Types 1 and 2

Types 1 and 2 sentences are those with the monomorphemic reflexive in finite and non-finite clauses. Response patterns from the experimental group did not show any significant difference whereas two patterns from the control group were supported by statistical significance. The native speakers LD bound the monomorphemic reflexive in finite clauses ($F(1, 198) = 54.52$, $p < 0.001$) and locally bound it in non-finite clauses ($F(1, 198) = 33.09$, $p < 0.001$).

Types 3 and 4

The response patterns for Types 1 and 2 recurred in the comparison of Types 3 and 4 with the polymorphemic reflexive in finite and non-finite contexts. The L3 subjects did not show a clear difference in the choice of the antecedent. By contrast, the results from the controls showed LD binding of the polymorphemic reflexive in finite clauses ($F(1, 198) = 29.15$, $p < 0.001$) and local binding in non-finite clauses ($F(1, 198) = 23.57$, $p < 0.001$).

Types 1 and 3

A similar pattern was observed in comparing the monomorphemic reflexive with the polymorphemic counterpart in finite clauses. There was no significant difference in the responses from both the learners and the native speakers, although both groups tended to select the LD antecedent more for the monomorphemic reflexive.

Types 2 and 4

A comparison of the monomorphemic reflexive with the polymorphemic one in the non-finite context revealed no significant difference in the responses from both the learners and the native speakers, even though both groups tended to prefer the LOC more for the polymorphemic reflexive.

Summary

In sum, the data collected from the L3 learners revealed significant local binding for monomorphemic and polymorphemic reflexives in most finite and non-finite structures, which is to be explored in details in the next section. The only exception was noted in Type 3 sentences, where both groups treated both LOC and LD/LOC options equally in the finite context for polymorphemic reflexives. This 'equal' preference, which requires further statistical support, might suggest a possible influence from their L1 (i.e. Tagalog) or from their L3 (i.e. Cantonese), triggering the learners to turn to the farther antecedent.

The control group, on the other hand, displayed both local and distant binding results across the test structures. They were observed to opt for the LOC for monomorphemic reflexives and the distant ones for the polymorphemic counterparts. Such patterns do not conform to the theoretical expectation that monomorphemic reflexives are more likely to be LD bound than polymorphemic ones. While this might require a look at the experiment per se, the response patterns should not be considered to be some kind of non-native or non-UG behavior since the status of finiteness in Cantonese is contentious per se. The distinctive patterns observed can simply imply that the finite/non-finite distinction in Cantonese might not manifest itself as what is proposed in the generative framework (which, as Tsang states (2003), seems to be a replica of the English distinction).[17]

Discussion

Should the predominant local binding patterns from the L3 learners be analyzed in terms of the key 'conditioning factors' presented earlier, two of them are worth discussing in the present study: typological proximity (which results in possible transfer from the languages involved) and status of a language.

The first factor that comes to the fore is typological proximity, with the focus on the similarities among the languages concerned (e.g. Cenoz, 2001; De Angelis & Selinker, 2001). The languages being examined in this study are Tagalog, English and Cantonese. As reviewed, Tagalog allows both local and LD binding, English only local binding, and Cantonese both local and LD binding. With the similar binding patterns between Tagalog and Cantonese, L1 transfer could have played a role. Traces of LD binding seemed to have turned up in the data, where some responses from the learners went for the farther antecedent or the ambiguous choice. However, the typological distinctions between the two languages seem to undermine such transfer: Tagalog being in the Austronesian language family but Cantonese belonging to the Sino-Tibetan family, and both having their distinctive linguistic settings. Rather, the significant preference for the LOC appears to imply the possible influence from their L2, i.e. English, rather than their L1. Again, this implication can be ruled out in that Cantonese belongs to the Sino-Tibetan family while English is a member of the Indo-European language family. The two languages, with their specific linguistic settings (e.g. phonology, morphology and orthography), can hardly activate each other. Hence, the interpretation of Cantonese reflexives can barely warrant the use of English.[18]

Typological similarity in turn leads to the emergence of another variable: L2/L3 status. The status of a language, as suggested in Williams and Hammarberg (1998) and Hammarberg (2001), concerns principally the linguistic roles of different languages involved in the acquisitional process and/or the status of a language at the community level. The linguistic status, however, appears not to be that obvious in the current study. While both English and Cantonese are 'foreign' languages for the L3 group, the two languages, as explained above, do exhibit their idiosyncratic patterns, which possibly weakens the possible role of English in L3 Cantonese.

Instead, the notion of 'status' can be interpreted in terms of some socio-linguistic criteria such as how often the learners use the target language or whether the learners need the target language for survival. In other words, this can be understood in the light of the role of the target language in the language repertoire of the learner.[19] Cantonese, the target language in the present study, seems to score nil in this respect. As shown by the responses from the L3 subjects in the questionnaire, Cantonese is mostly used only during their Chinese lessons. Tagalog and English play a more prominent role both outside their 'Chinese' classroom and in their daily life: Tagalog in the family and English for other lessons and in the territory.[20] Such modest influence of Cantonese on the L3 learners certainly hinders the acquisition of the language, possibly resulting in some non-target-like linguistic behavior.

What the data from the current study suggest can be a factor that is applicable to interpretation or comprehension of L3: 'minimal distance'. Instead of allowing both local and distant binding as in their source languages and/or the target language, the learners would assign the nearest antecedent for the reflexive most of the time, regardless of the nature of the clause or the type of reflexive involved. This in turn means that the interpretation of the reflexive would be fixed in a monoclausal context, without crossing any clause boundary. As Finer and Broselow (1986) explain, and Ying (2003) suggests, learners' interpretation of a reflexive can be affected by surface order and learners therefore avoid or prefer choosing a particular antecedent. The choice of the antecedent is thereby fixed by 'minimal distance' for the sake of instant comprehension of the message, co-indexing the reflexive with the nearest antecedent and ignoring the farther choices. As a result, a more conservative option, i.e. local binding (rather than LD binding), was preferred among the learners in the current study.[21]

Conclusion

This chapter has presented an investigation of the acquisition of Cantonese reflexives by L3 learners. Through a co-reference-judgment task, the L3 learners were found to locally bind the reflexives, regardless of the type of reflexive (monomorphemic/polymorphemic) and host structure (finite/non-finite). Instead of treating the response pattern as an outcome of their L2 (English), the notion of 'minimal distance' is proposed.

The possible role of 'minimal distance' can be further testified by involving other languages with the choice of LD binding.

Notes

1. The present review of the 1986 study is based on Finer (1991).
2. Korean differs from English in that it can have the 'farthest' governor for the reflexive. The Japanese binding system is the same as the Korean one while Hindi adopts a middle position (i.e. a TNS/INFL/subject can be the prospective antecedent).
3. Other than the generative framework, Ying (2003) investigates the interpretation of reflexive anaphora with Relevance Theory (RT). Focusing on the role of contexts in constraining the effect of 'minimal processing effort', she tested 50 Chinese learners of English on their processing of sentences with Verb Phrase (VP)-ellipsis in two experiments. In the experiment with the test sentences only, subjects were found to give 'sloppy' interpretations – the nearest noun phrases as the antecedents, implying the role of surface order in the interpretation. On the other hand, in the other experiment where referential and non-referential contexts were provided, subjects were observed to be influenced by referential contexts (but not non-referential ones) and opted for the strict interpretations – i.e. farther antecedents – for the elided constituents.
4. Christie and Lantolf (1998) work on the acquisition of Mandarin reflexives by the English learners in their study. However, a detailed account of the study is not included in this chapter since there is not any analysis done in terms of the finite/non-finite distinction.
5. These key reflexes of finiteness in the traditional accounts also exist in the generative account but are 'transformed'. 'Tense' stands on its own while 'Person' and 'Number', together with 'Gender', form AGR[eement]. In the pre-Minimalist stage, 'Tense' and 'Agreement' are the constituents of INFL[ection]. In other words, finiteness becomes linked to this functional category INFL (Haegeman, 1991; Radford, 1988; Rizzi, 1997). Following Pollock's analysis (1989), the Minimalist Program (MP) has the INFL split and English finiteness ties more closely with Tense Phrase (TP). The tense feature has its own projection TP. On the other hand, AGR is getting more vacuous in that its own projection AgrP is not where the agreement features are (not surprisingly, AgrP is deleted eventually). Instead, these agreement features (ϕ-features in Minimalist term) are assumed to be shared by a number of substantive and functional categories (V, N, T, v or even C). As to finiteness, it is under T, which is '[±finite], with further subdivisions and implications about event structures and perhaps other properties' (Chomsky, 1995: 240).
6. The transcription of all Cantonese examples in this chapter follows the romanization system devised by the Linguistic Society of Hong Kong (LSHK).
7. As pointed out by Tang (1989) for Mandarin reflexives, ambiguity of the nature of the polymorphemic reflexive can arise as a result. Adopting her view, we can arrive at two interpretations: a polymorphemic element (like the English one) – *keoi5zi6gei2* or a pronominal with the monomorphemic one which functions as the emphatic reflexive – *keoi5* + emphatic *zi6gei2*. However, we should note that the underlying structures of the two forms are different. While *keio5zi6gei2* is a polymorphemic reflexive, *keoi5* + *zi6gei2* are a combination of two parts. By definition, *keoi5* is an argument and *zi6gei2* is an adjunct to the argument. Thus, there should not be any confusion among the native speakers about whether or not it is an emphatic reflexive.

8. See Pan (1988) for a detailed discussion of LD binding of Mandarin polymorphemic reflexive, which is also applicable to the Cantonese counterpart.
9. Unless specified, the Tagalog examples were supplied and translated by Ms R. Misa, who is a native speaker of Tagalog studying a postgraduate programme at the Hong Kong Baptist University, and Ms S. Pillas, a Tagalog native speaker who is vice-chairperson of a Filipino organization in Hong Kong. Mr R. Ullah, another postgraduate student at the Hong Kong Baptist University, also helped invite his Tagalog students in the elicitation of Tagalog examples and interpretations (personal communication).
10. ERG = Ergative Case; INF = Infinitive.
11. While suffixes are principally used to indicate finiteness in English, different kinds of affix (including infixes and circumfixes) are involved in Tagalog, e.g. *s-um-ulat* 'wrote' and *i-sulat* 'to write'.
12. NOM = Nominative Case.
13. ABS = Absolutive Case; TOP = Topic; DIR = Direction Marker; REL = Possessive Marker.
14. The time interval was fixed after a pilot study with two other groups of native speakers and Tagalog learners of Cantonese.
15. The questionnaire is adapted from the one in Schönpflug (2000).
16. One Tagalog learner was excluded from the study as she failed to complete half of the listening task, resulting in 14 subjects in the experimental group.
17. Tsang (2003) and Sybesma (2004) are among some other accounts on the nature of finiteness in Cantonese.
18. The distinctiveness of the three languages, Tagalog, English and Cantonese, also possibly undermines the influence from another related factor, psychotypology (i.e. how the learners perceive such linguistic differences).
19. Unlike Hammarberg who discusses the role of the language in the speech community (i.e. status), the current study views 'status' as a variable that is more local to the learners.
20. Their use of English in the territory largely falls into the comprehension and production of the written form, which goes with the Chinese counterpart (e.g. road signs and announcements on public transport).
21. This in turn might have an implication on another 'conditioning factor', namely proficiency. The processing mechanism proposed helps the learners with an easy reference for interpretation and such convenience is expected to be overridden by improvement in the L3 subjects' proficiency, possibly resulting in more target-like behavior.

References

Andrews, A. (1985) The major functions of the noun phrase. In T. Shopen (ed.) *Language Typology and Syntactic Description: Clause Structure* (pp. 62–154). Cambridge: Cambridge University Press.

Bouvy, C. (2000) Towards the construction of a theory of crosslinguistic transfer. In L. Cenoz and U. Jessner (eds) *English in Europe: The Acquisition of a Third Language* (pp. 143–156). Clevedon; Buffalo: Multilingual Matters.

Cenoz, L. (2001) The effect of linguistic distance, L2 status and age on cross-linguistic influence in third language acquisition. In L. Cenoz, B. Hufeisen and U. Jessner (eds) *Cross-linguistic Influence in Third Language Acquisition: Psycholinguistic Perspectives* (pp. 8–20). Clevedon: Multilingual Matters.

Cheung, H.L.S. (1972) *Cantonese as Spoken in Hong Kong* [in Chinese]. Hong Kong: Chinese University of Hong Kong.

Chomsky, N. (1995) *The Minimalist Program*. Cambridge, MA: MIT Press.

Christie, K. and Lantolf, J.P. (1998) Bind me up bind me down: Reflexives in the L2. In S. Flynn, W. O'Neil and G. Marthohadjono (eds) *The Generative Study of SLA* (pp. 239–260). Hillsdale, NJ: Erlbaum Associates.

De Angelis, O. and Selinker, L. (2001) Interlanguage transfer and competing linguistic systems in the multilingual mind. In L. Cenoz, B. Hufeisen and U. Jessner (eds) *Cross-linguistic Influence in Third Language Acquisition: Psycholinguistic Perspectives* (pp. 42–58). Clevedon: Multilingual Matters.

Eckman, F. (1994) Local and long-distance anaphora in second-language acquisition. In E. Tarone, G. Gass and A. Cohen (eds) *Research Methodology in Second Language Acquisition* (pp. 207–225). Hillsdale, N.J: Lawrence Erlbaum.

Ernst, T. (1994) Functional categories and the Chinese Infl. *Linguistics* 32, 191–212.

Finer, D.L. (1991) Binding parameters in second language acquisition. In L. Eubank (ed.) *Point Counterpoint: Universal Grammar in the Second Language* (pp. 351–374). Amsterdam: John Benjamins.

Finer, D.L. and Broselow, E. (1986) Second language acquisition of reflexive binding. *Proceedings of the North Eastern Linguistic Society* 16, 154–168.

Flynn, S., Foley, C. and Vinnitskaya, I. (2004) The cumulative-enhancement model for language acquisition: Comparing adults' and children's patterns of development in first, second and third language acquisition of relative clauses. *The International Journal of Multilingualism* 1, 3–16.

Greenbaum, S. (1996) *The Oxford English Grammar*. Oxford: Oxford University Press.

Grimes, B.F. (2000) *Ethnologue: Languages of the World [electronic resource]*. Dallas, TX: SIL International.

Haegeman, L. (1991) *Introduction to Government and Binding Theory*. Oxford: Blackwell.

Hammarberg, B. (2001) Roles of L1 and L2 in L3 production and acquisition. In L. Cenoz, B. Hufeisen and U. Jessner (eds) *Cross-linguistic Influence in Third Language Acquisition: Psycholinguistic Perspectives* (pp. 21–41). Clevedon: Multilingual Matters.

Hirakawa, M. (1990) A study of the L2 acquisition of English reflexives. *Second Language Research* 6 (1), 60–85.

HKSAR (2007) Proportion of population (1) aged 5 and over able to speak selected languages/dialects, 1996, 2001 and 2006. On www at: http://www.bycensus2006.gov.hk/FileManager/EN/Content_981/a114e.xls. Accessed 08.08.2008

Hu, J., Pan, H. and Xu, L. (2001) Is there a finite vs. nonfinite distinction in Chinese? *Linguistics* 39, 1117–1148.

Huang, J. (1989) PRO-drop in Chinese: A generalized control theory. In O. Jaeggli and K. Safir (eds) *The Null Subject Parameter* (pp. 185–214). Dordrecht: Kluwer Academic Publishers.

Kwok, H. (1972) *A Linguistic Study of the Cantonese Verb*. Hong Kong: Centre of Asian Studies, University of Hong Kong.

Li, C. and Thompson, S. (1981) *Mandarin Chinese: A Functional Reference Grammar*. Berkeley: University of California Press.

Matthews, S. and Yip, V. (1994) *Cantonese: A Comprehensive Grammar*. London: Routledge.

Pan, H.H. (1988) Closeness, prominence and binding theory. *Natural Language and Linguistic Inquiry* 16, 771–815.

Pollock, J.Y. (1989) Verb movement, universal grammar, and the structure of IP. *Linguistic Inquiry* 20, 365–424.

Quirk, R., Greenbaum, S., Leech, G. and Svartvik, J. (1985) *A Comprehensive Grammar of the English Language*. London: Longman.

Radford, A. (1988) *Transformational Grammar*. Cambridge: Cambridge University Press.

Rizzi, L. (1997) The fine structure of the left periphery. In L. Haegeman (ed.) *Elements of Grammar: Handbook in Generative Syntax* (pp. 281–337). Dordrecht: Kluwer Academic Publishers.

Schönpflug, U. (2000) Word-fragment completions in the second (German) and third (English) language: A contribution to the organisation of the trilingual speaker's lexicon. In J. Cenoz and U. Jessner (eds) *English in Europe: The Acquisition of a Third Language* (pp. 121–142). Clevedon: Multilingual Matters.

Sybesma, R. (2004) Exploring Cantonese tense. In L. Cornips and J. Dœtjes (eds) *Linguistics in the Netherlands 2004* (pp. 169–180). Amsterdam: John Benjamins.

Tang, J.C.C. (1989) Chinese reflexives. *Natural Language and Linguistic Theory* 7, 93–121.

Tsang, W.L. (2003) The L2 acquisition of English finiteness by Cantonese learners – A generative approach. PhD dissertation, University of Cambridge.

Williams, S. and Hammarberg, B. (1998) Language switches in L3 production: Implications for a polyglot speaking model. *Applied Linguistics* 19 (3), 295–333.

Ying, H.G. (2003) L2 Learners' interpretation of reflexive anaphora in VP-ellipsis: A Relevance Theory perspective. In J.M. Liceras, H. Zobl and H. Goodluck (eds) *Proceedings of the 6th Generative Approaches to Second Language Acquisition Conference (GASLA 2002)* (pp. 346–351). Somerville, MA: Cascadilla Proceedings Project.

Yip, P.C. and Rimmington, D. (1997) *Chinese: An Essential Grammar*. London: Routledge.

Yip, V. and Tang, G. (1998) Acquisition of English reflexive binding by Cantonese learners: Testing the positive transfer hypothesis. In M-L. Beck (ed.) *Morphology and its Interfaces in Second Language Knowledge* (pp. 165–193). Amsterdam: John Benjamins.

Yuan, B.P. (1998) Interpretation of binding and orientation of the Chinese reflexive *ziji* by English and Japanese speakers. *Second Language Research* 14 (4), 341–358.

Appendix 1

Warm-up Sentences

(1) 阿三想阿四自己做功課
     aa3saam1 soeng2 aa3sei3 zi6gei2 zou6 gung1fo3
        Three   want   Four   self   do   homework
     'Ah Three wants Ah Four himself/herself (*self) to do homework.'

(2) 阿四佢自己提阿六交表
     aa3sei3 keoi5zi6gei2 tai4 aa3luk6 gau1biu2
     Four himself/herself remind Six   submit-form
     'Ah Four himself/herself reminds Ah Six to submit a form.'

(3) 林生覺得林太唔 錫佢自己
     lam4saan1 gok3dak1 lam4taai2 m4 sek3 keoi5zi6gei2
     Lam Mr   feel   Lam Mrs not love   herself
     'Mr Lam feels that Mrs Lam does not love herself.'

Test Sentences

(4) 阿二自己叫阿大煮飯
     aa3ji2 zi6gei2 giu3 aa3daai2 zyu2faan6
      Two   self   ask   Big   cook
     'Ah Two himself/herself asks Ah Big to cook.'

(5) 陳生提李生介紹自己
     can4saan1 taai4 lei5saan1 gaai3siu6 zi6gei2
     Chan Mr remind Lee Mr   introduce self
     'Mr Chan reminds Mr Lee to introduce himself (*self).'

(6) 陳生話陳太嚇親佢自己
     can4saan1 waa6 can4taai2 haak3can1 keoi5zi6gei2
     Chan Mr   say Chan Mrs scare   herself
     'Mr Chan says that Mrs Chan scares herself.'

(7) 阿三想阿四原諒佢自己
     aa3saam1 soeng2 aa3sei3 jyun4loeng6 keoi5zi6gei2
        Three   want   Four   forgive   himself/herself
     'Ah Three wants Ah Four to forgive himself/herself.'

(8) 阿大覺得 阿四 鍾意自己
     aa3daai2 gok3dak1 aa3sei3 zung1ji3 zi6gei2
        Big   feel   Four   like   self
     'Ah Big feels that Ah Four likes himself/herself (*self).'

(9) 阿三話阿二佢自己洗衫
     aa3saam1 waa6 aa3ji2 keoi5zi6gei2 sai2saam1
        Three   say   Two   himself   wash clothes
     'Ah Three says that Ah Two himself washes clothes.'

(10) 阿六唔 知阿三鬧佢自己
aa3luk6 m4 zi1 aa3saam1 naau6 keoi5zi6gei2
  Six   not know Three   scold himself/herself
'Ah Six does not know that Ah Three scolds himself/herself.'

(11) 阿二叫阿三照顧佢自己
aa3ji2 giu3 aa3saam1 ziu3gu3 keoi5zi6gei2
  Two ask   Three   take care himself/herself
'Ah Two asks Ah Three to take care of himself/herself.'

(12) 阿四信阿大滿意自己
aa3sei3 seon3 aa3daai2 mun5ji3 zi6gei2
  Four believe Big   satisfy self
'Ah Four believes that Ah Big is satisfied with himself/herself
    (*self).'

(13) 阿二叫阿四 挑戰 自己
aa3ji2 giu3 aa3sei3 tiu1zin3 zi6gei2
  Two ask Four   challenge self
'Ah Two asks Ah Four to challenge himself/herself (*self).'

(14) 阿六想阿三自己去
aa3luk6 soeng2 aa3saam1 zi6gei2 heoi3
  Six   want   Three   self   go
'Ah Six wants Ah Three himself/herself to go.'

(15) 王太 提陳太介紹佢自己
wong4taai2 tai4 can4taai2 gaai3siu6 keoi5zi6gei2
Wong Mrs remind Chan Mrs introduce herself
'Mrs Wong reminds Mrs Chan to introduce herself.'

(16) 阿三知阿五嬲自己
aa3saam1 zi1   aa3ng5 nau1 zi6gei2
  Three   know Five   angry self
'Ah Three knows that Ah Five is angry with himself/herself (*self).'

(17) 阿二勸阿六買個電腦俾自己
aa3ji2 hyun3 aa3luk6 maai5 go3 din6nou3 bei2 zi6gei2
  Two persuade Six   buy   CL computer for self
'Ah Two persuades Ah Six to buy a computer for himself/herself
    (*self).'

(18) 阿六信阿四滿意佢自己
aa3luk6 seon3 aa3sei3 mun5ji3 keoi5zi6gei2
  Six   believe Four satisfy himself/herself
'Ah Six believes that Ah Four is satisfied with himself/herself.'

(19) 老大佢自己想阿二 知錯
lou5daai2 keoi5zi6gei2 soeng2 aa3ji2 zi1co3
Old Big   himself/herself want Two admit-wrong
'Old Big himself/herself wants Ah Two to admit his/her mistake.'

(20) 李太話李生嚇親自己
      lei5taai2 waa6 lei5saan1 haak3can1 zi6gei2
      Lee Mr say Lee Mrs scare self
      'Mrs Lee says that Mr Lee scares himself (*self).'

(21) 阿三想阿六原諒 自己
      aa3saam1 soeng2 aa3luk6 jyun4loeng6 zi6gei2
      Three want Six forgive self
      'Ah Three wants Ah Six to forgive himself/herself (*self).'

(22) 阿二覺得老大鍾意佢自己
      aa3ji2 gok3dak1 lou5daai2 zung1ji3 keoi5zi6gei2
      Two feel Old Big like himself/herself
      'Ah Two feels that Old Big likes himself/herself.'

(23) 阿三叫阿二 挑戰佢自己
      aa3saam1 giu3 aa3ji2 tiu1zin3 keoi5zi6gei2
      Three ask Two challenge himself/herself
      'Ah Three asks Ah Two to challenge himself/herself.'

(24) 阿四話阿六佢自己好辛苦
      aa3sei3 waa6 aa3luk6 keoi5zi6gei2   hou2 san1fu2
      Four say Six himself/herself very exhausting
      'Ah Four says that Ah Six himself/herself is exhausted.'

(25) 阿四唔知阿二嬲自己
      aa3sei3 m4 zi1 aa3ji2 nau1 zi6gei2
      Four not know Two angry self
      'Ah Four does not know that Ah Two is angry with himself/herself
      (*self).'

(26) 阿三叫阿六照顧自己
      aa3saam1 giu3 aa3luk6 ziu3gu3 zi6gei2
      Three ask Six take care self
      'Ah Three asks Ah Six to take care of himself/herself (*self).'

(27) 阿二勸阿四 買本字典俾佢自己
      aa3ji2 hyun3 aa3sei3 maai5 bun2 zi6din2 bei2 keoi5zi6gei2
      Two persuade Four buy CL dictionary for himself/herself
      'Ah Two persuades Ah Six to buy a dictionary for himself/herself.'

(28) 老大知 老二鬧佢自己
      lou5daai2 zi1 lou5ji2 naau6 keoi5zi6gei2
      Old Big know Old Two scold himself/herself
      'Old Big knows that Old Two scolds himself/herself.'

Note: The italic numbers show the filler sentences.
Key to the transcription: CL = classifier

Appendix 2

Response Sheet

Instruction: In each question, can you identify the person (or people) who the reflexives '自己' or '佢自己' refers to by **circling ONE of the given choices**?

Example: 阿三話阿四佢自己會嚟

| | (a) | 阿三 | (b) | 阿四 | (c) | 阿三 / 阿四 | (d) | 唔知道 |

(1) (a) 阿三   (b) 阿四   (c) 阿三 / 阿四   (d) 唔知道

(2) (a) 阿四   (b) 阿六   (c) 阿四 / 阿六   (d) 唔知道

(3) (a) 林生   (b) 林太   (c) 林生 / 林太   (d) 唔知道

(4) (a) 阿二   (b) 阿大   (c) 阿二 / 阿大   (d) 唔知道

(5) (a) 陳生   (b) 李生   (c) 陳生 / 李生   (d) 唔知道

(6) (a) 陳生   (b) 陳太   (c) 陳生 / 陳太   (d) 唔知道

(7) (a) 阿三   (b) 阿四   (c) 阿三 / 阿四   (d) 唔知道

(8) (a) 阿大   (b) 阿四   (c) 阿大 / 阿四   (d) 唔知道

(9) (a) 阿三   (b) 阿二   (c) 阿三 / 阿二   (d) 唔知道

(10) (a) 阿六   (b) 阿三   (c) 阿六 / 阿三   (d) 唔知道

(11) (a) 阿二   (b) 阿三   (c) 阿二 / 阿三   (d) 唔知道

(12) (a) 阿四   (b) 阿大   (c) 阿四 / 阿大   (d) 唔知道

(13) (a) 阿二   (b) 阿四   (c) 阿二 / 阿四   (d) 唔知道

(14) (a) 阿六   (b) 阿三   (c) 阿六 / 阿三   (d) 唔知道

(15) (a) 王太   (b) 陳太   (c) 王太 / 陳太   (d) 唔知道

(16) (a) 阿三   (b) 阿五   (c) 阿三 / 阿五   (d) 唔知道

(17) (a) 阿二   (b) 阿六   (c) 阿二 / 阿六   (d) 唔知道

(18) (a) 阿六   (b) 阿四   (c) 阿六 / 阿四   (d) 唔知道

(19) (a) 老大   (b) 阿二   (c) 老大 / 阿二   (d) 唔知道

(20) (a) 李太   (b) 李生   (c) 李太 / 李生   (d) 唔知道

(21) (a) 阿三   (b) 阿六   (c) 阿三 / 阿六   (d) 唔知道

(22) (a) 阿二   (b) 老大   (c) 阿二 / 老大   (d) 唔知道

(23) (a) 阿三   (b) 阿二   (c) 阿三 / 阿二   (d) 唔知道

(24) (a) 阿四   (b) 阿六   (c) 阿四 / 阿六   (d) 唔知道

(25) (a) 阿四   (b) 阿二   (c) 阿四 / 阿二   (d) 唔知道

(26) (a) 阿三   (b) 阿六   (c) 阿三 / 阿六   (d) 唔知道

(27) (a) 阿二   (b) 阿四   (c) 阿二 / 阿四   (d) 唔知道

(28) (a) 老大   (b) 老二   (c) 老大 / 老二   (d) 唔知道

Appendix 3

問卷 **Questionnaire**

個人資料 **Personal information**

(1) 年歲*Age* _____

(2) 性別*Gender* 男Male 女Female

(3) a) 國籍*Nationality* _____

    b) 出生地*Country of birth* _____

(4) 學校*School name* _____

(5) 母語 *Mother tongue* _____

(6) 語言學習次序*Sequence of languages learned*:

    1. _____   2. _____

    3. _____   4. _____

語言運用現況 **Current language use**

(7) 你跟誰講廣東話？

With whom do you speak Cantonese?

o-------------- o ----------- o ------------o

	很少	有時	時常	常常
父母 Parents	seldom	sometimes	often	very often

o-------------- o ----------- o ------------o

	很少	有時	時常	常常
兄弟姊妹 Siblings	seldom	sometimes	often	very often

o-------------- o ----------- o ------------o

	很少	有時	時常	常常
好朋友 Best friend(s)	seldom	sometimes	often	very often

o-------------- o ----------- o ------------o

	很少	有時	時常	常常
朋友 A friend	seldom	sometimes	often	very often

o-------------- o ----------- o ------------o

	很少	有時	時常	常常
同學 Classmate(s)	seldom	sometimes	often	very often

o-------------- o ----------- o ------------o

	很少	有時	時常	常常
中文老師 Chinese teacher(s)	seldom	sometimes	often	very often

o-------------- o ----------- o ------------o

其他老師	很少	有時	時常	常常
Other teachers	seldom	sometimes	often	very often

語言學習背景 Language learning history

(8)   廣東話*Cantonese*

1-2-3-4-5-6-7-8-9-10-11-12-13-14-15-16-17-18   歲years of age

在學習廣東話的期間畫上交叉。

Mark those years with a cross ✗ in which you actively learn/learned Cantonese.

(9)   英文*English*

1-2-3-4-5-6-7-8-9-10-11-12-13-14-15-16-17-18   歲years of age

在學習英文的期間畫上交叉。

Mark those years with a cross ✗ in which you actively learn/learned English.

(10)   母語*Mother tongue*

1-2-3-4-5-6-7-8-9-10-11-12-13-14-15-16-17-18   歲years of age

在學習母語的期間畫上交叉。

Mark those years with a cross ✗ in which you actively learn/learned your mother tongue.

語言選好 Language preferences

(以1,2,3 列出各語言的選好 Indicate the order of preference for the languages with 1, 2 and 3.)

(11)   你喜歡講那種語言？   _____ 母語First language
Which language do you prefer to speak?   _____ 廣東話Cantonese
                                               _____ 英文English

(12)   你喜歡聽那種語言？   _____ 母語First language
Which language do you prefer to listen to?   _____ 廣東話Cantonese
                                               _____ 英文English

語言能力 Language competence

廣東話Cantonese

o-------------- o ----------- o ------------o

	不太好	好	很好	像母語般
(13) 你懂得講廣東話嗎？ *How well do you speak Cantonese?*	not very well	well	very well	like my first language

o-------------- o ----------- o ------------o

(14) 你明白廣東話嗎？　　　不太好　　好　　　　　　很好
像母語般

How well do you　　not very　　well　　very well　like my
understand Cantonese?　well　　　　　　　　　　　　first
language

英文English

(15) 你懂得講英文嗎？　不太好　好　　很好　　像母語般
How well do you speak　not very　　well　　very well　like my
English?　　　　　　　well　　　　　　　　　　　　first
language

(16) 你明白英文嗎？　　　不太好　　　好　　　很好　　像母語般
How well do you　　not very　　well　　very well　like my
understand English?　well　　　　　　　　　　　　first
language

語言運用 **Automatisation in language use**
(在一種語言旁畫上交叉Mark the appropriate language with a cross **✗**.)

(17) 你較易說出那種語言？　　　　　　　　　廣東話Cantonese
In which language do you speak more easily?　英文English

(18) 你較易運用那種語言數數目？　　　　　　廣東話Cantonese
In which language do you count more easily?　英文English

☺ 謝謝你的幫忙 ☺

Thanks a lot for your help!